*Idea and Act
in Elizabethan Fiction*

Idea and Act in Elizabethan fiction

BY WALTER R. DAVIS

PRINCETON UNIVERSITY PRESS

PRINCETON, NEW JERSEY

1969

Publication of this book has been aided by
the Whitney Darrow Publication Reserve Fund
of Princeton University Press

This book has been composed in Linotype Granjon

Printed in the United States of America
by Princeton University Press, Princeton, New Jersey

Second Printing, 1971

THIS BOOK IS FOR

Mark
Alison
Peter
Catherine
Elizabeth

Two statements about this study are necessary to an understanding of its nature. First, its scope is limited to original sixteenth-century English fiction novelistic in length (though in no other respect), a category of fiction which, unlike the realistic novella, has paradoxically proved so anomalous to historians of the novel. Therefore, many kinds of fiction produced in the period will be almost totally ignored, most notably translations of the *Amadis de Gaula* cycle and others, the novella, and the jest book. Second, this book cannot be construed as an overall history of Elizabethan fiction. It is rather a study of what I take to be the central endeavor of that fiction, that is, the testing of ideas of value by means of experience in a manner much like that outlined by Wallace Stevens in "Of Modern Poetry." I have explored the various versions of this endeavor by types: the accommodation of ideas and experience in pastoral romance, their conflict in courtly fiction, their disjunction in Neo-Hellenic romance, the destruction of ideas by experience in satirical fiction, and the use of experience to structure systems of value in middle-class fiction. Therefore, even though Chapters 4 through 7 suggest by their sequence the outline of a history, it is only an outline, not strictly chronological (Chapter 3 would probably be placed between 5 and 6 in a chronicle), and one which the introduction of material I have deliberately excluded would alter.

Wherever possible, I have taken the texts I discuss from reliable modern editions; otherwise, I have used the earliest available editions. In either case, I have not hesitated to modernize quotations slightly for purposes of readability by regularizing *i* and *j, u* and *v,* and by expanding unusual contractions.

Without an Arts and Humanities Grant from The University of Notre Dame for the academic year 1966-67, I would not have had the leisure to complete this study (which was actually begun as long ago—so it seems now—as 1962). I owe thanks to Richard A. Lanham, A. L. Soens, Merritt Lawlis, and Joan Webber for their continued interest in this study and for their encouragement; to Charles Crupi and (especially) David Kalstone for several concrete suggestions for the improvement of my original manuscript; to Linda Peterson of Princeton University Press for her great care in helping to make the manuscript fit to print; and to my wife for whatever peace I have enjoyed during the process of composition. I also owe thanks to my former colleagues Robert J. Allen and Donald Gifford, with whom, some time ago, I discussed the problems of early fiction. My greatest debt, however, is to my students: to the students of English S 110 at Williams College in 1957 and 1959, and to those of English 58 at Notre Dame from 1961 to the present. I shall always be grateful for their enthusiastic response and fresh approaches to the fiction we read together, and especially for their persistence in finding books like *Euphues* and *Rosalynde* interesting. It was not until this study had reached completion that I realized my great debt to Erich Auerbach's *Mimesis*, which has shaped, through the years, so much of my thinking about fiction.

For permission to quote copyrighted material I wish to thank Random House, Inc., publishers of *Last Tales* by Isak Dinesen, and Alfred A. Knopf, Inc., publishers of *The Collected Poems of Wallace Stevens*. I also wish to thank the editors of *Studies in English Literature* for allowing me to reprint parts of an article that originally appeared in Volume V of their journal in my Chapter 3.

W.R.D.

The University of Notre Dame

CONTENTS

*Idea and Act
in Elizabethan Fiction*

The poem of the mind in the act of finding
What will suffice. It has not always had
To find: the scene was set; it repeated what
Was in the script.
                        Then the theatre was changed
To something else. Its past was a souvenir.
It has to be living, to learn the speech of the place.
It has to face the men of the time and to meet
The women of the time. It has to think about war
And it has to find what will suffice. It has
To construct a new stage. It has to be on that stage
And, like an insatiable actor, slowly and
With meditation, speak words that in the ear,
In the delicatest ear of the mind, repeat,
Exactly, that which it wants to hear, at the sound
Of which, an invisible audience listens,
Not to the play, but to itself, expressed
In an emotion as of two people, as of two
Emotions becoming one. The actor is
A metaphysician in the dark, twanging
An instrument, twanging a wiry string that gives
Sounds passing through sudden rightnesses, wholly
Containing the mind, below which it cannot descend,
Beyond which it has no will to rise.
                        It must
Be the finding of a satisfaction, and may
Be of a man skating, a woman dancing, a woman
Combing. The poem of the act of the mind.

Wallace Stevens, "Of Modern Poetry"

CHAPTER I

On Reading Early Fiction

The reading—not to mention the study—of fiction produced during the many centuries before 1750 has long been hampered by the unjustified assumption that early fiction ought to have something to do with the modern novel. Historians of fiction have usually limited their interest in fiction before Defoe to whatever elements they can cite as having "led" toward the modern novel; and even Walter Allen, while insisting that there were no novels before Defoe, tends to imply that authors before Defoe were trying (and failing) to produce novels.[1] As an astute reviewer of the only recent study of Elizabethan fiction points out, histories of fiction assume too casually that to trace antecedents of the modern novel and to write the history of early fiction are the same thing.[2]

Northrop Frye by no means overstates the case when he writes,

> The literary historian who identifies fiction with the novel is greatly embarrassed by the length of time that the world managed to get along without the novel, and until he reaches his great deliverance in Defoe, his perspective is intolerably cramped. He is compelled to reduce Tudor fiction to a series of tentative essays in the novel form, which works well enough for Deloney but makes nonsense of Sidney. . . . Clearly, this novel-centered view of prose fiction is a Ptolemaic perspective which is now too complicated to be any longer workable, and some more relative and Copernican view must take its place.[3]

[1] Walter Allen, *The English Novel: A Short Critical History* (London, 1954); see pp. 25-26.

[2] Merritt Lawlis, review of Margaret Schlauch's *Antecedents of the English Novel, 1400-1600* (Warsaw and London, 1963), in *Journal of English and Germanic Philology*, LXIV (1965), 297.

[3] Northrop Frye, *Anatomy of Criticism: Four Essays* (Princeton,

Frye posits four distinct forms of prose fiction: the romance, which is so close to myth that its characters approximate psychological archetypes; the confession or fictional autobiography, which intellectualizes and projects inner experience; the satirical anatomy, which deals with mental attitudes rather than with characters and therefore tries to present "a vision of the world in terms of a single intellectual pattern";[4] and the novel. Of these forms, romance, the most important quantitatively and qualitatively, is the only one besides the novel to have received much critical attention.

One of the first to draw attention to the romance was William Congreve, who, in the preface to his fine little mock-romance *Incognita* (1692), contrasted the wonderful improbabilities of this form to the familiar delight of the novel. One of the latest is Richard Chase, who, in his perceptive study *The American Novel and Its Tradition,* has drawn many deep contrasts between novel and romance. While the novel attempts to render reality in detail, he writes, the romance refuses to do so; while the novel relies on probability, as Congreve said, the romance strives for the wonderful. Character is of such prime importance in the novel that some critics of the form—E. M. Forster, for instance[5]—go so far as to lament the necessity of telling a story at all; the romance, on the other hand, is concerned with action to such an extent that the romancer's characters possess little palpable reality and sometimes become, as Frye states, "stylized figures which expand into psychological archetypes."[6] The novel, with its characters rooted firmly in specific social contexts, explores the general through particular aspects of human life, such as the problems of the American in Europe or the difficulty of love among the rural gentry; the romance faces generic concerns—problems of

---

1957), pp. 303-4. See also Wayne C. Booth, *The Rhetoric of Fiction* (Chicago, 1961), Chap. 2.

[4] Frye, p. 310.

[5] E. M. Forster, *Aspects of the Novel* (London, 1927), pp. 44-48.

[6] Frye, p. 304.

good and evil, of man in the universe—in a direct, almost abstract way. The settings of romance are therefore open, almost cosmic, rather than being restricted to circumscribed societies. The romance's drive toward the generic accounts, too, for its association with symbolic forms; romance frequently exhibits vestiges of the mythic, while the time-conscious novel is wedded to history.

Not only are the settings different, but they are presented differently. What is important to the novel is not so much a relevant setting as (what James saw) someone's sense of the setting, setting as conveyed through a meaningful human intelligence. The romantic setting is deliberately distinct from the human characters and forms a separate, often symbolic, backdrop for their activities. As with the relation of character to setting, so too with that between character and character. A character in a novel will have multiple relations to other characters, and these will be complex and, above all, personal relations typified by such emotions as love or hate. Romance characters, however, "will not be complexiy related to each other or to society or to the past. Human beings will on the whole be shown in ideal relations—that is, they will share emotions only after these have become abstract or symbolic," or ritualistic.[7] Romance and novel really focus on different kinds of relations. Novelistic relations center on sharing, interaction, and change; romantic relations tend instead to be a matter of the arrangement of elements that remain separate and unaffected by one another. A romantic setting may symbolize the mind of a hero without his ever being aware of this fact, or characters may observe analogues to themselves in others without ever joining those others in love or friendship.

The concept of ritual arrangement suggests some underlying connection between several traits of romance: the stress on an almost "pure" action, the direct presentation of archetypal

[7] Richard Chase, *The American Novel and Its Tradition* (New York, 1957), p. 13.

concerns of human existence, the creation of a setting foreign
to human character, and the distant kinds of human relations
that go on within such a setting. For in all these we see a very
close connection between elements that are at the same time
irrevocably separate and distinct. We shall find in a consideration of the effects of the romance some reasons—and some
rationale—for the connection and disjunction found coexisting
at its center. One of the most eloquent spokesmen for those
effects and their purposes is Isak Dinesen, who is so often
concerned to define the ways in which her traditional art dif-
fers from modern novelistic fiction. She calls her art the art of
the "tale" or "story," a much more inclusive genre than romance, since it includes Old Testament narrative and the
satirical tales of Boccaccio as well; her comments therefore
apply to early fiction in general.

In "The Cardinal's First Tale," which serves as an introduction to *Last Tales,* she defines her purpose and method
through a story. The story, which is set in the latter part of the
eighteenth century when the novel is coming into its own,
seeks to align the priest as father-confessor with the storyteller,
for both try to answer for their audiences the question "Who
am I?" Cardinal Salviati answers a lady's question about his
identity by telling her a story, the story of his life. He dwells
only on the characters of his father (a dry old religious fanatic)
and his mother (a romantic and artistic woman), their relationship, and the circumstances of his birth. He is one of a set
of twins, but he does not know which—Atanasio, destined to
the church, or Dionysio, destined to be an artist (obviously he
is both). He tells nothing of his thoughts or psychological
makeup, only of his relation to his context, his parents, his
time. The lady recognizes his character in the story but objects
that "He no more looks to me quite human, and alas, I am
not sure that I am not afraid of him." He replies:

"Madame," he said, "I have been telling you a story. Stories
have been told as long as speech has existed, and *sans* stories

the human race would have perished, as it would have perished *sans* water. You will see the characters of the true story clearly, as if luminous and on a higher plane, and at the same time they may look not quite human, and you may well be a little afraid of them. That is all in the order of things. But I see, Madame," he went on, "I see, today, a new art of narration, a novel literature and category of belles-lettres, dawning upon the world. It is, indeed, already with us, and it has gained great favor amongst the readers of our time. And this new art and literature—for the sake of the individual characters in the story, and in order to keep close to them and not be afraid—will be ready to sacrifice the story itself.

"The individuals of the new books and novels—one by one—are so close to the reader that he will feel a bodily warmth flowing from them, and that he will take them to his bosom and make them, in all situations of his life, his companions, friends, and advisers. And while this interchange of sympathy goes on, the story itself loses ground and weight and in the end evaporates. . . . the literature of individuals, if we may call it so—is a noble art, a great, earnest and ambitious human product. But it is a human product. The divine art is the story. In the beginning was the story. At the end we shall be privileged to view, and review, it—and that is what is named the day of judgment."[8]

The contrast implies that while in the novel the characters are humanized, made like us, a mirror for the reader, in the tale this is not so; there the characters are bigger than life and put the reader into relation with the strange, the nonhuman that is greater than life. Thus in a novel we see ourselves, but in a tale we see our relation to our context—to the universe, the greater life around us. This distinction is related to another: the story draws a clear narrative line, but the more the novel becomes involved with character, the more blurred the narra-

---

[8] Isak Dinesen, *Last Tales* (New York, 1957), pp. 23-24.

tive line, until at last it disappears entirely. The value of narrative line seems to be that it has something to do with putting us into relation with other things, perhaps in that it shows the interaction of a man with the universe or other men. Furthermore, such narrative, in relating the diverse by action, is by implication an analogue of divine story, of man's relation to the divine from Genesis to Revelation.

The cardinal goes on to suggest more:

"The story," he took up the thread, "according to its essence and plan, moves and places these two young people, hero and heroine—together with their confidants and competitors, friends, foes and fools—and goes on. They need not distress themselves about material for the burnt offering, for the story will provide. It will separate the two, in life, by the currents of the Hellespont and unite them, in death, in a Veronese tomb. It provides for the hero, and his young bride will exchange an old copper lamp for a new one, and the Chaldeans shall make out three bands and fall upon his camels and carry them away, and he himself with his own hand shall cook, for an evening meal with his mistress, the falcon which was to have saved the life of her small dying son. The story will provide for the heroine, and at the moment when she lifts up her lamp to behold the beauty of her sleeping lover it makes her spill one drop of burning oil on his shoulder. The story does not slacken its speed to occupy itself with the mien or bearing of its characters, but goes on. It makes the one faithful partisan of its old mad hero cry out in awe: 'Is this the promised end?'—goes on, and in a while calmly informs us: 'This is the promised end.'"

"O God," said the lady. "What you call the divine art to me seems a hard and cruel game, which maltreats and mocks its human beings."

"Hard and cruel it may seem," said the Cardinal, "yet we, who hold our high office as keepers and watchmen to the story, may tell you, verily, that to its human characters there is salvation in nothing else in the universe. If you tell them—you compassionate and accommodating human readers—that they may bring their distress and anguish before any other authority, you will be cruelly deceiving and mocking them. For within our whole universe the story only has authority to answer that cry of heart of its characters, that one cry of heart of each of them: '*Who am I?*'"

The novel works by analysis: we see ourselves in a character whose mind and heart are explored by psychological analysis in a limited social context. A tale, on the other hand, works by a special kind of relation. With its emphasis on events in time and on the ambiguity of any human act within that continuum, it tells us who we are by placing us in the universe which is so puzzling to us, by placing us in relation to the other (just as, for example, Odysseus established his identity —his name—by doing something to Polyphemus). In this view, the difference between novel and early fiction is like Gilson's distinction between the modern concept of *personality,* an individual mind which psychology can analyze in isolation, and the Christian concept of a *person,* based on the examination of the human condition in relation to the earth and its Creator, which Christian philosophy provides.[9] It is the latter —the definition of the human person through his relations with a foreign context—that concerns the teller of tales. This is what the cardinal's tale of himself accomplished, and this is what his work with the lady achieved:

"In the course of our talks together all these fragments have been united into a whole. Oh, not into an idyll—I am well aware that I am in for a *furioso*—but into a harmony without a discordant note to it. You have shown me myself! I might tell you that you had created me, and that I had come to life under your hands, and surely it would have been both

[9] Etienne Gilson, *The Spirit of Mediaeval Philosophy,* trans. A.H.C. Downes (New York, 1940), Chap. X.

happiness and pain to have been thus created. But it is not so; my happiness and my pain are greater still, for you have made me see that I was already created—aye, created by the Lord God Himself and issued from His hands. From this hour, what on earth or in heaven can harm me? To the eyes of the world, it is true, I am standing at the edge of an abyss, or walking in a blizzard in wild mountains, but the abyss and the blizzard are the work of God and are infinitely and magnificently beautiful!"

The tale has placed her in a world both frightening and good, but above all real.

The storyteller's concept of definition, of identity, as existing only in the relation among various distinct elements pervades Dinesen's work, whether it be in the attempt to establish the human identity of a Scottish giantess by relating her to a monumental statue of St. Peter, or a young nobleman's attempt to find himself by confronting the peasant who should perhaps bear his title. Many of her stories record the process of a character's establishment of his own identity in terms of another person, as in "The Young Man with the Carnation" or "A Consolatory Tale," where the writer's relation to the public that brings him into being becomes clarified by a tale of an Oriental prince who meets his complex double in order to realize that rich and poor, man and woman, life and death are each "two locked caskets, of which each contains the key to the other."[10] From the close connection of the disjunct, too, comes the typical structure of Dinesen's tales. For her tales are usually nests of stories, where several diverse actions impinge on one another to illuminate, by their special area of likeness, some central vision. As Wallace Stevens wrote, "If resemblance is described as a partial similarity between two dissimilar things, it complements and reinforces that which the two dissimilar things have in common. It makes it bril-

[10] Dinesen, *Winter's Tales* (New York, 1942), p. 312.

liant."[11] An excellent example is "Tales of Two Old Gentlemen" in *Last Tales,* wherein a set of brief stories told against
a background of contradance and waltz unfolds, within the
stories themselves and through their interactions, a vision of
life as both orderly and paradoxical.

Dinesen's work is valuable in its insistence on dialogue
between the strange and the familiar in romance; from some
such attempt to join the two result many of the features of
romance that we noted earlier. Obviously, a mythic sense of
an unrationalized but acceptable connection between human
life and the realms beyond it fosters and impels such fiction.
And the emotion of wonder—an emotion which possesses us
like the tragic emotions instead of yielding to our control like
the delight of recognition called forth by the novel—is a fitting
response to the spectacle of the human and the not-human in
converse. Such converse must exist in the realm of the marvelous, the even remotely possible; its setting must be unrestricted, and must be especially designed to include elements
beyond human society and human ken. Finally, the focus must
not be on the mind of a man, but on his relationships. What is
always essential is some connection between two or more distinct elements or realms—usually the human and the nonhuman—even while their disjunction is just as strongly established. A setting, far from being projected through a hero's
mind, seems foreign and frightening to him; yet it may turn
out to be a mirror of his mind. The hero may meet men, hear
their stories and depart from them forever without ever acting
on the perception that they are his images. The separate elements are always driving toward some ritualistic relation.

In order to get a sense of the many forms of converse
between the strange and the familiar in early fiction—along
an idea of its differing purposes and means—we shall examine
in some detail two stories, one a classical Latin satirical work,

[11] Wallace Stevens, *The Necessary Angel: Essays on Reality and the
Imagination* (New York, 1951), p. 77.

the other a medieval English romance. We shall find several differences between them, but at the same time we shall see strong evidences of a coherent and continuous tradition, with shared aims and techniques. One of the earliest examples of Western prose fiction, the *Metamorphoses* or *Golden Ass* of Apuleius (second century A.D.), exhibits certain striking resemblances to Dinesen's work. Among these is the use of nests of stories as a means of widening the hero's self-awareness, proving thereby the necessity of the naked fictional activity of seeing one's self in the stories of others separate from the self. Therefore, it is essential to trace in the *Metamorphoses* the hero Lucius' progressive reactions to stories; we shall later have occasion to compare his progress to that of a second hero, the Balin of Malory's *Le Morte D'Arthur*.

Lucius begins his story thus: "I fortuned to travel into Thessaly, about certain affairs."[12] On the road to the city of Hypata there, he meets one Aristomenes in the midst of a quarrel with a friend about magic; Lucius defends Aristomenes' belief in magic, adducing as evidence the fact that while a lump of cheese almost choked him the other evening, he once saw a man swallow a whole sword by magic. After asserting that anything is possible in this world, he begs Aristomenes to tell him his story. Aristomenes begins: once, when business affairs took him to Hypata, he met his old friend Socrates, who, having left his wife and been given up for dead, was living the life of a fearful outcast with the witch Meroe. Aristomenes scoffed at his fear of Meroe and his belief in her magic powers. Socrates told him his story: a while ago, after he had been robbed on the road, he found his way to Hypata, where the witch Meroe at first took him in as her lover and then enslaved him by magic. Later, after Aristomenes had persuaded Socrates to escape her and had taken him to an inn to rest, Meroe entered their room, opened Socrates' throat with a sword and

[12] Apuleius, *The Golden Ass*, with the translation of William Adlington (1566), ed. S. Gaselee (London: Loeb Classical Library, 1915), p. 5.

blocked it with a magic sponge (thus strangely the lump in Lucius' throat and the sword reappear), while Aristomenes crouched beneath his bed as if metamorphosed into a tortoise. When Socrates miraculously arose the next day, the two proceeded to run away from Hypata; but Socrates, who grew paler with every step, died when he leaned over a stream for a drink and caused the sponge to fall out. Earlier, when Aristomenes had noted his paleness during lunch, Socrates had replied that the bread "did so stick in my jaws that I could neither swallow it down nor yet yield it up" (just as the cheese had stuck halfway down Lucius' throat). Grief at the death of Socrates, together with fear of Meroe's further revenge, has caused Aristomenes to leave his wife and home and to wander, a frightened outcast, through Thessaly. At the moment Aristomenes' story ends the three arrive at the gates of Hypata, and Lucius enters.

Once established at Hypata, Lucius goes to a dinner party, where he hears another story about magic and witchcraft. The episode is launched by a burst of laughter from the company at a chance allusion to another guest, Thelyphron, who thereupon tells his story. The tale begins with Thelyphron's volunteering, out of brash curiosity, to safeguard a corpse from mutilation by witches, and ends with his realization that it is he himself (his name being the same as the corpse's) who was mutilated: he stands above the corpse looking out on a ring of laughing faces—like the ring of laughing faces which encircles him again at the end of his tale. His whole life, it seems, has been a repetition of this scene of a crowd laughing at the folly exhibited in his razed face. Afterward, Lucius' hostess insists that he prepare a joke for the next day's festival of laughter. He promises to do so, and, unwittingly, immediately does. Returning home tipsy, he mistakes three enchanted wineskins for bandits and bravely "slays" them; the next day he is seized by the law and subjected to a great mock-trial for murder in the amphitheater. He pleads, weeps, and lies, until at last he is made to uncover the "corpses." The episode ends

with Lucius standing above the three uncovered "corpses,"
surrounded by a sea of laughing faces.

Hypata is a sort of charmed circle, the realm of sex, magic,
absurdity, and puzzling laughter. The center of all sorts of
strange legends, Hypata really involves a view of life—the
combination of wonder, fear, and irresistible attraction toward
something probably illicit and certainly not understood which
is typical of the uninstructed. This is Lucius' reaction upon
entering:

> I was in the midst part of all Thessaly, where, by the com-
> mon report of all the world, is the birthplace of sorceries
> and enchantments, and I oftentimes repeated with myself
> the tale of my companion Aristomenes whereof the scene
> was set in this city; all agog moreover (being moved both
> by desire and my own especial longing) I viewed the whole
> situation thereof with care. Neither was there anything
> which I saw there that I did believe to be the same which
> it was indeed, but everything seemed unto me to be trans-
> formed into other shapes by the wicked power of enchant-
> ment, in so much that I thought the stones against which I
> might stumble were indurate and turned from men into
> that figure, and that the birds which I heard chirping, and
> the trees without the walls of the city, and the running
> waters were changed from men into such feathers and leaves
> and fountains. And further I thought that the statues and
> images would by and by move, and that the walls would
> talk, and the kine and other brute beasts would speak and
> tell strange news.[13]

The peculiar kind of action this metamorphic atmosphere
produces is one wherein people unwittingly imitate others.
The parallels in the nest of stories we have related seem
strangely causative, as if hearing another person's story neces-
sitated going through a similar experience, as if the story
spread bad luck. The lump in Lucius' throat seems almost to

[13] *The Golden Ass*, p. 49.

call up the choking in Aristomenes' story; Aristomenes ends
in a condition similar to that of Socrates merely because he
observed him; and Lucius replaces Thelyphron on the scaffold, exposed to public laughter, the day after he has heard his
story. The effect of unwilled imitation is peculiarly central to
a feeling for the absurdity of life. For men are thereby shown
to be mimics without being aware of it, design is shown to be
all too pervasive but to operate like a clockwork mechanism,
where men are cogs rather than co-actors; and people observe
the strangeness of their analogous lives without being able to
account for it in the least. To be uninstructed, unaware of the
real nature of life, is to repeat absurdly, over and over, the folly
of others in your own actions. The nest of stories therefore
illustrates Lucius' involvement in the folly of the world, for it
is in Hypata that he is transformed into a jackass.

There is one further analogous story fixed at Hypata, a
story which underlies all the others and draws them into a
general relation (just as the statues representing the tale pull
every object in the garden where they stand into proper perspective). This is the tale of Actaeon, that emblem of curious
lust whose desire to see Diana naked caused the goddess to
transform him into a stag. It is the group of statues illustrating
this myth that Lucius' hostess points out as a warning to him
just before he rushes forth to ingratiate himself with the nym-
phomaniac witch Pamphile. The comic hero immediately turns
away to act out his own supreme analogue to all the stories of
curiosity and lust for things beyond understanding that have
led up to this one; and suffers for it as did Aristomenes, Socrates, Thelyphron, and Actaeon. Hoping to turn himself into
an owl as Pamphile has just done and thus to soar up to the
gods (with a power he can see only as a means to the satisfaction of his lust), Lucius manages to steal some magic ointment
from her and smears it all over himself. But it is the wrong
ointment, and he becomes, instead of an owl, an earthbound
jackass, that pariah and emblem of ignorance whose only posi-

tive attribute is sexual. Lucius has become absolutely what he
was metaphorically.

It is in the midst of Lucius' sufferings as a jackass that
Apuleius places the next important story, the famous tale of
Cupid and Psyche. This tale has three referents, two of them
as a result of its position in the work as a whole and a third
of its symbolism. First of all, it is a consolatory tale told by a
hag to Charite, a young girl stolen from her lover on her wedding day; it both offers to her the possibility of rejoining her
lover by toil just as Psyche did (a possibility she later realizes)
and dignifies her situation by putting it into the universal
terms of painful love between the human and the divine, so
that she is able to accept it. To Lucius, who overhears the
tale told to Charite (and thus becomes bound to her later), it
represents a mirror image of his present situation and foretells
his future in terms of another's. Just as Lucius allowed his
inordinate desire for a debased kind of knowledge of the
supernatural to reduce him to the bestial form which leaves
him subject to the vicissitudes of fortune, so too Psyche, bereft
of her divine lover by her attempt to acquire forbidden knowledge of him, must seek reunion by wandering through the
world in yearning and toil. And just as Psyche's willing acceptance of pain shows the virtue which restores her to her
lover in heaven, so too will Lucius' forbearance and final
renunciation cause the goddess Isis to restore him to manhood
and finally to raise him to participation in her nature.

In addition to these two meanings of the story arising from
the context of its telling, there is a third which overarches
them, for the tale is an allegory of the human condition. The
human soul, possessed by an impertinent desire to know the
divinity which has raised it from the body and nourished it,
commits an act that alienates the divine; it can reunite itself
with divinity only by bearing patiently the life of fallen man
and enduring human toil, which it dedicates to its beloved.
Because this tale is a central statement of man's case, elements
from it—especially details derived from its setting—keep crop-

ping up throughout the rest of the book.[14] And it is the analogy between this allegorical statement of the soul's plight and Lucius' asshood that raises his situation to a new and illuminating level. For it shows that asininity is an image of the present state of mankind (bestial, but longing for the divine in all its wrongheaded ways) and hints that his curiosity was an imperfect version of what—purged of selfishness—is really a desire for communion with the divine. Therefore, the story implies that credulity may be purified by means of severe experience into faith, in the case of both Lucius and mankind.

The tale of Cupid and Psyche represents a moment of illumination for Lucius, for the important act of seeing himself in Psyche (and next to Charite), instead of merely acting out her story unaware, has the effect of placing him in a universal scheme and thus indirectly puts him into relation with the absolute. Hence, after the tale his asshood ceases to be a merely privative state and becomes instead symbolic of the human condition. He accepts his state, becomes willing and helpful to others, and, most important, uses his asinine shape to further an exploration of the human condition it signifies. As he himself says later, "I do now give great thanks to my assy form, in that by that mean I have seen the experience of many things, and am become more experienced (notwithstanding that I was then very little wise)."[15] The experiences—both Lucius' own and those he observes (the two tend to blend in this part of the book, since he is primarily a central intelligence)—are of the sordidness of the human unilluminated by the divine. In the course of his adventures he sees several illustrations of the bestiality of the human mind acceding to its own untempered desires: the nasty assboy, the treacherous Thrasyllus, the disgusting eunuch priests, the adulterous baker's wife, the sadistic nobleman, the incestuous counselor's wife,

[14] Compare the description of Cupid's palace (p. 200) with Actaeon's sculptured cave (p. 54) and with the construction of Mount Ida in the amphitheater (p. 526).

[15] *The Golden Ass*, p. 421.

and finally the poisoner so pointlessly evil that she is condemned to be torn apart while mating with a beast in public.

In their emphasis on human bestiality, these episodes form
a ghastly parody of Lucius' shape and the experience that
imprisoned him in it, for his theme has broadened under the
light of Cupid and Psyche to include inordinate human desire
in itself (something like the Christian idea of sin as *cupiditas*),
rather than any particular manifestation of it such as curiosity or lust for power. There is no aura of the supernatural or
of magic here, only down-to-earth fabliaux and records of the
horribly immediate operations of the human mind. In keeping
with the severely limited human context, there is an insistent
tone of infernal futility; everything falls of its own weight,
whether it be the little societies which continually disintegrate,
(the stud farm, the bakery, the company of priests), or the
individual histories which all follow a pattern of ironic reversal (the murderer murdered, and so forth). After the tale
of Psyche, the unilluminated life takes on the character of a
pointless cycle of unending revenge, dissolution, and waste.

The reaction of the ass to these experiences is most important. Instead of seeing life with wonderment and fear, he can
view these episodes only with abhorrence—an abhorrence
which both results from and produces a progressive detachment
from the humanly bestial (in contrast to his earlier dumb
involvement). For these events are conducted in the clear and
astringent atmosphere of his instructed sight instead of in the
confused and clouded view of the uninstructed. This clarity
is accompanied by an ethical development in Lucius; he became a moralist immediately after the tale of Psyche, and he
now sees clearly that human life is not endowed with a vague
magic of its own but is a deadly drab affair when left to itself.
Therefore, it is his final refusal to indulge in a bestial act with
a poisoner (in an amphitheater where people mimic the gods
and act like animals) that prepares him for prayer and the
final rewarding vision of the goddess Isis, who alone can transform him back into his human shape. It is in an atmosphere

redolent of spring and the fertile sea that Isis opens to him the full reality that is beyond human sight; in her he recognizes the essential One beyond all particular manifestations of divinity and virtue, and through her he gains knowledge of the providence which stands behind fortune. To know these things is to be truly a man with an accurate vision of his place in the real, and Lucius therefore ends his life as a barrister who leads his quotidian life in the light of the absolute.

In his reactions to the series of analogous tales that proliferate around his, Lucius proceeds from unwitting mimicry, through the "interpenetration" of seeing himself in others, to a detached moral observation of human faults like his own. As he becomes less involved with the circumstances of events, he really becomes *more* fully involved with them mentally; and this development charts his unfolding relation to the absolute— from ignorant suffering under the paradoxical justice meted out to him, through a complex examination of the human condition in himself and a resulting alignment of his view of life with a revelation of the divine, to final direct contact with the divine. It is of crucial importance for early fiction that a satisfactory denouement can come about only by a revealed knowledge of a true idea of humanity in a cosmic context, and that such knowledge can be received only after events have led toward a willingness to see the self in others.

Malory's tale of Balin shows a surprising degree of correspondence with the Latin work produced some thirteen centuries before it. For instance, the tale of Balin uses narrative analogy extensively, but the analogous episodes concern the hero rather than others like him, and are in fact the products of his actions. Therefore he does not observe relations and derive a sense of design from them, but rather discovers by experience the ambiguity of human action in a peculiarly supernatural context; therefore, too, the tale is always pressing toward some mysterious transcendent view of life rather than to a perception of a kind of clear, higher order.

Balin's first act both sets his subsequent adventures in motion and fixes the pattern they are to follow. Balin proves his purity of motive by drawing the sword and thus freeing the damsel from it. But when she asks him to give it back to her, he refuses (after all, doesn't it belong to him by right?); she thereupon reveals the destructive nature of the sword, for with it Balin shall slay the man he most loves. His only response is the terse fatalistic phrase which crops up again and again in his story: "I shall take the aventure."[16] Then, as is doomed to happen time after time throughout his story, the situation in which Balin has involved himself is immediately subjected to a complex series of revaluations as the context of the deed enlarges. The Lady of the Lake appears to accuse the damsel of falsehood, Balin of murder; after Balin refutes the charge and chops off her head for allegedly slaying his mother (thereby losing Arthur's favor), Merlin reveals that the damsel was indeed false, and goes on to prophesy the full self-destruction of Balin. Balin's excess has, we see, led him into an incredibly tangled skein of appearance and reality, good and evil—so tangled, in fact, that death alone can release him from it. He, by his own free act, has set the pattern of his life: hereafter, he will do a deed of sudden justice that seems obviously right in his own eyes, will just as suddenly see the context enlarge itself beyond his narrow personal view to show the opposite, that the deed was in fact wrong; he will then see his action as essentially self-destructive, but will only be able to accept all this as fate, as right though suicidal.

Immediately after Balin's departure from Arthur's court, the orgulous knight Lanceor, who envies his success with the sword, accosts him and forces a combat. He gets his just deserts when Balin slays him with the first blow. But then Lanceor's lady bursts in upon the scene and kills herself for grief. Suddenly the case is altered; even Lanceor was beloved. And the context broadens further, as a dwarf comes to sketch in the social and political implications of the deed (Lanceor was one

[16] *The Works of Sir Thomas Malory*, ed. Eugene Vinaver (London and New York, 1954), p. 47. Cited below as *Malory*.

of Arthur's best knights), King Mark the romantic (Lanceor and his lady were ideally true lovers), and Merlin the supernatural (this deed prefigures the Dolorous Stroke). In this almost impossibly broad context, the deed of self-defense becomes a crime, and Balin is seen to have progressed one step further toward his destined self-destruction; as Merlin says, "thou haste done thyselff grete hurte."[17]

Balin can only accept the consequences and push on to his next analogous adventure, the slaying of the wicked knight Garlon in revenge for his many treacheries at the castle of Garlon's brother Pellem. When Pellem snatches up a weapon and pursues Balin through the castle in revenge, the desperate Balin grabs a spear he finds in a strange room and smites Pellem with it. Immediately "therewith the castell brake roffe and wallis and felle downe to the erthe. And Balyn felle downe and myght nat styrre hande nor foote, and for the moste party of that castell was dede thorow the dolorouse stroke."[18] Three days later Merlin comes to raise him and to reveal that the spear was the spear of Longius, the castle that of the Grail King, and his predestined stroke the means of turning the country into a wasteland that will not be redeemed until the coming of Galahad. His ironic mission completed, Balin rides away a pariah, cursed throughout the countryside for his just deeds. With Garnish of the Mount the pattern asserts itself yet once more. Again we see the seemingly simple act of justice, as Balin shows Garnish his lady embracing another and tells him to kill them. Again, the broader context shows that what seemed to be a good act was really wrong, for Garnish realizes at once the depth of his love and the extent of his remorse and kills himself. Whereas the Dolorous Stroke represented the apex of Balin's destructive urge and actually merged him with his victims in the rubble, with the death of Garnish the action turns more decisively inward on him. All along Balin has done to others what he will soon do to himself

---

[17] *Malory*, p. 54.
[18] *Malory*, p. 64.

—that is, he has bereaved people of their dearest friends—but Garnish is a more obvious victim-double of Balin than the others, for he slays with his own sword the one he loves most and then destroys himself. In accord with this fact, Balin's response for the first time turns from mere fatalistic acceptance to a deeper one; he feels guilt, and steals away from the scene in awe and fear. He seems, moreover, to feel his doom closing in on him, and in his despair is eager for it to descend.

The next and final version of the pattern is the supreme analogue, the fulfillment of the type that has been asserted again and again. Here what had been implicit or metaphorical becomes direct and literal. Whereas before he had pushed a simple, inadequate idea of justice beyond limits, he here deliberately crosses the border that no knight must cross alone; and whereas earlier his self-destruction had been implicit in his destruction of others, now the two are inextricable. Balin has come to see that he, who had thought of himself as the judge, is really the criminal, that the meting out of simple and violent human justice is abominable to the divine; and so, as he hears a horn blow the mort, he remarks to himself, "That blast . . . is blowen for me, for I am the pryse, and yet am I not dede."[19] When the pattern reasserts itself, it is final: Balin mortally wounds a man, then discovers that it is his brother and double Balan and that he himself is fatally wounded.

Each analogous episode of the tale of Balin pushes toward the same point: that when the curtain dividing limited human insight from a fuller view of reality is lifted, human action is revealed to be terribly different from what it seemed, the world more complex and strange than we know. As the episodes proceed serially, ideas of reality are progressively redefined, so that straightforward action is seen first as destructive and then as essentially self-destructive. The pattern is a tragic one, rather like that of *Oedipus*. A man's error in attempting

[19] *Malory*, p. 67.

to push limited human capabilities into realms beyond their normal bounds leads to his self-destruction and the realization that "it is not for no knyght alone to ryde toward this castel." Tragic, too, is the final feeling that when life has been revealed in this new and brighter light it is accepted as both terrible and unfalteringly right, above all as *real*. Malory's tale of Balin, like Apuleius' book, moves toward a new placement of the human, and it works toward its goal by establishing relations both within episodes, by expanding contexts of meaning, and between them, by means of analogy. But it is concerned with pushing contexts always outward toward the absolute without ever reaching it, so that it ends with a vision of life still mysterious, not understood, but felt as right.

So it is with Malory's work as a whole. Recent criticism has relieved us of much of the timidity with which we used, under the watchful eye of Eugene Vinaver, to approach the question of the wholeness of *Le Morte D'Arthur*,[20] and we can now look at the work, as printed by Caxton, as a total design rather than as a collection of short fiction. When we do so, we find a large design analogous to that of Balin's tale. What the coming of Arthur meant to Britain was the superimposition of a human order on the lust and chaos of Uther Pendragon's world; the reign which began at Pentecost was above all a moral order, based on religious values and implemented by force of arms. As this reign spread with the Round Table, it became a civilization. Its human elements increased, and its roots in the sacred became attenuated. It solidified into a secular code where feelings were paramount and social reputation arose as a prime motivating force; the most sophisticated development of the code was of course courtly love, which, in the

[20] See especially *Essays on Malory*, ed. J.A.W. Bennett (Oxford, 1963); *Malory's Originality: A Critical Study of "Le Morte Darthur*," ed. R. M. Lumiansky (Baltimore, 1963); and Charles Moorman, *The Book of Kyng Arthur: The Unity of Malory's "Morte Darthur"* (Lexington, Kentucky, 1965).

person of Lancelot, at once held together the humanistic civilization that produced it and threatened this civilization from within. There is, therefore, an almost Thucydidean sense of the hybristic overextension of an entire civilization when the quest of the Grail comes to test the Round Table: "hit shall nevermore be sene here," says Christ in a vision, "And knowyst thou wherefore? For he ys nat served nother worshipped to hys ryght by hem of thys londe, for they be turned to evyll lyvyng."[21] The coming of the Grail momentarily rends the curtain between the human and the divine. It redefines knighthood as something nearer the priesthood than the warrior's or the courtier's code, redefines the meaning of deeds according not to their temporal results but to their symbolism, what they are in God's eye; and it shows reality to be something irradiated by divine purpose rather than a set of bittersweet human experiences.

The absolute destroys human order in the interest of a superhuman order; it ruins Lancelot, decimates the Round Table, and ends by totally dissolving Arthur's bright civilization. Arthur's response to all this is reminiscent of Balin's and similar to the lady's reaction in "The Cardinal's First Tale." Implicit in this attitude are both horror and a conviction of the rightness of thus placing human action in a divine context:

> "Sertes," seyde the kynge, "we ought to thanke our Lorde Jesu Cryste gretly that he hath shewed us thys day at the reverence of thys hyghe feste of Pentecost". . . . "Alas!" seyde kynge Arthure unto sir Gawayne, "ye have nygh slayne me for the avow that ye have made, for thorow you ye have berauffte me the fayryst and the trewyst of knyghthode that ever was sene togydir in ony realme of the worlde. For whan they departe frome hense I am sure they all shall never mete more togydir in thys worlde, for they shall dye many in the queste."[22]

[21] *Malory*, pp. 735-36.
[22] *Malory*, pp. 634-35.

⟨ II ⟩

Among the several points of similarity between Apuleius and Malory (and Dinesen too), we might single out two as having especial importance for an approach to early fiction. First, both endeavor to relate the human to the nonhuman; it is therefore as important to inspect their worlds of value, their settings, and their implied or explicit concepts of order, as it is to analyze their characters. Second, their main technique for exploring such a relation is analogy, that prime instrument for extending the known into the unknown along the great chain of being. Hence we must be as alive to analogy in early fiction as we are to its use in the multiple plots of Elizabethan drama, and we must be prepared to find analogies of various sorts: between one action and another, between human affairs and the divine, between man and the cosmos in which he operates.

The differences between the two are mainly historical, and we can describe them best in terms of the different apprehensions of the absolute which they reflect. Apuleius shared the intellectual milieu of the Greek romances of the third and fourth centuries, most of which seem to have originated as cult books asserting the power of a particular god or goddess.[23] Both Greek romance and *The Golden Ass* demonstrate the rightness and order of an unintelligible universe by making the movements of blind fortune eventually issue in the triumph of right. The characteristic rhythm of Heliodorus' *Aethiopica* and Achilles Tatius' *Clitophon and Leucippe*—a rhythm of the separation of two lovers and their eventual reunion in a moment closely associated with theophany—both proves the rightness of such a concept of order and gives it a structure. *Daphnis and Chloe* is an especially clear example, since it puts its protagonists into relation with the absolute both directly (by showing that their whole development is foreordained

---

[23] See Moses Hadas, ed., *Three Greek Romances* (New York, 1953), p. 8.

by Eros and carried out by the immanent deities of the earth)
and indirectly (by making them reproduce in their own lives
the maturation cycle of the earth). The seasonal plot structure,
whereby Daphnis and Chloe pass through two cycles of desire
in spring, torment in summer, and fruition in autumn, acts as
a supreme analogue to their self-discovery; and thereby it
defines the true nature of that discovery in the context of this
world's great design.

Whereas classical fiction asserts that "the gods are, order is,"
medieval romance, which depends on a firmly established but
frequently inscrutable God, asks "What is God? What is His
true order?" The progressive revision of ideas of order that
we discovered in Malory can be found in many other works
as well. In Chaucer, we find various forms of it in "The Wife
of Bath's Tale," "The Franklyn's Tale," and most explicitly
in "The Knight's Tale," where Theseus' final speech shows
that apparent injustice is really part of a divine order which
includes both union and separation, love and death, and that
"life's pattern is itself a reflection, or better a reproduction, of
the order of the universe."[24] Similarly, in *Sir Gawayn and the
Grene Knyght* the hero must move out of the self-contained
human society of Arthur's court into the brute nature of its
other-than-human alter ego, the Green Chapel, in order to
realize the necessity for give and take, for including in all
human constructs a sense of the mysterious universe which
both suckles such constructs and antagonizes them. This is
the kind of plot implicit, too, in the successive redefinitions
of Beatrice and Amor in *La Vita Nuova,* or in that strange
work derived from Dante, the *Ameto* of Boccaccio, whose
hero discovers that what he received as erotic excitement was
really an education in the seven virtues, and that, in a life
redefined as symbolic, Venus is the symbol of the trinity.

The characteristic action of classical fiction began when
the protagonist was driven off his intended course by a storm

[24] Charles Muscatine, "Form, Texture, and Meaning in Chaucer's
Knight's Tale," *PMLA*, LXV (1950), 920.

or some other nonhuman force, that of medieval fiction when the knight issued forth from his castle into some unknown realm of nature. The action of Renaissance fiction begins when the hero accepts a concept. For in a Renaissance world reoriented toward ideals by the Humanists (a process which in Renaissance Neoplatonism ended by making the absolute seem an "It" instead of a "Thou"), and thus generally tending to replace metaphysics with ethics and to stress virtuous action as the end of life,[25] the central questions change to "What is the true Idea of humankind? What ideals of human conduct are valid?" And we have a mode of fiction which submits ideas of value or order to the test of experience. It is in the light of their responses to ideas—and their techniques for conveying such responses—that we shall therefore examine the major writers of Renaissance English fiction.

[25] See, e.g., Hiram Haydn, *The Counter-Renaissance* (New York, 1950), pp. 51-64; and Eugene F. Rice, Jr., *The Renaissance Idea of Wisdom*, Harvard Historical Monographs, XXXVI (Cambridge, Mass., 1958), Chap. 6: "The Transformation of Wisdom from Knowledge to Virtue."

CHAPTER 2

Acting Out Ideas in Sidney's Theory

The *Defence of Poesie* is of unique importance to the study of Renaissance English fiction, because it alone of the Elizabethan critical treatises squarely faces the problem of imaginative fiction. "It is not ryming and versing that maketh a Poet . . . but it is that faining notable images of vertues, vices, or what els, with that delightfull teaching, which must be the right describing note to know a Poet by" (10-11),[1] Sidney wrote, and he insisted that prose romances such as Heliodorus' *Aethiopica* and *Amadis de Gaula* were as truly poems as was the *Aeneid*. For Sidney, poetry was fiction, an activity "distinct from history on the one hand and from lying on the other."[2] Therefore he did not, as did Lodge and most of his codefenders of poetry, conceive of fiction as a lie that covers truth like a cloak or veil, so that "under the person of Aeneas in Virgil the practice of a diligent captaine" may be discerned.[3] Rather, since the essential business of the poet is simply the creation of those fictions called lies, truth is found within the lie—if that is what it is— by looking at it directly rather than by peeking under it: "wisdom and temperance in *Ulisses* and *Diomedes,* valure in *Achilles,* friendship in *Nisus* and *Eurialus*" (15).[4] The value of poetry or fiction resides in itself, not in something it points to; and Sidney tried to show that this was so by stripping from the concept of "feigning" the associations of lying or cloaking the truth, by restoring to it its original meaning of

[1] Parenthetical references are to Albert Feuillerat's edition of *The Defence of Poesie,* in *The Prose Works of Sir Philip Sidney* (4 vols.; 2nd printing; Cambridge, 1962), Vol. III.

[2] C. S. Lewis, *English Literature in the Sixteenth Century* (Oxford, 1954), p. 319.

[3] Thomas Lodge, *Defence of Poetry,* in *Elizabethan Critical Essays,* ed. G. Gregory Smith (2 vols.; Oxford, 1904), I, 65.

[4] For this contrast between "under" and "in," see A. C. Hamilton, *The Structure of Allegory in The Faerie Queene* (Oxford, 1961), p. 22.

"making,"[5] and by demonstrating what such making meant.

Just how high Sidney's claims for poetry are, and just how great a task he sets for the architectonic science, can be seen only by close attention to certain key passages in the *Defence*. First, his formal definition of poetry, which initially seems a typical Renaissance conflation of Aristotle, Horace, and Plutarch:[6] "*Poesie* therefore, is an Art of *Imitation:* for so *Aristotle* termeth it in the word μίμησις, that is to say, a representing, counterfeiting, or figuring forth to speake Metaphorically. A speaking *Picture*, with this end to teach and delight" (9). But what is unusual about such a definition is that Sidney, in his care to define and redefine the act of mimesis, fails to specify just what it is that the poet imitates. And his successive rephrasings move yet further from the idea of copying, toward the idea of producing an affective image. To put the act of figuring forth in these terms is to give it such preeminence as to make it nearly autonomous; and, in fact, it is Sidney's purpose here to show "how high and incomparable a title" the name of "a Maker" is. As Arthur Barker writes, "his definition of poetry (or proposition) does not tell us precisely what poetry imitates: we have to find that out for ourselves from reading his full defence responsively."[7] Of course there must be an object of imitation, no matter how little Sidney chose to tell us of it in his definition. What is it? Is it men in action, as in the original *Poetics*? Or is it nature, as in the commonly

---

[5] Robert J. Clements has shown how the verb *fingere*, which originally was merely a translation of "ποιεῖν," "to make," had acquired by the time of Vida the connotation of "veiling or cloaking": *The Peregrine Muse: Studies in Comparative Renaissance Literature* (Chapel Hill, N.C., 1959), pp. 7-8. See also C. M. Dowlin, "Sidney's Two Definitions of Poetry," *Modern Language Quarterly*, III (1942), 579-80.

[6] On the prevalence of such conflations, see Bernard Weinberg, *A History of Literary Criticism in the Italian Renaissance* (2 vols.; Chicago, 1961), I, 139.

[7] Arthur E. Barker, "An Apology for the Study of Renaissance Poetry," in Carroll Camden, ed., *Literary Views: Critical and Historical Essays* (Chicago, 1964), p. 39; see also Hamilton, p. 24.

received Renaissance generalization of Aristotle (for instance, in Hamlet's "the purpose of playing . . . is to hold, as 't were, the mirror up to nature") ? By no means; it turns out that the object of poetic imitation does not exist in nature at all, but only in the mind of the poet. Poetry becomes, for Sidney, the animation of a Platonic Idea: "La mimesi in Sidney ha una netta impronta neo-platonica, è neo-platonizzata, e, intanto, essa sempre supero l'oggeto, l'oggetto imitato, per un impulso che le imprime l'Idea, una figura di perfezione e di assolu-tezza."[8]

This fact comes out explicitly in a passage where Sidney lists the arts which, he says, all have nature for their object: "There is no Art delivered unto mankind that hath not the workes of nature for his principall object." The astronomer, the arithmetician, the natural philosopher, the musician, the moral philosopher, the historian, the grammarian, the logician "compassed within the circle of a question," the physician, even the metaphysician, are merely "Actors & Plaiers, as it were of what nature will have set forth." But this is not true of the poet: "Onely the Poet disdeining to be tied to any such subjection, lifted up with the vigor of his own invention, doth grow in effect into an other nature: in making things either better then nature bringeth foorth, or quite a newe . . . so as he goeth hand in hand with nature, not enclosed within the narrow warrant of her gifts, but freely raunging within the Zodiack of his owne wit" (8). The last image in the passage is not merely the microcosmic commonplace of Elizabethan thought. It goes further, implying that if there is a microcosm of the mind, this is enough. The mind contains all that the poet needs of nature. Or, again, "to imitate [poets]

---

[8] Luciano Anceschi, *L'Estetica dell' empirismo inglese*, I, *Da Bacone a Shaftesbury* (Bologna, 1959), 21. For Platonic and Neoplatonic strains in the *Defence*, see Lewis, pp. 318-22; Hamilton, pp. 15-29; Dowlin, passim; and the two following studies: Irene Samuel, "The Influence of Plato on Sir Philip Sidney's *Defense of Poesy*," *Modern Language Quarterly*, I (1940), 383-91, and F. M. Krouse, "Plato and Sidney's *Defence of Poesie*," *Comparative Literature*, VI (1954), 138-47.

borrow nothing of what is, hath bin, or shall be, but range onely reined with learned discretion, into the divine consideration of what may be and should be" (10). What is possible: this is the object of imitation, and this is found in the universe of the poet's mind. Sidney here asserts, in contradiction to Plato, that the poet *does* perceive Ideas, and that he has them within his mind ready to send them forth as images of reality. They come to the poet by inspiration from God, who "creates *ex nihilo* and contains the Ideas within Himself,"[9] and who, in the most daring passage of the *Defence,* is made not only the sponsor but the type of the poet:

> Neither let it be deemed too sawcy a comparison, to ballance the highest point of mans wit, with the efficacie of nature: but rather give right honor to the heavenly maker of that maker, who having made man to his owne likenes, set him beyond and over all the workes of that second nature, which in nothing he sheweth so much as in Poetry; when with the force of a divine breath, he bringeth things foorth surpassing her doings. (8-9)[10]

Poetry is totally Platonic: Platonic in its origins, since it goes beyond Nature to Ideas for imitation, and Platonic in its status, since it mediates between Ideas of things as they should be and the material, things as they are. But it is Christian too, for the poet as a little God not only possesses and shows Ideas, but he bodies them forth, he creates, in word and image, flesh for the divine Idea. And it is noteworthy that Sidney does not mean "Incarnation" only figuratively. The poet and God are both makers, yes; but further, their creations both have real substance. He handles the implication by comparing the poet

[9] Hamilton, p. 25.

[10] For the analogy between the poet as maker and God, see, e.g., Puttenham, *The Arte of English Poesie,* ed. Gladys Doidge Willcock and Alice Walker (Cambridge, 1936), p. 3; Paolo Beni, quoted by Baxter Hathaway in *The Age of Criticism: The Late Renaissance in Italy* (Ithaca, 1962), p. 21; and Guarini, in *Literary Criticism: Plato to Dryden,* ed. Allen H. Gilbert (New York, 1940), p. 506.

to *Natura naturans:* "Neither let this be jestingly conceived, bicause the works of the one [Nature] be essenciall, the other in imitation or fiction: for everie understanding, knoweth the skill of ech Artificer standeth in that *Idea,* or fore conceit of the worke, and not in the worke it selfe. And that the Poet hath that *Idea,* is manifest, by delivering them foorth in such excellencie as he had imagined them" (8).

So far, this amounts to little more than an assertion of the truth of the imagination. But Sidney continues: "which delivering foorth, also is not wholly imaginative, as we are wont to say by them that build Castles in the aire: but so farre substancially it worketh, not onely to make a *Cyrus,* which had bene but a particular excellency as nature might have done, but to bestow a *Cyrus* upon the world to make many *Cyrusses.*" Poetry thus completes the analogy with the original creation by reproducing in each kind. The vision of the good ruler in poetry gives birth to good rulers; a prince, seeing the image or Idea of the good ruler in Cyrus, loves it, and strives to make himself conform to this pattern.

Sidney means all this soberly. When he avers, after comparing the poet to God, that "these arguments will by few be understood, and by fewer graunted," and proceeds to "a more ordinarie opening" of poetry, we perhaps expect him to diminish his claims. But he does nothing of the sort; he merely restates them in a more logical manner with more temperate diction. His division of poets into religious, philosophical, and "right Poets," the purpose of the latter being merely to "make to imitate," reestablishes stress on the pure act of *making* in itself. Again, the difference between the maker and the other poets is like the earlier distinction between the other arts and poetry: pure fictive poetry has no object in nature. While the other poets "counterfeit onely such faces as are set before them," the right poets, "having no law but wit, bestow that in colours upon you, which is fittest for the eye to see"—and that is "what may be and should be" (10). Poetry's "incarnation" of the Idea in an image is here presented through an analogy not with the divine, but with the painter who "painteth not *Lucre-tia* whom he never saw, but painteth the outward bewty of such a vertue." It is in this way that the visionary maker of poetry combines in himself the two functions suggested by the Greek and Roman names for him: the poet makes in the world of matter an image of what he envisions as *vates* or prophet.[11] Here, too, the reproductions or births which the created work of poetry yields receive concrete definition: poetry, by creating a Cyrus, teaches men "to take that goodnes in hande" by delight in it. Sidney closes his "more ordinarie" section on definition and division by rephrasing the original definition in such a way as to gather up many of the implications we have explored. It is, he says, "that faining notable images of vertues, vices, or what els, with that delightfull teaching, which must be the right describing note to know a Poet by" (11). "Imitation" has become the embodiment of Ideas, "faining notable images" of virtues and vices.

Sidney's claims for poetry or fiction—in both his visionary and his ordinary version—are high indeed. But if we go on to his weighing of the poet's, the philosopher's, and the historian's works, we see that these claims are made not so much for poetry in isolation but for poetry as the chief arm of wisdom, which is entrusted with an enterprise of great moment. For Sidney shares the common Renaissance assumption that it is the task of wisdom to repair the harm done by the fall of man; it must restore man, so far as possible, to the state of original justice, or threefold subjection of the body to the soul, the lower soul to the rational soul, and the whole man to God.[12] In a passage remarkable for its rondo structure, Sidney redefines successively the position of wisdom after the fall.

[11] See John Buxton, *Sir Philip Sidney and the English Renaissance* (London, 1954), p. 4: "Sidney describes the poet as a combination of *vates*, divinely inspired seer, and poet, or maker."

[12] A. L. Soens, in the introduction to his forthcoming edition of *The Defence of Poesie* (University of Nebraska Press), attributes this concept of the end of poetry to the Pléiade, especially Du Bellay and L'Hospital; see, e.g., Du Bellay, *L'Olive*, CXII.

First: "This purifying of wit, this enriching of memorie, enabling of judgement, and enlarging of conceit, which commonly we cal learning, . . . to what immediate end soever it be directed, the finall end is, to lead and draw us to as high a perfection, as our degenerate soules made worse by their clay-lodgings, can be capable of" (11). In the second appearance of the theme, the denigration of the body is reduced and the whole process is presented more optimistically: "to knowe, & by knowledge to lift up the minde from the dungeon of the bodie, to the enjoying his owne divine essence." And, in the last statement, it appears that man can reascend to God by his own virtuous action after his mind has been irradiated by wisdom: "so yet are they all directed to the highest end of the mistresse knowledge, by the Greeks ἀρχιτεκτονικη, which stands as I thinke, in the knowledge of a mans selfe, in the Ethicke and Politique consideration, with the end of well doing, and not of well knowing onely . . . . the ending end of all earthly learning, being verteous action" (11-12). To know yourself is to know your own divine essence, which we may identify with the Idea of mankind; and virtuous action is the means by which you put yourself in phase with such an Idea of your nature. The task set before the architectonic knowledge, then, is that of twofold purification, operating on both the intellective and the appetitive parts of the rational soul: first, a purification of the wit or understanding by showing it true good and evil; second, a purification of the will by moving it to follow the good and avoid the evil.[13] The dual aim appears again and again in Sidney's discussion of man and wisdom: "our erected wit . . . and . . . our infected wil"; "to move men to take that goodnesse in hande . . . and teach to make them know that goodnesse whereunto they are moved." And, of course, his aim in this section of the discourse is to prove that poetry both teaches the good and moves men toward it more effectively than either philosophy or history: "as vertue is the

[13] See Barker, p. 40: "'Poetry energizes the will . . . but it does so by irradiating the mind in all its rational powers.'"

most excellent resting place for al worldly learning to make his end of, so *Poetry,* being the most familiar to teach it, and most Princely to move towards it, in the most excellent worke, is the most excellent workeman" (21–22).

How does the fiction of poetry teach the good more effectively than either the precepts of philosophy or the records of history? In a comic debate modeled on the pastoral singing match where the moderator steals the prize from both contenders, Sidney awards the laurel to the poet for the same reason Aristotle did: poetry avoids the pitfalls of both philosophy, which presents principles abstractly and not vividly, and history, which shows the mere unprincipled concrete. Poetry is more concrete than philosophy, more philosophical than history, for it synthesizes both; it is, in a word, the concrete universal. But Sidney's is a peculiar form of the concrete universal, since for him the universal is real, the realm of Ideas. The poem is therefore not so much the concrete example of a universal phenomenon as it is the concrete image of a universal Idea. Therefore, when he handles Aristotle's statement about the universal in literature (16), he gradually shifts from "what is fit to be said or done, either in likelihood or necessitie" to the matter "as it should be" to "a perfect patterne" or Idea rather like "the example or the Idea of the true prince" which Fabrini found prescribed in Horace.[14] For the Platonist, material reality, and therefore a poem expressing it, is the image of an Idea: "Still the arts are not to be slighted on the ground that they create by imitation of natural objects; for, to begin with, these natural objects are themselves imitations; then, we must recognize that they give no bare reproduction of the thing seen but go back to the Reason-Principle from which Nature itself derives."[15] Occasionally Renaissance critics

[14] Giovanni Fabrini, *L'Opere d'Oratio* (1556), pp. 380v-81; quoted by Weinberg, I, 181.

[15] *Enneads* V.viii.1, trans. Stephen McKenna in the third edition of his *Plotinus,* rev. B. S. Page (New York, n.d.); cited by C. S. Lewis, p. 320.

used Plotinus' insight to build a definition of poetry as the explicit imitation of Ideas. This is the case with Ronsard, for instance: "l'invention n'est autre chose que le bon naturel d'une imagination concevant les Idées & formes de toutes choses qui se peuvent imaginer tant cellestes que terrestres, animées ou inanimées, pour apres les represent, descrir, & imiter";[16] or Agnolo Segni, in a passage that comes very close to Sidney's: "Poetry joins the one part and the other [history and philosophy], recounting things past or present, not as they are or were, but similar to their Ideas, and showing the Ideas not in themselves, but in things which have been and things which are."[17] And one finds similar statements in Tomitano, Maggi and Lombardi, and Giacomini.[18]

Moreover, Renaissance thinkers frequently merged the Aristotelian universal and the Platonic Idea as Sidney did. Thus Tasso wrote that "the poet does not spoil truth, but he seeks it in a perfect form, supposing in place of the truth of particulars that of universals, which are Ideas";[19] and Fracastoro explained that while other writers imitate the particulars, the poet "imitates not the particular but the simple idea clothed in its own beauties, which Aristotle calls the universal."[20] It was, in fact, usual for the Italian critics—such as Capriano, Segni, and Buonamici—to assume, casually, the identity of universals and Ideas.[21] Thus, if poetry is more concrete than philosophy and more philosophical than history, it is because

---

[16] *Abbregé de l'Art poëtique françois*, in *Oeuvres complètes*, ed. Paul Laumonier (17 vols.; Paris, 1914-60), XIV, 12-13.

[17] *Ragionamento sopra le cose pertinenti alla Poetica* (1581), pp. 65-66; quoted by Weinberg, I, 31.

[18] See *ibid.*, I, 265, 270, and 323, respectively.

[19] *Apologia . . . in difesa della sua Gerusalemme Liberata*, quoted by Weinberg, II, 1011-12; see also Weinberg's comment on Tasso's Platonism in I, 341.

[20] *Naugerius, sive de Poetica Dialogus*, trans. Ruth Kelso, University of Illinois Studies in Language and Literature, IX, 3 (Urbana, 1924), 60.

[21] See Hathaway's discussion of this phenomenon, in *The Age of Criticism*, pp. 138-43.

it, like the world of created nature, is an image of an Idea. For Sidney, the concrete is the image.

The image achieves considerable importance in Sidney's theory of poetry. He constantly employs Plutarch's concept of the poem as image or picture: "a speaking picture," "faining notable images," "a perfect picture," "pictures what should be," "painting men," "figuring forth good things," "see those beasts well painted." It enters his *Defence* preeminently when he is illustrating the possibilities which poetry teaches: "*effigium justi imperii,* the pourtraiture of a just Empyre under the name of *Cyrus*," "that picture of love in *Theagenes* and *Chariclea*," "the lofty image of such worthies most inflammeth the mind with desire to be worthy," "let but *Sophocles* bring you *Ajax* on a stage," "*Vespacians* Picture," "the tale of *Turnus* having planted his image in the imagination." Now, the image is important to Sidney first of all because it is clear, exact, and striking. Thus the poet "yeeldeth to the powers of the minde an image of that whereof the *Philosopher* bestoweth but a wordish description, which doth neither strike, pearce, nor possesse the sight of the soule so much, as that other doth" (14). The image is also transcendent because it is unbounded, and proliferates meanings which the discursive reason cannot hope to encompass. Plotinus wrote:

> . . . the wise of Egypt . . . indicated the truth where, in their effort towards philosophical statement, they left aside the writing-forms that take in the detail of words and sentences —those characters that represent sounds and convey the propositions of reasoning—and drew pictures instead, engraving in the temple-inscriptions a separate image for every separate item: thus they exhibited the absence of discursiveness in the Intellectual Realm.[22]

Hence, for Dionysius, Plotinus, Ficino, Christoforo Giarda, and others the image was closely associated with the divine;[23]

---

[22] *Enneads* V.viii.6.
[23] See E. H. Gombrich, *"Icones Symbolicae*: The Visual Image in

even Ben Jonson wrote that "Picture is the invention of
heaven, the most ancient and most akin to nature."[24] The
vision of the mystic was not verbal; the divinely inspired
dream came through the gate of the eye, not the ear;[25] the
hieroglyphs and symbols of the divine mysteries were images
to be decoded by the reason in words; the angels know by
image, intuitive knowledge proceeding directly by sight rather
than being gained by reason and words as is discursive knowledge. The sight was therefore at the top of the hierarchy of
the senses in the works of Ficino, Castiglione, and practically
every other Renaissance author.

The fact that the image is both clear and transcendent explains its preeminence for Sidney's theory. For the image,
while it embodies the Idea in concrete form, also leads the
mind from the concrete to the Idea. Moreover, in the act of
receiving an image the intellectual and the emotional are inseparable. Sidney writes that the grounds of wisdom "lie darke
before the imaginative and judging power, if they bee not
illuminated or figured forth by the speaking picture of *Poesie*"
(14), and to illuminate is both to make clear and to move. As
Hamilton writes, "Sidney defines the work of the right poet
in terms of the *image* which can move our infected will."[26]
This fact helps to explain the manner in which poetry accomplishes the second great task of the architectonic science, the
purification of the will in order to move men to strive for
perfection. Obviously, the second purpose of poetry, to delight
as well as teach, takes care of this:

> For hee doth not onely shew the way, but giveth so sweete
> a prospect into the way, as will entice anie man to enter into
> it: Nay he doth as if your journey should lye through a faire

---

Neo-Platonic Thought," *Journal of the Warburg and Courtauld In-
stitutes*, XI (1948), 163-92; see also Tasso, in *Literary Criticism*, ed.
Gilbert, p. 476.

[24] *Timber or Discoveries*, ed. R. S. Walker (Syracuse, 1953), p. 34.
[25] See Hathaway, p. 383.
[26] Hamilton, p. 26 (italics mine).

vineyard, at the verie first, give you a cluster of grapes, that full of that taste, you may long to passe further . . . . hee commeth to you with words set in delightfull proportion, either accompanied with, or prepared for the well enchanting skill of *Musicke,* and with a tale forsooth he commeth unto you, with a tale, which holdeth children from play, and olde men from the Chimney corner; and pretending no more, doth intend the winning of the minde from wickednes to vertue. (19–20)

It is by involving men's actions in their perception of the ideal that the poet moves them to desire what they see. And his chief means for doing this is the image. Imagery, the figuring forth of Ideas in flesh, both teaches clearly and moves men toward that which is so brilliantly presented to their perception.

To realize this is to dispel a misunderstanding about Sidney's concept of delighting. It sometimes seems as though Sidney's is the sugar-coated-pill theory into which the Horatian tradition frequently descended, as when he compares the poem to rhubarb hidden in sweets. But this is not really so. The function of delight is to make one seek out the good he sees in a poem; it does not precede the teaching, but operates along with it to propel man toward the good of wisdom.[27] For poets "imitate both to delight & teach, and delight to move men to take that goodnesse in hand, which without delight they would flie as from a stranger; and teach to make them know that goodnesse whereunto they are moved" (10). There is no teaching without delight, for that would fail to operate effectively on the desire for the good. And there is no delight without teaching, for that would reduce delight to a tickle in

[27] Harry Berger puts the matter differently, but comes to a similar conclusion when he writes of the sugar-coated-pill metaphor: "Where medieval theories of art are always conjunctive—pleasure *plus* profit— or disjunctive—pleasure, ornament, vividness *here,* allegory, philosophy, theology, worship *there*—the enlightened Renaissance understanding of the metaphor is *profit inside pleasure*" ("The Renaissance Imagination: Second World and Green World," *The Centennial Review of Arts and Science,* IX [1965], 43).

the ribs—and a tickling in the ribs it is not, as Sidney's interesting distinction between the delightful and the laughable insists. Delight and knowledge of the good are, in fact, inseparable. We must notice what Sidney classifies as delightful: "words set in delightfull proportion," or harmony.

> . . . delight wee scarcely doo, but in thinges that have a conveniencie to our selves, or to the generall nature: Laughter almost ever commeth of thinges moste disproportioned to our selves, and nature. Delight hath a joy in it either permanent or present. Laughter hath onely a scornfull tickling. (40)

Proportion, order (the chief value of numerous verse), the permanent: what gives delight is, of course, beauty. And, for the Platonist, the good is the center of the circle whose circumference is beauty. What moves men, in short, is delight in beauty, the outward form of the good which teaches them. Just as the image which is the poem combines the cognitive and the emotive, so teaching and moving, knowing and delighting, are inseparable.

An analogy to poetry suggests itself in these terms, and it comes to the surface in the sentence following the one we last quoted: "For example, wee are ravished with delight to see a faire woman, and yet are farre from beeing mooved to laughter." Sidney often speaks of poetry in the same terms as those in which Ficino, Benivieni, and Castiglione speak of love: it is the power that draws men out of their bodies toward the divine Idea of the good by the impact of beauty. Thus David, in Sidney's terms, "sheweth himselfe a passionate lover of that unspeakable and everlasting bewtie, to be seene by the eyes of the mind" (7). The "grounds of wisdom . . . lie darke before the imaginative and judging power, if they bee not illuminated or figured forth by the speaking picture of *Poesie*" (14), just as in love, according to Plotinus, "that beauty is dead until it take the light of The Good, and the soul lies supine, cold to all, unquickened even to Intellectual-Principle there before it.

But when there enters into it a glow from the divine, it gathers strength, awakens, spreads true wings."[28] Poetry is able to "lift up the minde from the dungeon of the bodie, to the enjoying his owne divine essence" (11), just as love makes the soul turn "to the beholding of her owne substance, as it were raised out of a most deepe sleepe, openeth the eyes that all men have, and few occupie, and seeth in her selfe a shining beame of that light which is the true image of the Angelick beautie partened with her."[29] Or, more directly, Sidney says that fiction operates thus: "who could see vertue, woulde bee woonderfullie ravished with the love of her bewty," which poetry shows forth (25). Poetry is, therefore, like love in its being and operation. It exists, like love, as intermediary between the concretely actual and the Idea; it acts, like love, to draw men from the actual to the Idea. It is, in short, the mediator of two worlds.

The concept of the mediate position of poetry helps to make better sense of a frequently misunderstood passage in the *Defence*:

> Now, for the *Poet,* he nothing affirmeth, and therefore never lieth: for as I take it, to lie, is to affirme that to bee true, which is false. . . . But the *Poet* as I said before, never affirmeth, the *Poet* never maketh any Circles about your imagination, to conjure you to beleeve for true, what he writeth: he citeth not authorities of other histories, but even for his entrie, calleth the sweete *Muses* to inspire unto him a good invention. In troth, not laboring to tel you what is, or is not, but what should, or should not be. (29)

At first glance, this passage seems to be an adumbration of I. A. Richards' "pseudo-statement"; but it is not exactly that, for there is more than an emotional assent involved, and the poet's statement is characterized as more prescriptive than

[28] *Enneads* VI.vii.22.
[29] *The Book of the Courtier*, trans. Sir Thomas Hoby (London: Everyman's Library, 1928), pp. 318-19.

descriptive. What Sidney is doing in this passage (as elsewhere in his fight to distinguish fiction from fact on the one
hand and from lying on the other) is attempting to define
the kind of statement fiction, as the presentation of an Idea or
ideal *as if* it were actual, makes. The reader is to believe in the
reality of the fictive image but not in its actuality, and his best
response will be to make the real and the actual coincide in
his own life. The golden fictional world, Barker writes, "in-
duces the reader to imitate the poet's effort, through which
he 'doth grow in effect into another nature'. . . . That other
nature is, as Sidney implies elsewhere, human nature as it
ought to be and might be but in this world is never likely
quite to be; but it is the process of effort in time that matters."[30]
The "patterns" of a Cyrus or an Achilles force men to make
them real; it is for this reason that, Sidney asserts, the feigned
Cyrus as he should be is more valuable than the supposedly
real Cyrus in Justin, the feigned Aeneas of Virgil better than
the real Aeneas in Dares Phrygius.

Therefore, when Sidney discusses the various kinds of poetry,
what he stresses is the way they offer different potential images
of life. Each of the genres, he shows us, holds up for our edification an image of the possible perfection or imperfection
of existence. A few of the genres—notably the Pindaric lyric
and the heroic—are exemplary, and present us with ideals to
follow. Many of the others operate more indirectly and more
interestingly upon us. The satiric, for instance, makes a man
laugh at folly and hence at himself, unless he avoids folly.
Comedy shows error in such a ridiculous way "so as it is impossible that any beholder can be content to be such a one"
(23). By doing so it implements self-knowledge, since nothing
can better open a man's eyes "then to see his owne actions
contemptibly set forth." The various literary genres, Sidney
insists, present rather than affirm; through them, "wee get as
it were an experience" (23). A man sees himself by placing
himself potentially in a feigned notable image of humility or

[30] Barker, p. 41.

greatness or folly or wickedness or tyranny. He then either
seeks or avoids this image in his own life, thus either consent-
ing or refusing to make that image real. We come to know
ourselves by seeing our relation to an image of an Idea of
humanity.

Fiction thus becomes hypothesis, an intellectual construct
exhibiting greater clarity, simplicity, and unity than we observe in experience. It does not pretend to be a depiction of
the actual, yet it claims intense relevance, since through it we
explore and even change the actual. Harry Berger terms the
hypothetical world created by Renaissance fiction a "hetero-
cosm" or second world, which is "potentially an image of
either or both" the actual and the ideal.[31] More's "Utopia,"
for example, is an image of neither the actual Europe of
More's day nor a purely ideal state, but rather something in
between, a "possible-ideal" of the better place Europe might
become.[32] Berger finds that "the hypothetical or imaginary
kosmoi posited by the mind" become increasingly important
intellectual tools in the sixteenth and seventeenth centuries,[33]
important not only (or even chiefly) for literature, but for the
social and physical sciences as well—for Castiglione's Urbino,
Gilbert's magnetic terella, Copernicus' hypothetical world system, Bacon's model-world of the mind, for example. The
Renaissance, in fact, explored the actual world by creating
hypothetical worlds.

Fiction that faces such a task can be of many kinds. Open
any book of Renaissance fiction, and the variety and relevance
of its ways of developing hypotheses become apparent. A story
can itself imitate, for example, the process of working by
hypothesis, as in the sixth tale of Barnabe Riche's *Riche his*

[31] Berger, p. 49.

[32] See H. A. Mason, *Humanism and Poetry in the Early Tudor
Period* (London, 1959), p. 126.

[33] Berger, p. 45. See his entire discussion of hypothetical thinking,
pp. 36-52; Hathaway, p. 308; and also E.M.W. Tillyard's brief discussion of "the Elizabethan hovering between equivalence and metaphor" in *The Elizabethan World Picture* (London, 1943), p. 92.

Farewell to Militarie Profession (1581), where Gonsales explicitly puts a set of inherited precepts to the test. A story can contain in its own action an analogue to the effect Sidney imagined the fictional hypotheses to have: in Riche's third tale, Lucilla's exhibition of the Idea of chastity in her person changes Don Hercules from lecher to benefactor, and in the fourth tale the ideal love of Fineo and Fiamma has a similar effect on the king of Tunis.[34] A different approach to the same kind of thing can be seen in the plot of the court masque, wherein, for example, the newly married couple can see acted out on the stage the Idea of marriage embodied in a myth, the hope being that they will then act out this Idea in their own lives. Such fiction may present images of virtue or vice directly or indirectly; it may present a more or less ordinary man becoming, or failing to become, a kind of ideal image. It may represent an ideal world, or a series of worlds hierarchically arranged according to whether they veer toward the actual or the ideal, as in *The Faerie Queene* or *Utopia*. In any case, such fiction will remain as close to Ideas, ideals, or ideas as to actions; and it will thus, instead of rendering for us the probabilities of life as we know it, attempt to enlarge our sense of the possibilities of life. It will dwell in the various areas of contact between things as they are and things as they might be, and it will end by presenting to our minds some potential adjustment between the two.

Sidney's thesis, in sum, is that to make fiction is to feign notable images, and that feigning is equivalent to presenting an image of the possible. By casting his emphasis on this process, Sidney points out the exploratory rather than the imitative function of fiction; he makes us see that fiction can be an act of speculation, an excursion into the realm of what is possible in human existence.

[34] These three tales are all adaptations from Cinthio's *Gli Hecatommithi* (1565), from III,5; VI,3; and II,6, respectively; see *Rich's Farewell to Military Profession*, ed. Thomas Mabry Cranfill (Austin, Texas, 1959), p. xxii.

⟨ II ⟩

If the end of fiction as the Elizabethans conceived it was to discover the area of contact between the ideal and the actual in life, then one of the most important means by which such a "fore-conceit" issued into actual narrative was a peculiarly strong sense of role-playing. For whatever the causes—"oral residue" or a sense of the spoken word behind the written word,[35] or traditions of oratory like the "ethical" appeal—we find common to much Elizabethan poetry and prose the sense that to write is essentially to speak, to speak essentially to act out a part. Such a histrionic sense of writing can be found in Sidney's *Defence of Poesie,* for example, which is conceived as an oration by a speaker who is capable of a whole range of vocal tones;[36] but it is most prominent in the pamphleteers.

L. C. Knights posits that the popular pamphleteer was, first and foremost, not an expositor, much less a dialectician, but rather an entertainer or an actor: "popular writing is largely, like verbal fencing, an exhibition of skill, and the writer, like an improvisator on the stage, takes care to call attention to a particular display of agility."[37] Thus the speaker's sense of himself often causes him to burst out in self-encouragement, self-gratulation, scornful triumph, even glee: "Py, hy, hy, hy! I cannot but laugh, Py, hy, hy, hy, hy! I cannot but laugh to think that an old soaking student in this learned age is not ashamed to be so impudent."[38] Such a sense of the self naturally leads to a close relation to the audience, and in reading "Martin Marprelate" or Nashe we often feel that the author is

[35] See Walter J. Ong, S.J., "Oral Residue in Tudor Prose Style," *PMLA,* LXXX (1965), 145-54; for the general background of oral and visual approaches to style, see Marshall McLuhan, *The Gutenberg Galaxy: The Making of Typographic Man* (Toronto, 1962).

[36] See Kenneth Orne Myrick, *Sir Philip Sidney as a Literary Craftsman* (Cambridge, Mass., 1935), Chap. II.

[37] "Elizabethan Prose," in *Drama and Society in the Age of Jonson* (London, 1937), p. 311.

[38] "Martin Marprelate," *Hay Any Worke for Cooper,* in *The Marprelate Tracts,* ed. W. Pierce (London, 1911), p. 217.

addressing us directly, the way a clown on the stage might. He will turn suddenly from his matter to fire a question at a member of the audience—"And what say you Boyes, the flatteringest hope of your moothers, to a *Porch of Panim Pilfryes, Pestred with Prayses*"; to communicate an ironic confidence— "Harke in your care, hee had a very faire Cloake with sleeves, of a grave goose turd greene; it would serve you as fine as may bee"; to twit him in an aside—"Gentle Readers (looke you be gentle now since I have cald you so)"; or to demand an opinion—"My masters, you may conceave of me what you list, but I thinke confidently I was ordained Gods scourge from above for their daintie finicalitie."[39] He is always beside us, answering our questions, inviting our comments, telling us to question, to laugh, to weep, to applaud.

When a pamphleteer confronts his audience this directly, he is assuming a fictional situation, setting a scene, arranging an audience, and adopting a mask. In short, he conceives of himself as an actor deliberately playing a role: "Hollow there, give me the beard I wore yesterday. O beware of a gray beard, and a balde head: for if such a one doo but nod, it is right dudgin and deepe discretion. But soft, I must now make a grave speach."[40] Some writers concentrated on scenario: in the Marprelate pamphlets the scene is usually a street where Martin, the homely wit, has come upon one of his opponents, Bridges or Cooper, and starts to berate him. The readers are the spectators of the confrontation, which may at any moment develop from flyting into fisticuffs: "And hold my cloak, there, somebody, that I may go roundly to work."[41] Others concen-

[39] Gabriel Harvey, *Pierces Supererogation*, in *The Works of Gabriel Harvey*, ed. Alexander B. Grosart (3 vols.; London: The Huth Library, 1884-85), II, 276; Thomas Nashe, *Strange Newes, Of the Intercepting Certaine Letters*, in *The Works of Thomas Nashe*, ed. Ronald B. McKerrow and reprinted with supplements by F. P. Wilson (5 vols.; Oxford, 1958), I, 288; Nashe, *The Unfortunate Traveller, Works*, II, 217 and 226.

[40] *Pappe with an Hatchet*, in *The Complete Works of John Lyly*, ed. R. Warwick Bond (3 vols.; Oxford, 1902), III, 403.

[41] *The Marprelate Tracts*, p. 230.

trated on gradual shifts of role, like the writer of *Pappe with
an Hatchet,* whose extensive wardrobe of beards—a gray beard
for sententious speech, a soldier's "pikede vaunt" for insult,
and so forth—determined his changes of tone. Open to them
all was a great range of roles, whether informal ones like that
of the modest orator or clearly defined fictional personalities
like those of "Martin Marprelate," "Cuthbert Cunny-Catcher,"
or "Piers Penniless."

Similarly, one of the salient characteristics of the poetry of
the period is its liberal use of masks. The Elizabethan poet
was an actor in the sense that when he wrote he was conscious of working in a certain tradition or genre which
demanded its own kind of mask. At one time the poet assumed
the pose of a simple shepherd and attempted to reproduce
the shepherd's characteristic interests and a selection of his
diction; at another he became the epic bard or the rough satyr
castigating vice. If he wrote a sonnet, he had first to become
"The Lover" like Petrarch, using high evocative imagery to
express hyperbolic attitudes. The reader therefore senses behind the poem an effort of mimesis, the poet gesturing as
speaker. Sometimes, too, the speaker assumes a mask within
the poem only to drop it near the end, as in Sonnets 47 and 74
of *Astrophel and Stella* or in Drayton's "Since ther's no
helpe."[42]

As with the activity of the writer himself, so too with the
action he dictates for his hero. The action of Elizabethan and
Jacobean drama, for example, often amounts to its hero's self-
conscious acting out of a role he has conceived for himself.
Whether he explicitly adopts a disguise, as so often is the case
in comedy, or whether he merely conceives of life itself as
histrionically exalted, as in tragedy, the Elizabethan hero is an
actor. As D. A. Traversi writes, "there is a sense, common in
Elizabethan stage heroes and villains, of the speaker playing

---

[42] On Sidney's sonnets, see Richard B. Young, *English Petrarke:
A Study of Sidney's "Astrophel and Stella,"* in *Three Studies in the
Renaissance* (New Haven, 1958), pp. 23-24 and 7-8.

up to a dramatically acceptable picture of himself" with the kind of fine histrionic self-awareness by which he actually "*sees* himself in a dramatic light."[43] Richard III, for example, starts his play with the naked determination to prove a villain, and proceeds through displays of his virtuosity in that role to entrapment in it and final Stoic endurance of its consequences. Similarly, in the ritual dedication of Act III, Scene 3, Othello gives up the role of honest trusting soldier and husband ("Farewell: *Othello's* Occupation's gone") and takes upon himself another, that of the instrument of divine vengeance, which he must act to the end. The classic case is Hamlet's, the bulk of whose play is about little else but the examination of roles: the pain of assuming a role alien to one's nature, the uses of the mask of madness, the proper role of action in comparison to others, and, finally, the relation of the role to providence.

Often the role represents a meaningful distortion of the character's real personality or situation, as in the satiric roles of Kent and Edgar in *Lear,* Giovanni in *The Malcontent,* and Flamineo in *The White Devil.*[44] A striking example of this is Bosola, who seeks an adequate form for his life in the chaotic world of *The Duchess of Malfi* and finds it (he uses insistent images of creation) in the ambivalent role of executioner and instructor which he plays out in the man-made world of horrors at Malfi. The tension he experiences in the role is an index of his attitude toward himself, and out of it comes his own tragic purpose. Beatrice-Joanna in *The Changeling,* Perkin Warbeck, and Vindice in *The Revenger's Tragedy* are ironic examples of histrionics, especially the last, whose successive masks—"Piato" and the caricature "Vindice," the malcontent scholar—really define his degeneration as he becomes

---

[43] D. A. Traversi, *Shakespeare: The Last Phase* (London, 1954), p. 7.

[44] See M. C. Bradbrook, "Shakespeare and the Use of Disguise in Elizabethan Drama," *Essays in Criticism,* II (1952), 159-68, esp. p. 163: "Hamlet's coarseness and Edgar's wildness are parts of themselves, but they are more than merely that."

submerged in the world's means in order to effect a worthy
end. He becomes what he plays.

Several aspects of the concept of dramatic action as histrionic are worthy of note here. For one thing, the function
of the role is to extend the normal possibilities of action for
the character involved in it.[45] In comedy, the role usually
allows the character to exceed the limitations of social position,
as it does for Florizel, or for Lacy in *Friar Bacon and Friar
Bungay;* or of sex, as it does for Portia, Julia, and Viola. Jonson's *The New Inn* offers even further extension to its hero,
for the two hours of circumscribed play set up at the Inn
permit Lovel to go beyond his real-life status as aging cynic
into a role expressing what he really is, the ideal true lover.
In tragedy, the role takes the hero beyond normal ethics, from
his proper self into a daring new self outside, if not above,
good and evil. Such extension by role-playing is a method of
bringing the hero-actor into contact with ideals of the self or of
humanity. Tragedy is always moving outward to test the furthest limits of life, while comedy always celebrates some ideal
necessary to human solidarity. Thus Faustus deliberately rejects the standard limited roles of scholar, physician, and divine in order to try out the new role of man-god, while Portia
dons the disguise of advocate in order to make explicit the
qualities of mercy and self-sacrifice by which men make their
lives together worth living.

It is because they touch ideals that these histrionics become
significant—the tragic hero's failure significant in defining
human limits, the comic hero's successful disguise significant
because through it he experiences such things as love and
humility. But the role must be given up at the end of the play,
for while it extends the possibilities of action for the hero it
also cramps his normally various personality into a strict and
narrow channel of purpose. The role distorts to tell the truth
or accomplish the purpose, and hence the hero hastens towards
the point where it can be destroyed. The tragic mode merges

[45] See *ibid.*, p. 160.

the role and the full self at the hero's death, as in Othello's last act; the comic insists on a ritual undressing, of which Prospero's return to common humanity is a striking example.

Role-playing is an exploration into the dimensions of the self, for as George Mead writes, "the self belongs to the reflexive mode. One senses the self only in so far as the self assumes the role of another so that it becomes both subject and object in the same experience."[46] The role can express the self, isolate and develop a single aspect of the self, or even change the self. Most frequently, as we have seen, it opens up new ethical possibilities for a person, either in circumventing normal morality or in rising above the normal level of nobility. We can see the former possibility offering itself in moments of choice as depicted by Euphuistic fiction, the latter in the transitions of romantic plots.

Near the beginning of Lodge's *Rosalynde* (1590), when Saladyne debates with himself whether to follow his father's deathbed injunction to foster his younger brother Rosader or to disregard it and seize the estate for himself, he sees his choice as one not merely between two courses of action, but also between two opposite roles: his proper role of natural son and protective elder brother and the unnatural role of self-seeking villain. Beneath the two roles lie polar ethical bases: "to content thee with thy fortunes" or "to aspire to higher wealth,"[47] the traditionally approved ethic of humility or the immorality of self-love. Since he has defined his case in this way, Saladyne cannot merely do a wrong thing, he must commit himself to *being* a villain. He pursues the latter role to his full failure in it and his consequent bitterness, until Rosader saves him from the lion and then invests him with a new pastoral role of the cherishing lover.

[46] George H. Mead, *Movements of Thought in the Nineteenth Century*, ed. Merritt H. Moore (Chicago, 1936), p. 63.

[47] *Rosalynde*, in *The Works of Thomas Lodge*, ed. for the Hunterian Club by Edmond Gosse (4 vols.; Glasgow, 1883), I (separately paginated), 16.

Rhegius, in Henry Chettle's *Piers Plainnes* (1595), goes through a more astringent experience. He is an essentially good man, the uncle and sage adviser of Queen Aeliana of Crete. Therefore, when he is assailed by an incestuous desire for his niece that he cannot bear to face directly, he turns to villainous shifts much as if he were taking up a dramatic part foreign to his nature. Consequently, it is significant, as well as instrumental to his purpose, that he does not act out his incestuous attempts *in propria persona*, but works through false dramatic performances, either by disguising himself—as the savage who tries to ravish Aeliana, for instance—or by setting up actions through his servant Dolon. Hence there exist throughout his story radical and ironic splits between his two selves, as when Aeliana in the hands of the savage "cried on her Unkle, invocating his helpe, that savagely attempted hir hurt."[48] The split exists in Rhegius' own awareness, too. On the one hand, he is able to fortify his resolution by "furnishing himselfe with sundry examples of most unnaturall and preposterous loves,"[49] examples that tempt him beyond limit and law: "Myrrha loved hir father, Byblis hir brother: this in the worlds eye was preposterous, to Nature not abhorring, to love agreeing: why shoulde not Love and Nature then commaund Lawe, seeing from them Law onely holdes hir cheefe positions."[50] On the other hand, he is always breaking out in shame at the base role he has chosen to play; in order to free the man from the role, it is necessary first that he fail and be exposed, and then that he rectify his passion by an honest love for Rhodope at the end.

Saladyne and Rhegius attempt to live out roles based on ideas of possibility that flout human solidarity, and they fail. But a more usual role held out for the hero was that of an ideal

[48] *Piers Plainnes Seaven Yeres Prentiship*, in *The Descent of Euphues: Three Elizabethan Romance Stories*, ed. James Winny (Cambridge, 1957), p. 137.

[49] *Ibid.*, p. 151.

[50] *Ibid.*, p. 154.

of human conduct above the normal. The frequent appearance of the latter possibility in chivalric romance, the meanest of the forms of prose fiction, testifies to its pervasive presence in Elizabethan minds. The hero of Richard Johnson's *Tom a Lincolne* (1607) is raised as the supposed son of the shepherd Antonio, but discovers, in play with his fellows, an idea of himself more appealing than that of shepherd: "he was chosen (in sport by them) for their lord or knight, and they to attend on him like dutiful servants; and though this their election was but in play, yet hee whose spirits were ravished with great and high matters, first procured them to sweare to him loyalty in all things, and to obey him as a king."[51] Tom's response is to attempt to act out this play of the chivalric ideal in life: "he persuaded them to leave that base and servile kind of life, seeking to serve in war,"[52] and they become a kind of Robin Hood band roaming throughout Barnesdale under a leader who has now assumed the identity of "the Red Rose Knight." Acting out chivalry in a nonchivalric context then becomes real, as Tom a Lincolne the Red Rose Knight joins the Round Table and eventually becomes "the perfect patterne of an exquisite souldier."[53] Tom has become the ideal figure he imagined for himself in play, and he turns out finally to have imagined the truth, when he is discovered to be King Arthur's illegitimate son.

Frequently, in the romances, role-playing becomes a means of education or purification. In *The Historie of Pheander The Mayden Knight* (ca. 1595) by Henry Robarts, for example, Prince Dionisius of Numedia pines ineffectually in his love for Nutania Princess of Thrace until he conceives a role for himself: disguised as the humble but wealthy merchant Pheander, he goes to Thrace, presents himself as Nutania's servant

---

[51] *The Most Pleasant History of Tom a Lincolne*, in *Early English Prose Romances*, ed. William J. Thoms (3 vols.; 2nd edn.; London, 1858), II, 242.
[52] *Ibid.*, pp. 242-43.
[53] *Ibid.*, p. 249.

to help her in her wars, is knighted by her as "The Mayden Knight," and defeats her enemies. Thus, as it were, he becomes again through his disguise the noble knight he really was at the start, but by acting out the attaining of this image all over again from the beginning in Nutania's service, he also becomes worthy of her love. Similarly, the noble Ornatus in Emanuel Forde's *Ornatus and Artesia* (ca. 1598) progresses from humble lover to rightful king by proving himself in a whole series of disguises, ranging from the virgin "Sylvia" to a "Palmer" to the noble "Phylastes."

⟨ III ⟩

Pre-novelistic fiction as a whole is interested in the intersection of the human and some other element; Elizabethan fiction is interested in intellectual constructs and it is fascinated by histrionics. We can gather up much of the material in the present chapter into four general propositions to be tested and modified in the pages that follow. First, the end of Elizabethan fiction is to put ideas of value or order into the context of experienced reality in order to observe their interaction. Second, the characteristic action of Elizabethan fiction is consequently some form of testing ideas of value by experience, the ideas so tested usually offering some potential image for man to mold himself into. The techniques by which such ideas are measured may vary, and range from explicit editorial comment to the mere neutral juxtaposition of incidents; but the sovereign technique lies in the nature of plot itself.

After Robert Greene had administered to his readers a dose of sage advice against love, he offered them a role to play in order to complete their education: "if these Aphorismes be too enigmaticall, become a Lover, and experience will quickly set thee downe a comment."[54] The dramatic role mediates between precept and experience, just as fiction, in Sidney's

---

[54] *Greenes Mourning Garment,* in *The Life and Complete Works in Prose and Verse of Robert Greene,* ed. Alexander B. Grosart (15 vols.; London: The Huth Library, 1881-86), IX, 200-201.

view, mediates between ideal and actuality. Our third proposition is, then, that the hero's conscious assumption of a dramatic role is essential to the testing of ideas in Elizabethan fiction. For the role—whether a disguise or merely a heightened self-awareness—is but the version of humanity that the idea submits concretized in a series of stylized actions. The role, by allowing the hero to do what is impossible in ordinary non-histrionic existence, becomes a way of experiencing the operation of a high idea in the self; and the hero can thus test the idea's validity in his own experience.

Our last proposition is this: the issue of this mode of action is the adjustment of the relation between ideas of reality and the experience of reality. It is in this way that Elizabethan fiction fulfills Sidney's idea of it as an act of speculation about the possibilities open to human existence. And it is in this way that the action of a hero—and the reaction of a reader watching him—may become

> The poem of the mind in the act of finding
> What will suffice.

CHAPTER 3

Pastoral Romance: Sidney and Lodge

There is considerable justice in the late C. S. Lewis' characterization of Elizabethan literature as "Golden," for it usually
works in the realm of golden ideals instead of in that of the
brazen world, and by this transformation submits "the shows
of things to the desires of the mind," as Bacon said.[1] Its
major genres—pastoral, epic, and sonnet—present positive
ideals rather than indulging negative emotions as satire does.
It is suffused with love, love conceived in the abstract rather
than submitted to the pressures of everyday life—a theme
which, as Everard Guilpin complained, had contaminated
almost every form of literature, even the "heroicke Poeme."[2]
Perhaps because of the analogy and connection between human and divine love in both the Platonic and Christian systems, love so conceived put man into contact with the absolute
and surrounded human life with a heady mythical aura. That
we see in erotic mythological epyllia like *Hero and Leander*
and *Venus and Adonis*; in the sonnet cycles, where the woman
is elevated to the status of a goddess; and in Spenser's romantic
epic, where love leads a knight toward the virtue he must
embrace. Its exaggeration can be inspected in the allusion-
stuffed *Moderatus* of Robert Parry, in which every character
and every action is related to several myths in a row.[3]

[1] C. S. Lewis, *English Literature in the Sixteenth Century*, pp. 64-65;
Bacon, *Of the Advancement of Learning*, ed. G. W. Kitchin (London:
Everyman's Library, 1915), p. 83.

[2] Everard Guilpin, *Skialethia, or A Shadowe of Truth, in Certaine
Epigrams and Satyres* (1598), sig. C1:

> The heroicke Poeme is lascivious,
> Which midst of *Mars* his field, & hote alarmes,
> Will sing of *Cupids* chivalrie and armes.

[3] Robert Parry, *Moderatus, The Most Delectable and Famous Historye of the Blacke Knight* (1595). Another good example of the
transformation of the brazen world into the golden by mythic anal-

Sidney's theory of fiction is most apposite to such a literature, for the quest for the area of agreement between the quotidian and the ideal elements in life that he posited in it would seem to be the major quest of the age's literature as well. The ideas submitted to experience in this theory offer several high images for man to take as his pattern, and the major technique of testing, that of playing a role expressive of the idea, exalts ordinary man by mimesis into the realm of the mythical. It is pastoral romance, the genre domesticated by Sidney himself, that pursues these goals most wholeheartedly and that therefore offers us the clearest examples of the Sidneian mode of fiction. From its origin in Theocritus, pastoral had always placed man in an ideally natural but abstract milieu, close to the gods and hence in contact with the supernatural or the ideal. And the use of disguise or confusions of identity, which had been a standard feature of pastoral romance since its abortive beginnings in *Daphnis and Chloe,* allows for a very explicit kind of role-playing.

Romance assumes, speculatively, the existence of pure motives within men and an ideally perfect world corresponding to these motives, whether that world be the "Faerie" of heroic romance or the "Arcady" of the prose pastoral romance. And romance seeks to establish how much of this ideal realm of action can find its way into the "Britain" of social reality. Renaissance pastoral romance formed a perfect vehicle for this adjustment of the actual and the ideal, because it always placed the real and the ideal side by side (often with the implication that the "real" was only apparent, the "ideal" really true). Its major implements in this enterprise were its dual setting and its dual presentation of character.

In the traditional setting of pastoral romance, we find two worlds juxtaposed: the actual world of human experience and a kind of inner circle, a purified abstraction of that world, or

---

ogies is afforded by Henry Chettle's description of Aeliana in *Piers Plainnes Seaven Yeres Prentiship* (in *The Descent of Euphues: Three Elizabethan Romance Stories,* ed. Winny, p. 134).

"Arcady." Thus we have Sannazaro's Naples and Arcadia, Montemayor's stylized Spain and fields of Ezla, Gil Polo's Mediterranean world and Ezla, Sidney's violent world of Asia Minor and the Arcadian retreat, Lodge's Bordeaux and the Forest of Arden.

The inner pastoral circle inherited from classical pastoral represented concretely a realization of more than the usual possibilities in life, or a life of conscious artifice. It always suggests the paradisiacal, whether explicitly—as when it is called "a second *Elisium*" or "*Natures Eden*"[4]—or implicitly, when it is described, like the godhead, by negatives asserting a peculiar state of stasis without cold or heat, without either direct sunlight or complete shade, a place of eternal becoming.[5] It is always presented as the place where the natural and the supernatural join, where heaven meets earth (often, concretely, as a place habitually visited by the pagan gods). Such a place is on the earth but not of the earth. Its peculiar status is conveyed by various means: sometimes it is removed into remote space and walled off either by men, as in Sidney's *Arcadia,* or by nature, as in the pastoral place of Melbancke's *Philotimus,* which is surrounded "with Pineapple & Cipresse trees, that armed were with prickes";[6] at other times a shrine is placed in its center, as is the case with the Cave of Pan in Sannazaro's *Arcadia,* the Temple of Diana in Montemayor's *Diana,* or the circular Temple of Diana in Markham's *English Arcadia.*

Descriptive passages stress wonderment at the supernormal or supernatural quality of the natural world perfectly assimilated to some ideal of order, of the mutable expressing the permanent, as in this passage from Sidney's *Arcadia:*

[4] Barnabe Riche, *The Straunge and Wonderfull Adventures of Don Simonides* (1581), sig. C2; Gervase Markham, *The English Arcadia, Alluding his Beginning from Sir Philip Sydnes Ending* (1607), sig. K3.

[5] See A. Bartlett Giamatti, *The Earthly Paradise and the Renaissance Epic* (Princeton, 1966), p. 84.

[6] Brian Melbancke, *Philotimus. The Warre betwixt Nature and Fortune* (1583), sig. Dd4v.

Do you not see how all things conspire together to make this country a heavenly dwelling? Do you not see the grasse how in colour they excell the Emeralds, everie one striving to passe his fellow, and yet they are all kept of an equal height? . . . Certainelie, certainely, cosin, it must needes be that some Goddesse enhabiteth this Region, who is the soule of this soile: for neither is any, lesse then a Goddesse, worthie to be shrined in such a heap of pleasures: nor any lesse then a Goddesse, could have made it so perfect a plotte of the celestiall dwellings.

Or this from Lodge's *Rosalynde:*

. . . round about in the forme of an Amphitheater were most curiouslie planted Pine trees, interseamed with Limons and Citrons, which with the thicknesse of their boughes so shadowed the place, that PHOEBUS could not prie into the secret of that Arbour; so united were the tops with so thicke a closure, that VENUS might there in her jollitie have dallied unseene with her deerest paramour.

Or, finally, this from *The English Arcadia:*

This Tempe was at first called *Natures Eden,* because in it was no part of mans workmanship; yet the worke in Arte more strange then the Art or work of man could correct; the trees did not overgrow one another, but seemed in even proportions to delight in each others evennesse: the flowers did not strive which should be supreme in smelling, but communicating their odours, were content to make one intyre sweete savour; the beddes whereon the flowers grew, disdained not the grassie Allies, but lending to them their lustre, made the walkes more pleasant: the faire ryver *Penaus* would at no time overflow his bankes to drowne their beauties, but with gentle swellings wash them like a deawie morning.[7]

---

[7] *The Prose Works of Sir Philip Sidney,* ed. Feuillerat, I, 57; *The Works of Thomas Lodge,* ed. Gosse, Vol. I, *Rosalynde* (the individual

More generally, the supernormal showed itself in the traditional topic of the strange cooperation or mingling of art and nature, man's art and God's art,[8] as in Sannazaro's Cave of Pan, Centorio's fountain, Guarini's or Sidney's central cave, or Riche's pastoral place, "furnished with all exquisit proportion, and disposition of Arte, fenced with the Walles of Nature."[9]

Theoretically, the meeting-place of the human and the supernatural was the realm of ideas—or Platonic Ideas—and Sidney, who transformed the Continental pastoral romance by consciously impregnating it with intellectual content, made this fact explicit:

> O sweet woods the delight of solitarines!
>
> . . . .
>
> Contemplation here holdeth his only seate.[10]

In his *Arcadia,* the setting becomes explicitly expressive of ideas. The inner pastoral circle becomes the realm of love and contemplation, the violent world around it, the realm of heroic action. For Riche's religious Don Simonides, the pastoral place atop a hill represents the meeting of earth and heaven, of life and the afterlife, where one casts aside the former for the latter: "heere, the onely place, whiche the Goddes have appointed for thy penance, where shakyng off thy worldly conceiptes, thou mayst be partaker of thy Unckle *Aristo* his Contemplation."[11] In the pastoral ending of William Warner's *Syrinx,* the closed circle is significant on two levels: generally, as the realm of true being cut off from the world of becoming

---

works are separately paginated), p. 39; Markham, *The English Arcadia* (1607), sig. K3.

[8] See Ernst Robert Curtius, *European Literature and the Latin Middle Ages,* trans. Willard R. Trask (New York, 1953), Chap. 10.

[9] See Sannazaro, *Arcadia,* ed. Michele Scherillo (Turin, 1888), p. 195; Ascanio Centorio, *L'Aura Soave* (Venice, 1556), p. 11; Guarini, *Il Pastor Fido,* trans. Fanshawe (London, 1647), p. 104; Sidney, *Arcadia,* in *Prose Works,* ed. Feuillerat, II, 7; Riche, *Don Simonides,* sig. D2.

[10] *Arcadia,* in *Prose Works,* II, 237.

[11] Riche, *Don Simonides,* sig. D3.

governed by fortune, and in personal terms, as the realm of the soul forgetting the body.[12] Robert Greene allegorizes the pastoral place in *Ciceronis Amor* by naming it "the vale of Love," whereas in the more realistic *Menaphon* it becomes the emblem of content:

> Content sitteth in thy minde as *Neptune* in his Sea-throne, who with his trident mace appeaseth everie storme. When thou seest the heavens frowne thou thinkest on thy faults, and a cleere skie putteth thee in minde of grace; the summers glorie tels thee of youths vanitie, the winters parched leaves of ages declining weaknes. Thus in a myrrour thou measurest thy deedes with equall and considerate motions.[13]

It is no exaggeration to say that in Elizabethan romances the pastoral land is first and foremost a symbol of an explicit ideal or desirable state of mind, and that the purpose of pastoral is to dramatize a state of mind by showing the correspondence between man's life and his natural context.

The plot of pastoral romance consisted generally of the hero's mere experience of two worlds: his entrance, full of the pain and turmoil he has contracted in the actual world, into "Arcady"; his experience of love and calm self-analysis in the inner pastoral circle; and his return to the outer world in harmony with himself. This action really amounts to the hero's observation of himself in two different contexts—an actual and an ideal one—or to his living two lives, one actual and one possible. To this traditional pattern correspond Sannazaro's *Arcadia,* Montemayor's *Diana,* Centorio's *L'Aura Soave,* Gil Polo's *Diana enamorada,* Sidney's *Arcadia,* and the English romances subsequent to Sidney's.

Such a plot demands that the hero play the role of his ideal

---

[12] William Warner, *Pan his Syrinx,* ed. Wallace A. Bacon, Northwestern University Studies, Humanities Series, 26 (Evanston, 1950), p. 184.
[13] *The Life and Complete Works in Prose and Verse of Robert Greene,* ed. Grosart, VI, 38.

or possible self to the full; and this central aspect of the action is always made explicit by the disguise that the hero must assume before he can enter the pastoral land. He must, in effect, relinquish his identity and become someone else. He must strip off his proper clothing, change his name, and put on the clothes and manners of a shepherd. But that "someone else" is really an image of the person that he, the hero, might become. Moreover, since the pastoral life expresses explicit ideas of value, the pastoral disguise signifies not only the discovery of a new aspect of the self, but the conscious acceptance of new values as well. The hero comes into contact with the absolute as he plays the part of The Shepherd of Humility, The Shepherd of Love, or The Holy Shepherd of Contemplation—much as, in a different context, the confused Montelyon enters the Garden of the Hesperides, to be reclothed in a ritual and to issue forth in his new identity as "The Knight of the Oracle" in order to carry a divinely ordained justice into the world of fact.[14]

The pastoral disguise expresses the values of the pastoral place, and that place is itself symbolic of a possible state of mind. The action of the hero in dressing himself as a shepherd and going to live in this place therefore constitutes an extensive exploration of his mind, especially touching the relation between what his mind is and the state it might achieve. That is precisely what such action meant to a later pastoral moralist:

> When he went to the pond, Thoreau struck an attitude and did so deliberately, but his posturing was not to draw the attention of others to him but rather to draw his own attention more closely to himself. "I learned this at least by my experiment: that if one advances confidently in the direction of his dreams, and endeavors to live the life which he has imagined, he will meet with a success unexpected in common hours". . . . *Walden*, subtitled "Life in the Woods," is

[14] Emanuel Forde, *The Famous Historie of Montelyon* (1640 edn.), sigs. R4-S.

not a simple and sincere account of a man's life, either in or out of the woods; it is an account of a man's journey into the mind.[15]

⟨ II ⟩

Sidney's own *Arcadia* is an explicit exploration of the possibilities of love.[16] As the description of Basilius' pastoral retreat as the unity of the diverse under "a Goddesse" of love (1,57) implies, the retreat is the realm of love. And the divers fortunes possible under the aegis of love are suggested both by the opening sentence, presenting the sun's love for the earth at the vernal equinox, and by the initial episodic contrast, which juxtaposes the shipwrecked heroes Pyrocles and Musidorous with the Arcadian shepherds Strephon and Klaius acting out their serene embodiment of Platonic theory of love. When Pyrocles and Musidorus enter the retreat, they feel that they are subjecting their personalities to a force which may very well change them completely; it is in this sense that they both feel "Transformd in shew, but more transformd in minde" (I,76) by their pastoral disguises. Their prevision of the changes love may effect is conditioned by theory, for the question they discuss as a prelude to entrance into the retreat is whether or not Plato's theory (as formalized by Ficino and popularized by Castiglione) of love as an induction to divine contemplation is true.

[15] E. B. White, "Walden-1954," *The Yale Review*, XLIV (1954), 15 and 16.

[16] Sidney's work exists in three separate states: the "Old" *Arcadia*, a manuscript draft written sometime between 1577 and 1580; the "New" *Arcadia*, an incomplete revision of Books I through III accomplished by about 1584 and published in 1590; and the *Arcadia*, combining the incomplete revision with the rest of Books III, IV, and V of the "Old" *Arcadia* (slightly revised), and published in 1593. The discussion of the 1593 *Arcadia* that follows is a digest of the author's *A Map of Arcadia*, contained in Walter R. Davis and Richard A. Lanham, *Sidney's Arcadia* (New Haven, 1965); see esp. Chaps. 3, 4, and 6. Parenthetical references by volume and page are to *Prose Works*, ed. Feuillerat.

Musidorus posits only two kinds of love: divine love and lust, the latter a passion full of discomforts, its end sensual pleasure, its status that of a pleasing delusion. For Pyrocles, however, human love exists between lust and divine love, as the effort of man to rise above the flesh; it has an end beyond pleasure which depends on the transfer of the emotion to ever higher objects of love: "in that heavenly love, since ther are two parts, the one the love it self, th'other the excellency of the thing loved; I, not able at the first leap to frame both in me, do now (like a diligent workman) make ready the chiefe instrument, and first part of that great worke, which is love it self" (I,80–81). The kind of love Pyrocles envisions has already been exhibited by Strephon and Klaius, whose love for Urania (after her departure) rose from desire to thirst for divine union; but the question before the heroes is whether such love may be achieved by nobles, and whether it may be accommodated to enjoyment of the beloved as well. The force of this theoretical dialogue is to make love synecdochic of the possibilities of existence, of rising from the flesh or falling further into the flesh. The theme of the relation of reason to passion that runs through the book projects the question of love into a question of justice or right proportion in the soul, and the pressures of state that make their appearance in the last two sections of the book make it also a question of justice in a state disrupted by individual passion. These possibilities are also extended by the sets of analogous episodes inserted into the plot: the effects of success and failure in love upon the integrity of the self in Book I, and the disruption of the self by passion and of the ordered state by passionate men in Book II.[17] Through both overt discussion and analogous episodes, the plot of *Arcadia* becomes a speculation about the possibility of reaching perfection in this life.

Role-playing transforms idea into act. The disguises that Pyrocles and Musidorus must assume in order to be admitted

[17] See further *A Map of Arcadia*, Chap. 5.

to the pastoral circle inhabited by their beloveds are themselves emblematic of suffering brought about by experience. Musidorus' disguise as shepherd subjects him to a ritual of humiliation at the hands of his beloved Pamela; and Mark Rose has well shown that Pyrocles' disguise as a woman (and as an Amazon disdaining the control of men, at that) signifies the overturn of reason by passion and the disruption of the theoretically structured state of things.[18] The disguises, moreover, represent an ironic extension of experience, since Musidorus, who had attacked love as base passion, is clothed in humility, while Pyrocles, the defender of love's divinity, figures passion. Disguise, as Sidney presents it, is double-edged. It is a way of extending the personality into experiences one has never encountered before, and hence offers ultimately to enlarge the self. Pyrocles will experience love as man and as woman, innocently and illicitly, in order to encompass fully the nature of love. But disguise also demands constraint, and reduces the range of actions possible to the undisguised personality. Hence Pyrocles cannot repulse Basilius' advances directly, but must put him off with his best approximation of feminine wiles; and Musidorus is forced into several frustrating gambits wherein he must play Musidorus through the mask of Dorus making love to Pamela through the clownish Mopsa: "making a contrariety the place of my memory, in her fowlnes I beheld *Pamelas* fayrenesse, still looking on *Mopsa,* but thinking on *Pamela. . . .* what soever I thought of *Pamela,* that I saide of *Mopsa*" (I,154–55). The crux of this play upon disguise is the comic scene (II,7ff.) between Pyrocles and Gynecia in the cave, where Pyrocles must run an exhausting gamut of roles ranging from lusting man (when he thinks Philoclea is inside the cave) to indignant virgin (when he finds it is Gynecia).[19]

Arcadia tends to present any human art or idea as poten-

---

[18] Mark Rose, "Sidney's Womanish Man," *Review of English Studies,* New Series XV (1964), 353-63.

[19] See the author's "Actaeon in Arcadia," *Studies in English Literature,* II (1962), 95-110.

tially ambiguous,[20] and it is therefore only natural that the heroes' life within the pastoral retreat of Arcadia should show them that the realm of love is the realm of heightened possibilities for good *or* evil, that love is a force rather than an ideal. It is base passion that first assails the heroes, both from without and from within. On the one hand, the lustful king Basilius (who actually believes Pyrocles to be a woman) and the queen Gynecia (who does not) pursue Pyrocles everywhere, while the silly Mopsa makes embarrassing overtures to Musidorus. On the other hand, the two heroes suffer feelings of "self-division" within themselves under the impact of love, and their minds thus become battlefields for the wars of reason and passion. So terribly have their minds been torn asunder by their experiences that, by the time they have won their mistresses—and, surprisingly enough, they do—they are more disturbed than ever, rather than content at last.

Love may be said to have triumphed rather early in the book, but it is a premature triumph. It occurs before the central questions about the nature and operation of love have begun to be solved, so that, ironically, the reader does not know whether to applaud or lament. Pyrocles and Musidorus love and are loved, but the question remains: What is love? It threatens to become brute passion, mere enjoyment rather than an incitement to virtue, for at the moments of supreme amorous success each of the heroes suffers a lapse of control. Passion seizes Musidorus as he is conveying Pamela out of Arcadia into Thessaly (there to establish the honorable liaison of marriage); one night, while she sleeps, he indulges himself in a banquet of the senses and almost ravishes her. And Pyrocles seems about to suffer complete mental collapse when, after experiencing a series of tormenting desires and amorous debates, he falls (like Troilus) in a swoon on his mistress' bed.

To the irony of premature fulfillment Sidney added the further—and counterbalancing—irony that the heroes' well-de-

---

[20] See *A Map of Arcadia*, pp. 174-79 and Lanham, *The Old Arcadia*, in *Sidney's Arcadia*, pp. 327-31.

served failures lead their minds toward the real perfections that love can bestow. The crisis of *Arcadia,* it is important to note, is not an amorous interview but a series of trials. The dialectic of the debates in Book III between the wicked Cecropia and her nieces Pamela and Philoclea, whom she tempts to disobedience and atheism, yields these conclusions: the world (including macrocosm, body politic, and microcosm) is orderly, not chaotic; its order is made possible only by an operation of divine providence; and one must act out his life in conformity with a belief in providence if he is to live happily and well. These values, while illuminating the moral life, have their origin and resting-place in an idea of love. For they make necessary humility, the self-sacrifice which can alone make love possible, and the virtues of the settled mind—such as temperance—as opposed to the fragile control over chaos incidental to virtues like continence, which take less seriously the imperative to impose order. And it is these values of life and love which the heroines transmit to their lovers at the latters' moments of failure: the men must remould their minds in conformity with providential order and act out their beliefs with patience, humility, and temperance, in order to face love successfully.

Richard A. Lanham writes that Sidney's romance "is not simply a rhetorical statement of the good old truths, though there are enough of them in it. Rather it shows how perilous a life those truths have in a world 'by love possessed.' "[21] Love turns out to be dual in its effect on "old truths" like patience and the ethical mean, for it can either overturn them completely or be harnessed in their service. Dual, too, is its effect on personality: left to itself, love encourages passion and self-division; if it is directed to the right woman, however, it can produce a new and vital conception of the self. Therefore the ending of *Arcadia* is ambivalent. On the one hand, in the trial scene which celebrates the restoration of order to the Arca-

[21] Lanham, *The Old Arcadia,* p. 331.

dian state, Pyrocles' father Euarchus condemns his son and his nephew, and explicitly repudiates their excuse of love, which, he asserts, is a disorderly passion. But on the other hand, Pyrocles and Musidorus are able to bear all this because of their resolution in the prison cell the night before. There we see the full fruition of their mistresses' instructions, for the heroes calmly give up their earthly lives in the hope of their souls' assimilation to the divine after death, and indulge in contemplation of that state: "voyde of sensible memorye, or memorative passion, wee shall not see the cullours, but lifes of all things that have bene or can be: and shall as I hope knowe our friendship, though exempt from the earthlie cares of friendship, having both united it, and our selves, in that hye and heavenly love of the unquenchable light" (II,166). What the heroes achieve in prison is, in fact, the original justice that Adam lost (and that Pyrocles emblematically repudiated by his disguise): the triple subjection of the body to the soul, of the passions to reason in the soul, and of the whole man to God.

Arcadia, in using plot as speculation, works through ideas of love in order to reject many of the traditional Platonic attributes of its power: it does not lead directly to mystic union, it can fall into *amor ferinus* at any point in its progress (especially when one seeks to unite its virtues with enjoyment of the woman as well), it never leaps from love of a particular woman to love of all beauty. But *Arcadia* does show how love can be the impetus to moral perfection in this life, and how the passions accompanying love can form a kind of purifying fire to aid such an endeavor. It is this difficult possibility of reestablishing natural justice in the soul by experiencing its opposite that *Arcadia* proffers to the Elizabethan world.

The modification of concept by experience enters the texture of Sidney's prose, where we often find structured expectations of the outcome of an episode belied by what actually happens. The many surprise scenes, for example, work by raising the character's—and the reader's—schooled expectations to a cer-

tain pitch and then allowing reality's intransigence to effect a
sudden reversal. The book opens with just such a scene,
wherein Strephon and Klaius' recital of the ideal operation of
Platonic love is suddenly broken off (I,8) by the appearance
of the shipwrecked Musidorus, who exhibits "what, in crude
fact, man has made of man."[22] The oppositions there implied
include theory against practice, love against hate or war, the
serene pastoral life against the heroic. A contrast of styles is
entailed, too—the balanced periodicity of pastoral speech
against the parataxis of events—and that contrast suggests, at
its outer limits, one between the ordered life of the mind and
the disorders of time, between the golden and the brazen.
Such is the case, as well, with Pyrocles' entrance into the cave
expecting a romantic love scene, and his finding instead the
threats of female lust (II,7); or with Musidorus' parallel scene
in the grove (II,27), where a serene and sensuous celebration
of love is broken off by the rude remnants of a peasant rebellion—an intrusion whose ironic effect is intensified by its sug-
gestion of the half-hidden tumult in Musidorus' own breast
at that moment. A highly detailed example of this particular
kind of reversal is the scene near the end of the first book
(I,119). The heroes and their ladies come to a fair field where
man's art has made nature into "a pleasant refuge then from
the cholericke looke of *Phoebus*." A delight to the senses, the
place leads naturally, it seems, to matters of love. Musidorus
(as Dorus) sighs and Pyrocles (as Zelmane), "taking the
hande of *Philoclea*, and with burning kisses setting it close to
her lips (as if it should stande there like a hand in the margine
of a Booke, to note some saying worthy to be marked) began
to speake these wordes. O Love, since thou art so changeable
in mens estates, how art thou so constant in their torments?
when sodainly there came out of a wood a monstrous Lion,
with a she Beare. . . ." Suddenly the control man's art has
imposed on the world of nature is broken by the fiercely

[22] See E.M.W. Tillyard, *The English Epic and Its Background*
(London, 1954), p. 303.

natural things that this art could not, for all its hopes, exclude; the love scene turns into a bloody fray which fully and unexpectedly fulfills Pyrocles' literary evocation of mutability, and that hand which supposedly marked a pretty speech points to real danger.[23]

Precept, even principle, frequently bows before experience in the recantation scenes that stud *Arcadia*—for example, in the comic recantation of Musidorus (I,114), where he ruefully gives up his textbook diatribe against love in the face of its mixed reality, or in the more pathetic scene (I,173) in which Philoclea ritually forswears her vow of virginity by moonlight. In the final scene of the romance we have a panorama of the difficult postures in which principles can trap their adherents: Euarchus held by his objective standard of abstract justice, Pyrocles and Musidorus by codes of unwavering friendship. The rigid principles issue in complete deadlock, but one that is broken by the absurdly real fact that Basilius, the supposed victim of murder, is not really dead. While Sidney in his plot holds out to his readers and his heroes the possibility of transforming one's life into a golden one, he is equally insistent in episode after episode on the difficult nature of the brazen reality upon which one must work. Ideas may possibly transform reality; what is certain is that they confront it.

⟨ III ⟩

Sidney was responsible for a radical shift in emphasis that made itself felt in all subsequent English pastoral romance; for he took the sometimes serene, sometimes lachrymose, but always sophisticated kind of emotional experience that the romances of Sannazaro, Montemayor, and their followers had imitated, and impregnated it with ideas. The remarkable fact is that most of this shift occurred while he was revising his first book, for the "Old" *Arcadia* contains the outline of

[23] I am indebted to David Kalstone's brilliant analysis of this scene in "Sidney's Arcadian Prose," a paper read before The Modern Language Association, December 28, 1967.

the plot we have recorded above without much of the intellectual depth supplied by the revised version. In revision, Sidney added long discussions and scenes of trial, like the lengthy captivity episode of Book III. He added over a dozen episodes that showed events in the main plot from a variety of angles and created a sort of thematic density whereby his romance's five books became small disquisitions on love, reason and passion, the nature of marriage, death both physical and spiritual, and justice, respectively. The transformation of his original romance into a work "at once a romance and a treatise"[24] naturally entailed some losses; the ventilation of the action by an occasionally wry first-person narrator disappeared, and many elements of the romantic comedy that Lanham finds in the first version, while still present in the second, had faded into the background.[25] Nevertheless, the resultant book, intellectualized and moralized, exerted a kind of radical influence upon subsequent pastoral romance that the first version could not have achieved. By forging the pastoral romance into a serious ethical tool, Sidney threw the focus upon theme, and the natural consequence of this act was a clearly articulated ideational structure.

While few English pastoral romancers after Sidney were able to follow him into an extensive and skeptical inquisition of ideas in fiction, all of them, whether or not directly influenced by him, have an interest in ideas that is lacking in their Continental counterparts. The English romances exhibit an overriding ethical drive and a lively interest in theme, whether that interest be expressed by extensive symbolism, inserted discussions of such matters as the active and contemplative lives or the nature of love, or merely through a perfunctory lecture by some hermit on the values of humility or simplicity. In order to see a spectrum of ideational slants made possible by Sidney's legacy—and to judge the various degrees of attain-

[24] R. W. Zandvoort, *Sidney's Arcadia: A Comparison between the Two Versions* (Amsterdam, 1929), p. 120.
[25] Lanham, *The Old Arcadia*, Chaps. 4 and 6.

ment involved—we shall examine briefly the work of three writers. The books they produced vary considerably in kind: Gervase Markham's *The English Arcadia* (published in two parts, 1607 and 1613) is a romance which continues Sidney's form and plot; John Dickenson's *Arisbas* (1594) is a collection of lyrics linked by a meager prose plot after the manner of Sannazaro's *Arcadia*; and Robert Greene's pastoral romances are modeled for the most part on Greek romance. The degree of dependence on Sidney varies, too, Markham's being largely a continuation of *Arcadia*, Dickenson's admitting its influence but imitating little more than its structure, Greene's showing little influence, and that indirect.

It is an interesting coincidence that the two romances written in imitation of Sidney's, *The English Arcadia* and *Arisbas,* maintain an unconscious decorum by themselves dealing with the imitation of an example. In them, the pastoral place is mainly a place where one comes into contact with supreme exemplars.

Gervase Markham's *The English Arcadia, Alluding his Beginning from Sir Philip Sydnes Ending* (1607) begins as a mere sequel to Sidney's romance, like Richard Beling's.[26] In it we are told that Helen took the nearly dead Amphialus to Corinth and cured him,[27] that they married and inherited the Laconian throne after Basilius' death, but that lately Helen has been accused of disloyalty to her husband. Musidorus has died and left Thessaly to his daughter Melidora; we hear nothing about Pyrocles, but the hero Adunatus or "Pyrophilus" (as he calls himself at the outset) is apparently his son. About halfway through the volume Markham develops new action, totally unrelated to Sidney's, in two episodes: Adunatus' uncompleted defense of Helen's constancy; and Adunatus' defeat of Diatassan, completed in the second part, whose title, *The Second and Last Part of the First Booke of the English*

[26] Richard Beling, *A Sixth Booke, to The Countesse of Pembrokes Arcadia* (1628).
[27] See Sidney, *Prose Works*, I, 495-98.

Arcadia (1613), shows how vast the proportions of the plot had grown in Markham's mind.

This new action is curiously literary, in that fulfillment of an action brings its hero into phase with a literary prototype. For example, when Helen brings the half-dead Amphialus to Corinth, she is greeted by a lugubrious masque of Hero and Leander which expresses her case: "As soone as she had set her foote upon the shore . . . there might she see upon the sands, *Leander* drowned, and *Hero* lamenting over him, in her Nunne-like and virgin-stained apparell . . . in her amazement [Helen] looked first upon *Hero,* then upon her selfe; after upon *Leander,* lastly upon *Amphyalus.*"[28] A similar example of action as the reliving of literary experience occurs at the beginning, where the shepherds Credulo and Carino, having mourned their full over Cinthia, call themselves "the truely loving *Strephon* and *Claius.*"

Adunatus' defeat of Diatassan, which fills the entire second volume and a goodly portion of the first, reads like a textbook case of literature's effect upon the reader as presented in *The Defence of Poesie,* to which Markham seems to allude when he quotes an opinion that Sidney's "contemplative labour first brought him to active worthinesse."[29] The episode falls into two parts, contemplative and active, a long story told to the hero and his consequent action in completing it. The hermit Eugenio, to whom the truth has come by divine revelation, tells the young questing Prince Adunatus how Thyrsis, forced by his sense of honor to fulfill an agreement made under duress, has given up his claim to his beloved Melidora and has used his bravery to win her for his deceitful rival Diatassan. Within the frame of the book, of course, the story is fact, not fiction; yet, like fiction, it strips away the deceptive appearances of life to show the truth clear and whole—a clarification

[28] *The English Arcadia,* sig. E3.
[29] *The Second and Last Part . . . ,* sig. A4v; compare *The Defence of Poesie, Prose Works,* III, 12: "the ending end of all earthly learning, being verteous action."

made possible only by the revelation allowed the poet-hermit Eugenio.

And the story, moreover, leads directly to virtuous action. It is left incomplete, for the next day Diatassan is to claim Melidora; but Adunatus, who has fallen in love with the virtues of Thyrsis, determines to help him. Eugenio treats the affair as a stage play:

> ... as for the conclusion, or making up of the last act in this stage-play of fortunes onely invention, I would have your selfe (my sonne) in it, not onely a vertuous spectator, but (when the tiranny of falshood shall adjudge truth to eternall banishment) such a worthy actor, that discovering the devouring covetousnesse of selfe-love, you may bring vertue back from exile, and defend it against all the assaults of envious mutability.[30]

He clothes Adunatus for his part, so that "playing the part not of a rude and barberous Heardes-man, but of a wittily conceited and learned Pastor, [you shall] enter into that worke which shall make your fame glorious for ever."[31] Thus disguised, Adunatus enters the story the next day in order to change the ending (as it were), challenges Diatassan and reveals his deceit, thus producing the eventual clarification and denouement. Adunatus sums up the effect this action has had upon him when he thanks Eugenio for bestowing a double benefit on him:

> ... first, by enriching his memory with a story so full of all the remarkeable notes of Fortunes most unsteady governement in the actions of mans life ... but especially by opening so faire a path to his honour and reputation, through which they might passe to the haven of their desires, by giving comfort to the miserable, and taking from the most vertuous, that most deceitfull abuse of false-hood.[32]

[30] *The Second and Last Part* . . . , sigs. N3-N3v.
[31] *Ibid.*, sig. N4.
[32] *Ibid.*, sig. M3v.

Here we see concretely how a "notable image" of virtue moves the spectator to act out the virtues given being in the story in order to assimilate himself to that image. The experience of the poem impels a man to act out the poem in his life.

The peculiarly literary pastoral circle of Tempe, where all diverse things live together in unity, is a place where things of this world are seen clarified and simplified, where the masks are stripped away to show truth shining in a perfect exemplar which one must imitate. And histrionics complete the action of ethical clarification: the imitative role created for Adunatus by Eugenio not only brought the story to a satisfying end, but also perfected Adunatus in heroic virtue, so that his transition from "vertuous spectator" to "worthy actor" by means of the role also represented the maturation of an unformed youth.

John Dickenson set out in *Arisbas, Euphues amidst his Slumbers* (1594) to rise to the heights of Sidney's *Arcadia*—as he put it, to "glance at the unmatchable height of his heroique humor," as Statius managed to do in the case of Virgil.[33] But even though he avowedly imitated Sidney's structure by beginning *in mediis rebus*[34] and by relating subplots to the main plot, *Arisbas* remains loose and digressive in form. It has a dramatic beginning (reminiscent of Sidney or of Greek romance) leading to narration of past events and an ending pulling more past events into the resolution; but instead of a middle, it has a series of digressions and miscellaneous poems (including a Humanist's progress of poetry). But Dickenson, a reputable Latin poet and one of the few followers of Sidney well enough trained in the classics to attempt quantitative meters in English, did restore to pastoral some of the mythopoeic sense it had possessed in Theocritus, Virgil, and Longus.

To Dickenson, Arcadia represents not so much a concept as a vision, the kind of vision of the divine and the human in

---

[33] *Prose and Verse by John Dickenson*, ed. Alexander B. Grosart (Manchester, 1878), p. 31.

[34] *Ibid.*, p. 28.

consort that must underlie any valid sense of the relevance of human experience to the absolute. Arcadia is the place where the gods disport themselves among men, the place where Pan resides, Diana hunts, the shepherds sing the myths of the gods, and where the two levels of being join in love. At its center stands a temple dedicated to Hyalus, a mortal boy of Arcadia beloved by both the goddess Pomona and the West Wind, Zephyrus. Their conflict over him, which temporarily defoliated Arcadia, was finally resolved by Hyalus' metamorphosis into a maiden and dedication as vestal virgin to Aeolus, god of the winds. It is at this temple, in a springtime ceremony, that the human plot of the book comes to resolution. Arisbas, disguised as a shepherd throughout his long hardships and wanderings, finally meets his lost beloved, Timoclea, who has passed through a series of melodramatic dangers at sea since their separation by disguising herself as a boy. When the long-separated lovers come together after their adventures on land and sea and Timoclea reveals herself to be a woman, the priest of the temple immediately points out an analogy:

> For next the rare hap of HYALUS whose memory we now celebrate, what other accident could so directly fit the feast of PARTHENIA? As his sexe was miraculously changed from a faire ladde to the fairest girle that ever lived in ARCADIA; so this lampe of royaltie, the Paragon of womans perfections, found in this place at this time, the onely occasion of disclosing of her disguise, and being supposed by all the mirror of our sexe, may now be tearmed the wonder of woman-kinde.[35]

It is true: what Hyalus suffered from the gods of air and land, Arisbas and Timoclea have suffered at the hands of fortune; and their happy transformation and reunion occur at the place and on the anniversary of Hyalus' metamorphosis. Indeed, upon Timoclea's arrival in disguise at Arcadia the shepherds had said of her "that eyther HYALUS beeing retransformed,

[35] *Ibid.*, p. 89.

had returned to grace ARCADIA, or CUPID shrowded in disguise of mortall shape, was come to fire their hearts with newe flames."[36]

What takes place in Dickenson's Arcadia is not contact with ideals of perfection or sets of values, but contact with the divine, the effect of such contact being chiefly the revelation (similar to that of Greek romance) that human life is an analogue of divine life. The world outside Arcadia is uninstructed and chaotic; Arcadia itself, filled with memorials of the gods' residence, is the place where humans discover both their connections and their likeness to the superhuman, and act out, unconsciously, that likeness. Their unconscious mimesis is emphasized by the seasonal structure of the plot, for hero and heroine act in phase with the earth governed and expressed by the gods, as did Daphnis and Chloe. Timoclea enters Arcadia in autumn, and remains quiet in her disguise at the temple all winter; Arisbas enters Arcadia at the vernal equinox; and the two are reunited amid the flourishing of spring.

Robert Greene's most searching use of pastoral occurs not in his actual pastoral romances, *Pandosto. The Triumph of Time* (1588) and *Menaphon Camillas Alarum to Slumbering Euphues* (1589), but in an interlude in his courtly romance *Ciceronis Amor. Tullies Love* (1589). This work is set in the countryside between Rome and the village of Arpinatum, in a place called "the vale of Love." The vale takes its name from a quasi-mythological love match accomplished there between the wealthy shepherdess Phillis and the lowly Coridon (an affair that prefigures the love of Terentia and Cicero in the main plot). Terentia, Cornelia, and Flavia relax in this pleasant spot and fall asleep after having heard the story of Phillis and Coridon. A handsome but witless young man, "Fabius the Foole" (who has been sent away from Rome in disgrace to work as a shepherd on his father's farm) comes upon the

---

[36] *Ibid.*, p. 52.

sleeping ladies. So struck is he by their beauty that a sudden intellectual awakening occurs: "from a grosse clowne hee became to be a Judge of Beautie,"[37] and then its worshiper. As Fabius says to Terentia later, "I speake this as being the man that from the cart live in the court, thus metamorphosed by your supernaturall beauties."[38]

The story, itself derived from *The Decameron,* also resembles Boccaccio's *Ameto,* with the exception that here the young man assumes his true identity as the son of a senator, rather than being transformed into someone different. His response to his change is twofold. First, it takes the form of a geographical motion: Fabius leads the ladies out of the countryside into Rome, his now properly noble sphere of action, never to return to Arpinatum. Secondly, at Rome he achieves a symbolic reclothing expressing his new status: "Loves arrowes thus piercing into the heart of *Fabius* whereinto never before any civill thought could enter, made such a Metamorphosis of his minde that not onely his Father & friends, but all *Roome* began to wonder at his sodaine alteration: for he required to be apparelled as the sonne of a Senator."[39] In this new status he joins the main plot near the end of the book, and takes part with the other two heroes, Cicero and Lentulus, in its happy denouement.

The pastoral place in *Ciceronis Amor*—"this earthly paradise" with its plenitude of "natures treasure" and its serene combination of opposites like art and nature—is deliberately and rather simply symbolic. It is "the vale of Love" and what happens there follows the standard Neoplatonic paradigm of the beautiful soul of a beautiful woman piercing a man's soul and raising it to contemplations higher than those of the flesh. Greene points the moral for his audience quite explicitly:

[37] Greene, *Works,* ed. Grosart, VII, 187. It should be noted that the episode of Fabius is almost a literal translation of the first part of *Decameron,* V,1, but that the original lacks the aura produced by Greene's mythical setting in "the vale of Love."

[38] *Ibid.,* VII, 207.

[39] *Ibid.,* VII, 188.

Here by the way courteous Ladies and brave gentlemen what shal I say of the transformation of *Fabius*? onely in my opinion this: that the high vertues of the heavens infused into this noble brest, were imprisoned by the envious wrath of Fortune, within some narrowe corner of his heart, whose bands went a sunder by love, as a Lord to mightie for fortune. *Cupid* the raiser up of sleepy thoughts dispersed those vertues into every part of his mind, obscured before with the eclipse of base thoughts.[40]

Greene here asserts unequivocally what Sidney explored and could accept only with modifications. Love raises Fabius, as it did Strephon and Klaius, to a higher form of life (though, be it noted, Fabius is noble from the first, whereas they rise from shepherds to become the equals of the noble). The Platonic Idea operates perfectly in experience.

In *Pandosto,* the problem solved by human action is that of love conceived as a social problem rather than as a philosophical one. The main value of the Sicilian pastoral circle is its very freedom from the operations of that fortune which alternately frowns and smiles on the hero and heroine·throughout the other portions of *Pandosto*'s world. "We shepheards are not borne to honor, nor beholding unto beautie," Fawnia declares, wherefore "the lesse care we have to feare fame or fortune."[41] To leave the Sicilian fields is to place oneself in that goddess' hands: "Ah, unfortunate *Fawnia* thou seest to desire above fortune, is to strive against the Gods, and Fortune. . . . haddest thou rested content to have bene a shepheard, thou needest not to have feared mischaunce."[42] The action of Dorastus and Fawnia in Greene's "Arcady" is therefore the accomplishment of a love which obliterates caste and status. The action, once Dorastus and Fawnia have fallen in love at first sight, proceeds dialectically to that end. It begins with the usual Euphuistic paired laments, Dorastus proclaiming

[40] *Ibid.*, VII, 188-89.   [41] *Ibid.*, IV, 282.   [42] *Ibid.*, IV, 308.

the humiliation of a lofty prince stooping to a shepherdess, Fawnia expressing the fear of a rustic wench aspiring to a prince. Their meeting suggests that the pastoral life offers a possible rapprochement of the high and low by means of an adjustment of appearance and reality. For after Fawnia has outlined the values of nature and content to Dorastus, she starts to redefine the gifts of fortune: "our greatest welth not to covet, our honor not to climbe, . . . rich in that we are poore with content, and proud onely in this, that we have no cause to be proud."[43] It is on this level of real mental nobility clothed in apparent material poverty that their love can prosper. Since the prince cannot wed the shepherdess, and the shepherdess refuses to become a concubine, the prince must approach her status by becoming a shepherd.

In *Menaphon,* produced a year later than *Pandosto,* the social freedom of the pastoral land has become its only value. As we shall see in our discussion of this book in Chapter 5, the cosmic dimensions provided by fortune are abandoned in *Menaphon,* the values of content exhibited by the shepherds are praised but cast aside and replaced by others, and the pastoral style is even mocked. All that remains is a kind of social no-man's-land, where a king, a princess, her husband and her son, and various shepherds—both ignoble and noble—can meet.

In the works of the three post-Sidneian pastoralists we have examined, we have a small spectrum of the kinds of value that could be located in the pastoral land and galvanized by the fact of the hero's disguise. The values are presented in a variety of ways and are more or less explicit: they may be expounded (as in *Pandosto*), revealed by theophany (as in *Arisbas*), or incorporated into an image or exemplar (as in *Ciceronis Amor* and *The English Arcadia*). They range in content from the metaphysical to the socio-economic. In *Arisbas* we have a

[43] *Ibid.,* IV, 283.

mythical vision of a seamless world, the "one" of metaphysics; in *Ciceronis Amor,* the Idea of love and its operation on the human soul; in *The English Arcadia,* a moral exemplar of self-sacrifice and justice; and finally, in *Pandosto,* we have concretized, rather than an ideal, a wish for complete social freedom. The possibilities of pastoral vision—which could embrace such divers matters as intellectual ideal, social imperative, ethical exemplum, and mythic vision—seem inexhaustible.

⟨ IV ⟩

Whereas Sidney showed increasing concern to make explicit the intellectual content of his pastoral, Thomas Lodge—the greatest writer of pastoral romance after Sidney—chose instead to stress the action of pastoral, the means of coming into contact with ideals rather than the ideals themselves. By putting his emphasis on the playing of roles, he took advantage of the potentialities of the genre as fully as Sidney had, but produced a totally different effect. His three pastoral romances, *The Delectable Historie of Forbonius and Prisceria* (1584), *Rosalynde. Euphues Golden Legacie* (1590), and *Euphues Shadow, The Battaile of the Sences* (1592), show an interesting progression in this regard.

At the beginning, Lodge was interested not in the values inherent in the pastoral land, but only in the quality of action possible within its confines. *Forbonius and Prisceria* is a brief, diagrammatic version of the pastoral action. Forbonius' love for Prisceria is thwarted by her parents, who send her away into the country. Forbonius, disguised as the shepherd Arvalio, comes to her there, and they open their hearts to one another. They are discovered by her father; but Forbonius persuades him that their marriage will compose the family feuds that separate them, and the lovers' subsequent marriage fosters social amity. It is a simple plot of separation in the city resolved by union in the country (a brief version of the *Aethiopica,* for Prisceria is the granddaughter of Theagenes and

Chariclea).[44] Unlike Sidney, Greene, and others, however, Lodge does not see the countryside as representing any ideal or Idea, but rather as an ambivalent place, redolent of amity but solitary as well, and therefore privative and unpleasant:

> . . . a place for the solytarinesse more fit for a *Tymon,* then convenient for a beautifull Ladie, the onely companie there being shepheards. . . . Thus from stately Court, from the regards of her sweet friend, from the plesures that follow the Citie, her companions were rurall maidens, her retinue frolicke shepheardes: whose slight capacitie not yeelding anie comfort to allaie the Gentlewomans sorrowings, made her (to her more hart griefe) continue her pensivenesse, and sup up her conceived sorrow in silence.[45]

The positive value of the countryside consists for Lodge in the freedom of action that masks permit there, as we can see in the scene where the lovers are united (a scene which will reappear, highly developed, in *Rosalynde*). Forbonius is sent to Prisceria disguised as the shepherd Arvalio, famous for singing, under the assumption that his sorrowful music will answer hers: they will join in the paradoxically solitary music that is the objective correlative of their common state of mind. Forbonius' expression of solitary grief will, by answering Prisceria's, lead to the end of solitariness. Forbonius manages this action by creating in his song a fiction for Prisceria to enter: the shepherdess Corinna loves Corulus, who first scorns her, then loves her, searches her out, and closes with her in marriage.[46] At the end of the song Forbonius detaches himself from it by contrasting his unhappy case to Corulus', and at that point it is only natural for Prisceria (who has recognized him) to step in and, by her love, to make Forbonius resemble his fictive hero. As the lovers progress from fiction to fact, Corinna and Corulus in the song become Prisceria the mourner

---

[44] Lodge, *Forbonius and Prisceria,* in *Works,* ed. Gosse, I, 54.
[45] *Ibid.,* I, 67.
[46] *Ibid.,* I, 70-76.

and Arvalio the singer, and finally Prisceria and Forbonius
the lovers. What Lodge has done in this brief scene is to suggest the kind of union that can arise between separate persons
when each takes a specific role in a fiction.

By the time of *Euphues Shadow,* Lodge has very little interest in disguise and role-playing: what happens in the pastoral
place is that an undisguised Philamour comes there to find
Philamis who, having taken upon himself the character of
the magician Climachus, leads Philamour to happiness. The
ideational content of the pastoral place, on the other hand,
receives considerable attention, chiefly through the old shepherd Celio. In conversation with Philamour, Celio outlines
the pastoral values and explicitly compares the place with the
curative pastoral retreats in Ariosto and Tasso.[47] And in an
appended piece, "The Deafe Mans Dialogue," Celio is detached
from the fiction in order to define the pastoral life as one removed from the worldly life and looking toward heaven. It
is here that his name becomes significant, as well as his symbolic deafness to the sounds of this world (this section also
resolves the conflict of the subtitle, "The Battaile of the Sences,"
by obliterating the senses). The quality of the pastoral world
as halfway house between this life and the next—contemplation conceived of as facing away from life toward death, as in
Don Simonides—leads to its mediate role in the action of the
book. This is the realm where the powers of human science
and magic control fortune and hence lead to the regeneration
of the unfortunate. Man here acquires by contemplation a
power analogous to God's "to revive the dead & commaund
the waters."[48] It is here that Philamis rescues Philamour from
despair and that both are rescued from death.

As in *Arcadia,* there are three fictional realms in *Euphues
Shadow*: the tragic world of human chivalry and cruelty (like
that of Malory), introduced in the long tale of Claetia which
fills the middle of the book; the courtly Euphuistic world of

[47] *Euphues Shadow,* in *Works,* II, 74.
[48] *Ibid.,* II, 84.

love and disappointment which opens it; and the pastoral world of natural magic and rebirth in which the story reaches its resolution. The courtly world stands between the other two, divided between tragedy and comedy. As in *Arcadia,* the courtly heroes hear about the tragic chivalric world, and enter at the end the comic pastoral world. And the three are bound together in analogy by the motif of the amorous quest. Rabinus' ritualistic quest, in which he must conquer three knights, kill three monsters, and so forth, in order to satisfy his cruel mistress Claetia, ends in tragedy for himself and his beloved. This quest immediately becomes an exemplum for the courtly group that hears its story. Harpaste (who disdains Philamour) is warned lest she suffer Claetia's fate,[49] but she refuses to heed the warning. She sends Philamour on a quest like Rabinus', commanding him to revive the supposedly dead Philamis and to enlarge a river for her love. When Philamour himself is revived from near-death in the pastoral world, Celio tells him a consolatory tale of the shepherd Calimander, who happily fulfilled such a quest with the help of Climachus (the disguised Philamis). Philamour then seeks out Climachus, and succeeds in making his quest the analogue of happy Calimander's rather than of Rabinus'. The plot of this book, beginning as an acting out of tragedy, ends, in the pastoral world of supernatural regeneration, by acting out a happy pastoral romance.

Rosalynde, Lodge's masterpiece, exhibits a much more subtle and highly developed sense of role-playing than *Forbonius and Prisceria* and at the same time is explicit enough about the values behind roles (though much less concerned with values than is *Euphues Shadow*) to make them fully significant.

The vitality of mimetic play in *Rosalynde* depends in part on the way Lodge handles the theme of art and nature. As in most pastoral romances, descriptions of Arden's scenery stress

---

[49] *Ibid.,* II, 48.

the combination of art and nature—for example, "a grove of Cipresse trees, so cunninglie and curiouslie planted, as if some Goddesse had intreated Nature in that place to make her an Arbour" (36).[50] The Forest of Arden is free from the taint of man's arts and hence "natural"; at the same time, it is ideal, completely unreal (since no such natural state has existed since the fall) and therefore "artificial." The country will present a natural ideal artificially, the city the vices of artifice in stylization: this is part of the tradition. But in *Rosalynde* the boundary between natural and artificial is blurred more radically and explicitly than in any other Elizabethan romance—so much so, in fact, that the blurring becomes thematic.

Such a possibility suggests itself when we consider the ways in which people behave in Arden. The inhabitants are divided into two groups: natives of Arden, like Coridon, Montanus, and Phoebe; and disguised members of the court, such as Rosalynde, Alinda, Rosader, and Gerismond. Within each group there are some rather surprising degrees of artifice. While the old shepherd Coridon comes as close as any character in the Elizabethan romances to the actual sixteenth-century rustic, Montanus and Phoebe (whose upbringing has never been shown to be any different from Coridon's) conduct their affairs in the highest courtly style, replete with sonnets, postures, and Euphuistic talk. And while Rosader's conduct as disguised shepherd is totally stylized, Rosalynde's is not at all, and Gerismond's pose as a Robin Hood figure allows him to exist in the relaxed greenwood milieu of vigor and plenty. Furthermore, there are several cases in which members of different groups are indistinguishable stylistically. Rosader's and Montanus' approaches to love operate on the same high level, their poetic styles are identical, and they speak the same Euphuistic prose—this despite the fact that one of them is a young nobleman playing a part while the other is a shepherd simply being himself. And Gerismond, the disguised king,

---

[50] Parenthetical references are to *Rosalynde, Works*, Vol. I.

speaks and acts in a less stylized fashion in his role than do the native Montanus and Phoebe.

The most radical example of the blurring of artificial and natural in a role is Rosalynde herself. She is the most fully disguised person in the plot—first as page, then as pastoral swain—yet her actions are the least stylized, the most spontaneous and free from conventional forms. In Arden, she shows more wit and common sense than anyone else. Behind her mask, she can approach her love for Rosader directly and humorously, reject Phoebe with dispatch and a homely image, and manage a denouement with delight and tact. Furthermore, her speech more closely approaches the colloquial in diction and syntax than does that of any other character in the book. Rosalynde's role suggests that the disguised characters who deliberately swathe themselves in artifice are no more stylized than the undisguised characters, and frequently act with less attention to conventions and codes than the others. A conscious pose may, in fact, be a way of being "natural," or true to yourself.

It is not the distinction between behaving normally and playing a part that matters in *Rosalynde,* but rather the nature of the part played. And that, in turn, depends on the different values inherent in the places where the parts are played out. The significant ideas represented by the two stages for miming, the city of Bordeaux and the countryside of Arden, are very clearly distinguished. For one thing, different kinds of events happen to people in Bordeaux and in Arden. Since Bordeaux is in the hands of a usurper, it is fittingly the realm of division and strife, where Torismond banishes Gerismond and later Rosalynde and his own daughter, and where he then oppresses Saladyne, who likewise has forced his brother into exile; where death rules over Sir John of Bordeaux and the victims of the Norman wrestler; and where constant violence erupts between brothers. The state of Arden under the true king is, in direct contrast, a place of union and mutual aid: Adam helps Rosader and Rosader saves Adam with the aid of Gerismond, who prevents them both from starving; Rosader saves Saladyne, Saladyne then saves Rosader, Rosalynde helps Montanus, and so forth. The values that cause these events appear clearly in Sir John's legacy at the opening of the book: "Climbe not my sonnes; aspiring pride is a vapour that ascendeth hie, but soone turneth to a smoake: they which stare at the Starres, stumble uppon stones. . . . Low shrubbes have deepe rootes, and poore Cottages great patience. Fortune lookes ever upward, and envie aspireth to nestle with dignitie. Take heede my sonnes, the meane is sweetest melodie; . . . levell your thoughts to be loyall to your Prince" (11). As his terms show, the court is ruled by the selfish pride later exhibited by Torismond and Saladyne, while the country exhibits the humility which opens the way to love and giving: Montanus' generosity in giving up Phoebe to Ganimede or Gerismond's largess proceeding from his content "with a simple cottage, and a troupe of revelling Woodmen for his traine." One very practical result of the contrasting values is that Bordeaux denies sustenance to the needy, while Arden is the inn where homely food is given to all who ask, whether it be at Gerismond's banquet or Alinda's cottage supper. Another evident consequence is the restriction of natural desires (and hence their complication) in the city, as against the peculiar liberty which allows one to act as he feels in the country. The contrast is felt especially in regard to love: in the city, Rosader's love for Rosalynde was obscured by his familial misfortunes, while the country allows him free expression and even offers trees on which to hang his sonnets. Rosalynde's love at court is complicated by her position—"But consider ROSALIND his fortunes, and thy present estate"—while in the freedom of Arden she can even become the wooer. Alinda relates the difference between city and country love to appearance and reality: "But sir our countrey amours are not like your courtly fancies, nor is our wooing like your suing: for poore shepheards never plaine them till Love paine them, where the Courtiers eyes is full of passions when his heart is

most free from affection: they court to discover their eloquence, we wooe to ease our sorrowes" (108). And she is right,
for pride is the result of illusions fostered by dumb fortune,
whereas humility represents the actual nature of humankind.

Two recurring terms, each with both personal and cosmic
applications, will help us to take the contrast to the general
level. These are fortune, referring both to individual luck and
the goddess Fortuna, and nature, meaning both one's human
nature and the creation. Bordeaux is the realm of fortune,
Arden the realm of nature. The forces are not exclusive, but
rather interact differently in each place: in the one fortune
suppresses nature, in the other nature operates freely to overcome fortune (just as, early in the pastoral tradition, Virgil's
eclogues demonstrated that human suffering was ameliorated
by the influence of the natural world). In the city, Fortuna
tempts Saladyne into villainy with her promises, makes love
impossible for Rosalynde, and keeps Rosader's natural nobility
obscure, causing him to exclaim: "Nature hath lent me wit
to conceive, but my brother denied me arte to contemplate
. . . those good partes that God hath bestowed upon me, the
envie of my brother dooth smother in obscuritie: the harder
is my fortune, and the more his frowardnesse" (17). Nature
can emerge here only in acts of extreme jeopardy (such as
Rosader's wrestling or his defense of the manor against law
and order) or in flight. In Arden, the goddess Fortuna frequently smiles, as when she leads Rosader to Gerismond, Rosalynde to Rosader, or Rosader to Saladyne. When she does not,
as when she seeks "to have a bout" with the lovers, using the
outlaws as her instruments, she is so successfully defeated by
the brotherly nature of Saladyne and Rosader that she turns
"her frowne into a favour" (92).

What Arden "means" is that in the natural world (the
world as it was intended to be at the creation, a world totally
unlike the one that it has become) one's true human nature
emerges. Saladyne's nature is not really villainous, as Torismond's is. Therefore, upon awakening from his dangerous

dream beneath the lion to find himself confronted by Rosader in Arden, he suddenly asks his brother for forgiveness and reforms. And his subsequent life in Arden, playing the part of a swain and wooing Alinda, is expressive of his true generous nature in a way that his "real-life" status as landowner and elder brother was not. The same is true of Rosader as a forester acting out his loyalty to his outlaw king and giving full vent to his loyalty to his supposedly absent mistress, or of Rosalynde playing the witty downright swain, or of Gerismond or Alinda. Each of the roles, it should be noticed, transforms the merely privative state of those who have lost their place in society into a positive ideal of unrestricted action. In this way playing a role becomes a transforming act: any disguise or conscious role which enables a character to adjust his life to the world of human and cosmic nature becomes, in effect, a means for expressing his true nature.

A consideration of the plot structure of Lodge's work will extend our understanding of the relation between the ideal and the disguise. In *Rosalynde* the usual plot—movement out of the civilized world into the pastoral world—amounts to quitting the realm of pride, discord, and a human nature clouded by appearances of fortune and entering the land of humility, love, and true nature. Since this is a multiple plot, we have several versions of such a movement. We have, first, the "envelope plot" of Gerismond and Torismond: the selfish brother usurps the good brother's throne and drives him to Arden, where he recovers, reconstructs a government on the natural Robin Hood model, and emerges to reinstate himself. The Saladyne-Rosader plot reinforces this one, paralleling it on the private level: the avaricious elder brother first oppresses and then exiles the good brother, but finally repents in response to the latter's generosity and reinstates him. The main amorous plot of Rosader and Rosalynde shows how love, dampened by the reversals of fortune administered by the selfish repressors Saladyne and Torismond, arises whole, fresh, and triumphant in the natural world. The two other love plots expand this

one: the Saladyne-Alinda plot parallels it but emphasizes social and economic conditions; the Montanus-Phoebe plot shows
the separation of lovers caused by Phoebe's pride yielding to a
union brought about by Montanus' triumphant humility and
Rosalynde's charity. All five plots are, of course, individual
variations on the single theme of a separation brought about
by selfishness yielding to a union wrought by love, which
arises so "naturally" in Arden. Or, as Lodge himself puts it:

> Heere Gentlemen may you see in EUPHUES GOLDEN LEGACIE,
> that . . . division in Nature as it is a blemish in nurture, so
> tis a breach of good fortunes; that vertue is not measured
> by birth but by action; that yonger brethren though inferiour
> in yeares, yet may be superiour to honours; that concord
> is the sweetest conclusion, and amitie betwixt brothers more
> forceable than fortune. (139)

Lodge wove his five variations together in a way most proper
to his theme. He divided his book structurally into two parts,
separation and reconstruction. The first part, as befits the theme
of separation, proceeds by large separate sections of parallel
plotting, a series of extrusions from the city to the forest like
those that occur in *King Lear*: first Rosalynde's banishment,
then Rosader's escape, and finally Saladyne's exile (Gerismond's banishment takes place before the story opens). The
second part, in keeping with the growth of unity, proceeds
by much closer interweaving, as Rosader, Saladyne, Alinda,
Montanus, Phoebe, and Rosalynde approach their unions in
the climactic scene at the end.

Now, the hinge on which the plot turns is the rapprochement of Rosader and Rosalynde; and that occurs in a delicate
interlude at the exact structural center, just after the final ex-
trusion of Saladyne and immediately preceding the first movement toward reconciliation, Rosader's discovery of Saladyne
and the lion. The central interlude is the most detached and
stylized incident in the whole book. Its language is heightened, for it is in verse, in a "wooing eclogue," that Rosader

and Rosalynde come together; and while Rosader is merely operating out of his woodland pose, though in verse, Rosalynde is stalking behind a whole system of masks—Rosalynde as Ganimede "playing" Rosalynde. Yet it seems that this very masking of identities and feelings is the only condition under which true feelings can come to light. For on this level Rosalynde feels that she can set aside maidenly modesty and act out the truth. Therefore the wooing éclogue begins with Rosader's frank persuasions matched by "Ganimede's" equally frank fears, proceeds to *stichomythia,* and ends in a harmony marked by the intimate sharing of a broken stanza:

ROSADER.

Oh gaine more great than kingdomes, or a crowne.

ROSALYNDE.

Oh trust betraid if *Rosader* abuse me.

ROSADER.

First let the heavens conspire to pull me downe,
And heaven and earth as abject quite refuse me.
Let sorrowes streame about my hatefull bower,
And restlesse horror hatch within my breast,
Let beauties eye afflict me with a lowre,
Let deepe despaire pursue me without rest;
Ere *Rosalynde* my loyaltie disprove,
Ere *Rosalynde* accuse me for unkinde.

ROSALYNDE.

Then *Rosalynde* will grace thee with her love,
Then *Rosalynde* will have thee still in minde.

ROSADER.

Then let me triumph more than *Tithons* deere,
Since *Rosalynde* will *Rosader* respect:
Then let my face exile his sorrie cheere,
And frolicke in the comfort of affect:
  And say that *Rosalynde* is onely pitifull,
  Since *Rosalynde* is onely beautifull. (79-80)

Questions about the relation of fact to fiction center on this eclogue. Before entering it, Rosalynde had tested the degrees of conventionality and sincerity in Rosader's love by this pretext:

> I pray thee tell me Forrester, what is this ROSALYNDE, for whom thou pinest away in such passions? Is shee some Nymph that waites upon DIANAES traine, whose chastitie thou hast decyphred in such Epethites? Or is shee some shepheardesse, that haunts these plaines, whose beautie hath so bewitched thy fancie, whose name thou shaddowest in covert under the figure of ROSALYNDE, as OVID did JULIA under the name of CORINNA? Or say mee for sooth, is it that ROSALYNDE, of whome we shepheards have heard talke, shee Forrester, that is the Daughter of GERISMOND, that once was King, and now an Outlaw in this Forrest of *Arden*. (62-63)

And the issue of the eclogue is, ironically, to turn fiction *into* fact:

> And thereupon (quoth ALIENA) Ile play the priest, from this day forth GANIMEDE shall call thee husband, and thou shalt call GANIMEDE wife, and so weele have a marriage. Content (quoth ROSADER) and laught. Content (quoth GANIMEDE) and changed as redde as a rose: and so with a smile and a blush, they made up this jesting match, that after proovde to a marriage in earnest; ROSADER full little thinking he had wooed and wonne his ROSALYNDE. (81)

Here, in the wooing eclogue, "fact" and "fiction," the "real" and the "ideal" merge, just as the restricted real-life identities of Rosader the youngest son of Sir John and Rosalynde the lost daughter of a deposed king blend into the larger versions of themselves which the roles of open rural lover and saucy swain (which may be characterized as the free dream-personalities of the lost) allow.

Such is the idealism of Lodge's book that it assumes both that a more idealistic version of the self is also a truer version of the self, and that to raise the situation by the use of masks to a level of supernormal freedom and ingenuousness is also to give more real and lasting solutions to its problems than would otherwise be possible. Hence, the wooing eclogue is the symbolic watershed of a plot where the problems of the unnatural "real" world are easily solved by a series of appeals to the true, natural, and "ideal" nature of each character. And the action of the eclogue is synecdochic of the entire plot, where one takes up a pose that expresses his real nature (allowing him freedom and loyalty, and therefore natural love), comes to terms with himself and others in that pose, and eventually drops it by returning to quotidian life. As the lovers use a formal song to test their love, so the whole of *Rosalynde* uses fictional roles as a means of testing the availability of an ideal of human conduct.

In *Rosalynde*, Lodge, like Sidney, attempted to explore and extend the possibilities of human existence. His thesis, the possibility that he explored, was that the world as we know it, with its selfishness and violence, is only the apparent world, whereas the real world is something we never see, an ideal of humility and love. Such a thesis presupposed a Platonic view of reality, and in order to test this view, Lodge created for each of his characters an artificial role of ideal generosity and self-sacrifice. To escape the heartless codes of Bordeaux, each character enters Arden under a mask, consciously adopted, finds his true self therein, and thus achieves meaningful discipline. Each of them therefore discovers his proper nature by acting it out dramatically. Gerismond the dispossessed acts out as Robin Hood the true nature of kingship, in giving sustenance to his subjects, Saladyne, in acting out the part of humble and loyal forester, discovers the true nature of an elder brother in protection and self-sacrifice. Rosader, who has no place in Bordeaux, acts out his unwavering loyalty to king and mistress in order to fulfill the part of a lover. And Rosalynde escapes from the ambiguity of Bordeaux to act out in Arden the role of the open and charitable swain and in this way to find for herself the true part of the beloved in frank and direct giving of herself. What Lodge accomplished here has been formulated for our time by William Butler Yeats: "There is a relation between discipline and the theatrical sense. If we cannot imagine ourselves as different from what we are and assume that second self, we cannot impose a discipline upon ourselves, though we may accept one from others. Active virtue as distinguished from the passive acceptance of a current code is therefore theatrical, consciously dramatic, the wearing of a mask."[51]

[51] William Butler Yeats, *Autobiography* (New York, 1938), pp. 400-401.

CHAPTER 4

Courtly fiction: Gascoigne and Lyly

To a limited but significant extent, the settings of the different kinds of Elizabethan fiction determine their different tonalities: the pastoral fields, the serene accommodation of ideal and actual; the large European and Asian landscapes of Neo-Greek romance, the cultivation of accident and absurdity; the urban settings used by Thomas Deloney and Henry Robarts, moral and mercantile earnestness; and the court of high society, cool irony and sophistication. The work of Gascoigne, Lyly, and the Euphuists, which we have designated "courtly fiction," does not have a tradition seventeen centuries long behind it, as does pastoral romance, but it does have antecedents—notably Chaucer's *Troilus and Criseyde*[1]—and it therefore tends to build with relatively recent material. Specifically Renaissance in its setting, rather than located in the timeless fields of Arcadia, it tends toward the topical. Its subject, like that of the pastoral romance, is love—love seen, however, not in the abstract, but in a setting where more common concerns of education, ethical norms, and the practical problems of life come to bear upon it. The court setting and the sophisticated tone proper to such a milieu combine to produce in this fiction a satirical rather than an idealistic attitude toward its main concerns.

The chief effort of courtly fiction was to cast a second and very critical glance at the assumptions of Tudor Humanism. The writers of this fiction were often courtiers or court entertainers, and thus exhibit the traits of the third generation of Humanists ("the humanist as courtier," in G. K. Hunter's phrase),[2] who used learning as the decoration rather than the

---

[1] See Percy Waldron Long, "From *Troilus* to *Euphues*," *Anniversary Papers by Colleagues and Pupils of George Lyman Kittredge* (Boston, 1913), pp. 367-76.

[2] G. K. Hunter, *John Lyly: The Humanist as Courtier* (Cambridge, Mass., 1962).

goal of life, and who therefore wove ideas into their work and modified them, rather than propounding absolute ideals of education, the ethical mean, or (in another vein) the Neoplatonic ideals of love. In submitting such Humanistic ideals to criticism, chiefly by showing their operation or failure to operate in everyday life, these writers were not only furthering a skeptical effort but developing a concept of the function and operation of fiction (one best represented by Sidney's concept of fiction) totally different from that of their forebears.

The attacks of Erasmus, Vives, and Ascham on the romances of Malory and others for glorifying "open manslaughter and bold bawdry" in their books make it clear that, for the early Tudor Humanists, the function of fiction was the direct presentation of ideal modes of conduct for the reader to incorporate into his life.[3] Their concept of fiction was, in short, straightforward exemplum, and the few fictional works produced between 1500 and the publication of Gascoigne's first work in 1573 amounted for the most part to treatises or dialogues using stories to prove a point: *The deceyte of Women, to the instruction and ensample of all men* (1547), *A lyttle treatyse called the Image of Idlenesse, conteynynge certayne matters moved betwene Walter Wedlocke and Bawdin Bacheler* (1559), and Edmund Tilney's *A briefe and pleasant discourse of duties in Mariage, called the Flower of Friendshippe* (1568). Therefore, there often seems to be merely a difference of degree between a book of instruction like Sir Thomas Elyot's *The Book named The Governor* (1531), where the tale of Titus and Gisippus from Boccaccio is inserted as "a right goodly example of friendship,"[4] and a nominal work of fiction such as Tilney's *The Flower of Friendshippe,* where various personages (including Vives and Erasmus) meet to tell

---

[3] See Robert P. Adams, "Bold Bawdry and Open Manslaughter: The English New Humanist Attack on Medieval Romance," *Huntington Library Quarterly,* XXIII (1959), 33-48.

[4] Sir Thomas Elyot, *The Book named The Governor,* ed. S. E. Lehmberg (London: Everyman's Library, 1962), p. 136.

brief tales about marriage which constitute a series of "learned *exempla* served up in Renaissance style."[5]

So closely are fiction and treatise related in the early Tudor period, in fact, that they almost exchange places: with fiction reduced to static exemplum, the fictive impulse can be seen vitally at work in books like *The Governor* or *Utopia,* where the reader engages in the exciting process of constructing a fictional ideal out of the shards of actuality. The clash between idealism and "realistic" defense of the status quo in the satirical dialogue of Book I of *Utopia,* for example, yields in Book II to the "urbane philosopher's" *tertium quid* between things as they are and things as they absolutely should be, the "possible-ideal" (that is, the closest version of the ideal that could actually be attained in the real world).[6] This, the realm of Utopia, is also the realm of fiction, which criticizes and redirects only by presenting an image of what is possible. The speculative image presented here is not "the best," but something better than the contemporary European situation, and is therefore hedged by irony as well as extended by satire. The process of reading *Utopia* (and this applies to Continental books like *Il Libro del Cortegiano* and to Book I of *Gargantua* as well) is the process of constructing an image, and follows a curve of transcendence—a transcendence of things as they are by things as they might be, of satire by myth, of dialogue by a single moving image.

Elizabethan courtly fiction, as we have said, does not construct ideals but rather tests them by acting them out in reality. It does so more directly than any other fiction of the period both because the ideals it tests are those constructed by the forebears of its readers and authors and because its settings have the distinct feel of the contemporary—even if Oxford is thinly disguised as "Athens" and London as "Naples." Whereas

---

[5] Schlauch, *Antecedents of the English Novel, 1400-1600*, p. 153.

[6] See H. A. Mason, *Humanism and Poetry in the Early Tudor Period* (London, 1959), p. 126.

Humanistic fiction was exemplary, this is the fiction of experience. Even the titles of these books advertise either direct experience or the subjection of ideas or qualities to experiential analysis: Lyly's *The Anatomy of Wit;* Robarts' *A Defiance to Fortune;* Greene's *Arbasto, The Anatomie of Fortune;* Melbancke's *Philotimus. The Warre betwixt Nature and Fortune;* Saker's *Narbonus. The Laberynth of Libertie;* and *Greens Groats-worth of Wit, Bought with a Million of Repentaunce.*

What there is of the exemplary in these books is negative, for they show the reader what *not* to do, and in so doing they satirize those who would live by rigid ideas. The hard schooling of experience often robs the naïve and usually bookish hero of hope, so that instead of the establishment of some ideal situation at the end, we have just the opposite: the spectacle of a defeated hero, bitter, disillusioned, and sometimes ruined. We have, for example, the bitter Euphues and Philautus, Gascoigne's F. J. leading the desperate life of a rake while his true love pines away, Riche's Don Simonides fleeing love and companionship, Saker's Narbonus brooding over his rejection by the ironically named Fidelia, Robarts' Andrugio retreating to a hermitage out of the reach of fortune, or Philotimus staring in disbelief at his ravaged face.

This is the literature of significant failure—significant because it shows the folly of trying to live out an actual life by adherence to rigid codes of action. Instead of beautiful structures of transcendence, we have the bathetic, a series of maps showing the various downward paths to wisdom.

George Gascoigne's *The Adventures of Master F. J.,* the first and one of the best works of original fiction of the Elizabethan period, presents a very full inquisition into the validity of a previous age's ideas. The book exists in two versions: the first, originally published in 1573, is an epistolary fiction set in England; and the second, published in 1575, a revision feigned to have been translated from the Italian, in which the setting becomes Italy and the narration becomes continuous.

While the first version is in many respects a better book, it is in the Italian setting of the second that Gascoigne's critique of ideas comes out more brilliantly.

Master F. J. comes close to acting out a play whose script was laid down in Castiglione's *Il Libro del Cortegiano.* The scene is set in Renaissance Italy, at the castle of the noble Lord of Velasco near Florence. Life there is leisurely, polite, and graceful, filled with banqueting, dancing, hunting, walking, polite visits, and—above all—conversation. There are informal courts of pastime, like those at Urbino, with the Lady Elinor presiding as the Duchess did, and Dame Pergo (a lady perhaps derived from Castiglione's Lady Emilia and exhibiting the same sort of biting pleasantness) acting as the goad to conversation. The questions decided there are rather like the medieval questions of love. We find, for instance, this sort of thing: "And one day passing the time amongst them, their playe grew to this end, that his Mistresse, being Queene, demaunded of him these three questions. Servant (quod she) I charge you, as well uppon your allegiance being nowe my subject, as also upon your fidelitie, having vowed your service unto me, that you aunswere me these three questions, by the very truth of your secret thought" (393).[7] The style of life at the castle of Velasco is, then, constricted within the bounds of the courtly code of conduct. Hence Ferdinando Jeronimi makes his properly adulterous approach to the Lady Elinor by the proper means of letters and sonnets, exhibiting himself pale and even ill with love, enlisting himself as the courtly servant of his *donna,* and reaping the ritual rewards of a *congé,* the *bezo las manos,* and the *zuccado dez labros.*

If the action exhibits in its style all the traits catalogued in a handbook of courtly love, the language in which it

[7] Parenthetical page references are to Vol. I of *The Complete Works of George Gascoigne,* ed. John W. Cunliffe (2 vols.; Cambridge, 1907). See Richard A. Lanham's brilliant analysis of the questions of love in "Narrative Structure in Gascoigne's *F.J.*," *Studies in Short Fiction,* IV (1966), 44-47.

is couched is the casual Neoplatonic-Petrarchan mode common to Renaissance courtly poetry. All of the clichés are there: the definition of beauty as proportion, color, and infused "comly grace" (389), the mistress as the embodiment of heavenly virtue ("the heavenly aspects whiche you represent," 418), love as contemplative delight in the mistress' virtues (431), Ficino's spiritual exchange of hearts ("since wee became one hart devided in two bodyes," 433), the kiss as the meeting of souls (393), and so forth. Ferdinando's amorous verse is—as the narrator candidly admits—uneven, but it is freely decorated with the standard, if exaggerated, Petrarchan conceits:

> But she (whome I doe serve) hir pearles doth beare,
> Close in hir mouth, and smiling shewe, the same.
>
> . . . .
>
> Since that hir sugred tongue the passage breakes,
> Betweene two rockes, bedeckt with pearles of price. (416)

Frank B. Fieler, in his study of the courtly elements in the book, concludes that F. J.'s "diction and conceits . . . are conventional, but at the same time pretentious, self-conscious, and bookish. What he desires is the conventional, but long outdated, servant-mistress relationship of the courtly romance."[8] It is perhaps necessary to add that the inhabitants of the Castle of Velasco are all too willing to give him what he desires.

It is good to insist that F. J.'s courtly approach to love is in part a function of his inexperience, for what actually happens in the book constantly gives the lie to his stiff, formal behavior. All of his finely styled action and speech, directed by traditional courtliness, Neoplatonism, and Petrarchism, leads to the following scene of consummation, which takes place when F. J. holds a nighttime tryst with Lady Elinor in the galley of the castle:

[8] Frank B. Fieler, "Gascoigne's Use of Courtly Love Conventions in 'The Adventures Passed by Master F. J.,'" *Studies in Short Fiction*, I (1963), 28.

The Dame (whether it were of feare in deede, or that the wylinesse of womanhoode had taught hir to cover hir conceites with some fine dissimulation) stert backe from the Knight, and shriching (but softly) sayd unto him. Alas servaunt what have I deserved, that you come agaynst mee with naked sword as against an open enimie. *Ferdinando* perceyving hir intent excused himselfe, declarying that he brought the same for their defence, and not to offende hir in any wise.

The Ladie beyng therewith somewhat apeased they began with more comfortable gesture to expell the dread of the sayd late affright, and sithence to become bolder of behaviour, more familiar in speeche, and moste kinde in accomplishing of common comfort. But why holde I so long discourse in describyng the joyes whiche (for lacke of like experience) I cannot set out to the full? (407)

The narrator of the 1573 version had left less to the reader's imagination, though his explicitness was hardly necessary:

But why hold I so long discourse in discribing the joyes which (for lacke of like experience) I cannot set out to the ful? Were it not that I knowe to whom I write, I would the more beware what I write. *F.J.* was a man, and neither of us are sencelesse, and therfore I shold slaunder him, (over and besides a greater obloquie to the whole genealogie of *Enaeas*) if I should imagine that of tender hart he would forbeare to expresse hir more tender limbes against the hard floore. Suffised that of hir curteouse nature she was content to accept bords for a bead of downe, mattes for Camerike sheetes, and the night gowne of *F.J.* for a counterpoynt to cover them, and thus with calme content, in steede of quiet sleepe, they beguiled the night.[9]

The passage is shocking, not because love has led to a frank

[9] Text in Gascoigne's *A Hundreth Sundrie Flowers*, ed. Charles T. Prouty, University of Missouri Studies, XVII (Columbia, Missouri, 1942), p. 69.

and eager consummation instead of to a contemplative union
with the divine—that was certainly common enough in both
literature and life—nor merely because of the hard reality
and even sordidness of their bed, but rather because of what
the narrator makes us see in his heroine and her affair at this
instant. He has suddenly become coarse, he assumes the comic
Chaucerian role of the naïf or the impotent (the 1573 narrator
even goes further in treating the reader as a big ballocky fellow
stuffed with masculine egotism). In his leering presentation,
he strips Elinor down to her shift to reveal the practiced
coquette, the "sensual comedienne"[10] possessing at the same
time enough hypocrisy, coyness, experience, and clearheaded
practicality to shriek "(but softly)." Words such as "courtesy"
become in this context euphemisms for four-letter words.

And the irony deepens when we read F. J.'s poem com-
memorating this "moonshine banquet," for he couches the
event in high, evocative, and even cosmic mythology:

> Dame Cynthia her selfe (that shines so bright,
> And dayneth not to leave hir loftie place:
> But onely then, when Phoebus shewes his face.
> Which is her brother borne and lendes hir light,)
> Disdaind not yet to do my Lady right:
> To prove that in such heavenly wightes as she,
> It fitteth best that right and reason be.
> For when she spied my Ladies golden raies,
> Into the cloudes,
> Hir head she shroudes,
> And shamed to shine where she hir beames displaies. (408)

Ferdinando's glamorous version of what we have just observed
makes only too patent the complete rift between the appearance of an ideal code of conduct and the reality of the needs
of the body satisfied crudely and summarily on the boards in
the Castle of Velasco.

[10] See Robert P. Adams, "Gascoigne's 'Master F. J.' as Original Fiction," *PMLA*, LXXIII (1958), 323.

The rift becomes even greater and much more comic in the scene in Ferdinando's bedchamber, where the lovers quarrel and break off their affair. Elinor comes to his bedside expecting to make love, not at all daunted by her suspicion that Ferdinando knows of her other lovers (after all, she seems to feel, there is "Goddes foyson there" still.)[11] But he in his courtly dream insists on "trouthe" between lovers, and demands that they discuss his doubts and her misdeeds. Such a discussion of course dampens her ardor, and Ferdinando, distressed at the growing heat of the scene, attempts a direct and forceful end of the discussion:

> The soft pillowes being present at al these whot speches, put forth them selves as mediators for a truce betwene these enemies, and desired that (if they would needes fight) it might be in their presence but one only blowe, & so from thence forth to become friendes againe for ever. But the Dame denied flatlye, alledging that shee found no cause at all to use such curtesie unto such a recreant: adding further many words of great reproche: the which dyd so enrage *Ferdinando,* as that having forgotten all former curtesies, he assayleth his enemies by force. (435)

Elinor is still speaking in terms of denying "courtesy unto such a recreant" while in fact she is trying to escape plain rape offered her by the courtier who himself began the scene with such high idealism about love; and Ferdinando has experienced the true nature of desires in his own breast, which he had thought to be only courtly respect.[12] After she has persisted in denying "courtesy" by jumping out of bed and running out of the room, the narrator coolly concludes, "I doubte not, but shee slept quietlye the rest of the night" (435).

[11] "The Miller's Prologue," *The Canterbury Tales,* Fragment A, l. 3165.

[12] See Fieler, p. 32: "The comic reversal of the seducer becoming the raped reflects in a dramatic manner the inadequacy of the convention, of F. J.'s fantastic ideals, in the face of flesh and blood reality."

The hard reality of sharp desire and cynical pretense beneath the courtly code is underlined by a series of bawdy in-
nuendoes which the narrator introduces, especially after the
consummation scene, to counterpoint Ferdinando's own Pla-
tonic-Petrarchan euphemisms. There is, for instance, the incident where Ferdinando stanches Elinor's "blood"; or all the
business of his "naked sword" (like Samson's "naked weapon"
or "tool" in *Romeo and Juliet*), which first frightens Elinor,
then presents itself "to the handes of Dame *Fraunces*," Elinor's rival for Ferdinando's favors, is at length "conveyed out
of Mistres *Fraunces* chamber, and brought unto hirs" (413),
and is at last restored to its proper male possessor. There is
likewise the bawdy scene between Elinor and her ugly secre-
tary, who "(having bene of long time absent, & there his quiles
and pens not worne so neere as they were wont to be,) did
now pricke such faire large notes, that his mistres liked better
to sing fa-burden under him, than to descant any longer
upon *Ferdinandoes* playne song" (436).

Bold and bawdy action and high Platonic talk exist side by
side in Gascoigne's book to show how fully love has degen-
erated into lust. Though the attitude taken toward this lapse
usually ranges from one of mordant comedy to irony, at the
end it turns tragic, for the outcome of the affair at Velasco is
that the bitter F. J. spends "the rest of his dayes in a dissolute
kind of lyfe" while Frances, totally abandoned, "dyd shortlye
bring hir selfe into a myserable consumption: whereof (after
three yeares languishing) shee dyed" (453). If we ask who is
at fault, our suspicions light first on Elinor, for she is the false
beauty against whom Bembo had warned, one whose "lavish
wantonnesse painted with dishonest flickeringes" causes many
men, "whom that manner delighteth, because it promiseth
them an easinesse to come by the thing that they covet," to
treat "cloked unshamefastnesse" as if it were true beauty.[13]
As the narrator says of her, "the highest flying faucon, doth
more commonly praye upon the corn fed crow & the simple

---

[13] Castiglione, *The Book of the Courtier*, trans. Hoby, pp. 311-12.

shiftles dove, then on the mounting kyte: & why? because the one is overcome with lesse difficultye then that other" (404). She is a multiple adulteress; and, while she is mannerly enough to enter the courtly affair, her harebrained vanity betrays her into giving such broad hints of her conquest that Ferdinando is hard pressed to keep the affair properly secret, as the code of "derne love" demands.[14] Yet Ferdinando is culpable too. He is not honest enough to take an easy conquest for what it is without exalting it into an ideal. He starts the affair, persists in taking it seriously despite all the counter-indications, and then clouds it by his unwarranted jealousy. And his conduct sorely disappoints Frances, whose relatively realistic estimate of him placed him at far above his real worth.

It is worth asking, in view of these considerations, whether *The Adventures of Master F. J.* is a critique of the characters or of the code. Is it that courtly love is a valuable ideal but that these people at Velasco are unworthy of its real if old-fashioned value? Or that these are normal if imperfect human beings caught up in a false and destructive code? If we hasten to choose the first alternative, then we reckon without two salient factors, the relevance of Frances and the role of the narrator.

The Lady Frances, with her wit, frankness, modesty, and warmth is an ideal of womanhood. Though she loves Ferdinando and eventually dies of unrequited love, she has too much pride and consideration for his desires to reveal her love. Her high sense of self-sacrifice and her wit combine in the role she plays in the adventures; for she becomes Ferdinando's confidante and furthers his affair with Elinor, in the hope that once he has discovered by experience the falseness of Elinor he will turn to her. She turns out to have overestimated the man she calls her "Trust." Yet, for all that, she is perhaps the only realist in the book, for she by no means closes her eyes to her beloved's imperfections and base conduct even though her hopes are betrayed. While Ferdinando deceives

[14] See Fieler, p. 30.

himself by casting a glamorous veil over base lust (as does Elinor, to some extent), Frances pursues an interestingly opposite tack: she sets up several fictional situations whereby the entrance into controlled experience becomes a means of making a person change his point of view. Thus what she calls her "experiment" with Ferdinando (403) is designed to help him to enter fully into the affair with Elinor, in order to show him what love of such a woman is really like. She formalizes this experiment by allegory, naming him her "Trust" (her trust in his ultimate goodness and wisdom), herself his "Hope" (first, hope of gaining Elinor by her aid; ultimately, hope of real happiness with Frances). If the experiment fails, it is not because it avoids the situation she is presented with. Later, too, Frances offers Ferdinando a tale of adultery in order to force him to see Elinor from her husband's imagined point of view, as a harlot, and hence to persuade him to give over his dishonorable action as the lover in the story did. His honor and reputation are always uppermost in her mind.

The difference between such a woman and Elinor is, as the narrator says, tremendous: "in their beauties no great difference: but in all other good giftes a wonderfull diversitie, as much as might betwene constancie & flitting fantasie, betwene womanly countenaunce and girlish garishnes, betwene hot dissimulation & temperat fidelity" (404). Yet, if Elinor is the false beauty, it does not necessarily follow that Frances is the ideal mistress for a courtly affair. She is too frank and familiar, too full of what is vulgarly termed "personality." In the descriptions of the two women, what is consistently stressed is Frances' personality and Elinor's status as a sex symbol or love-object, "very fayre, and of a very courtlike behaviour" (383). Elinor behaves on the surface as the courtly mistress, Frances as the friend or companion (who ironically possesses more delicacy of feeling than the mistress); Ferdinando is Elinor's subordinate, her "servant," but he is Frances' equal, playing "Trust" to her "Hope."

What Frances offers Ferdinando—and what her father in-

tended in inviting Ferdinando to his castle in the first place—
is the understanding and companionship of marriage. The
affair with Elinor therefore represents the disruption of a story
which should have been one of happy marriage. The constant
presence of Frances makes us follow the adulterous love affair
with the possibility of a better way always in mind. Thus we
see the story objectively and ironically, always aware of the
course it could have taken were it not for the destructive code
of adulterous love.

A contrast with the quite similar situation of Lancelot and
Elaine in *Le Morte D'Arthur* will make the effect more
pointed. For in spite of the obvious beauty and ideality of
Elaine and all she offers in contrast to the cruel mistress
Guinevere, who takes all and gives nothing, Malory is at one
with his hero in rejecting her and lamenting her attempt to
unsettle the adulterous roots of the Round Table by Christian
marriage. Gascoigne's narrator sees the case as just the opposite
—as the courtly code upsetting marriage—and in doing so
indicates the gap between medieval and Elizabethan attitudes
toward courtly love and codes of behavior in general. For
Malory, codes had a supernatural sanction and tested men. If
a man was ruined by love, he had had the satisfaction of serving an ideal, and if an affair failed, it was because of human
frailty. Gascoigne's view is more pragmatic: a code of behavior
(or an ideal place like Thélème or Utopia) is created by men
and for men; if it ruins a man, it is *ipso facto* wrong, and
must be discarded.

The case against the code of love is furthered by Gascoigne's
strategy of creating for his story a narrator totally at variance
with it. In the original version of 1573 the narrator had not
only a personality but a name, "G. T.": F. J. told his story
and gave his poems to G. T., who then recounted the tale,
supplying signed narrative links between poems and letters.
The manuscript was sent in turn to one H. W., who printed it
as a comic exemplum against those who "have enchayned

them selves in the golden fetters of fantasie."[15] The work
then had the form of a modern epistolary novel, in which the
reader was always aware that the narrator G. T. was shaping
by his attitudes the raw material supplied by the hero.[16] In
the revised version of 1575 the narrator has been absorbed into
the narrative as its central intelligence. Since everything save
the inserted letters and poems appears from his point of view,
the story as he sees it becomes the story as it really was, instead
of being merely material upon which he comments. Yet he
retains the distinct personality he originally possessed: he is
the reader's garrulous and intimate companion, never missing
an opportunity to confide his real opinions of the characters to
us, or to point out the latent comedy in a situation. He is an
honest, downright fellow, not always very quick-witted (as
when he misses the point of the analogy Ferdinando draws
between his Elinor and Helen of Troy, 415), especially when
it comes to the subtleties of courtly love. For he is inexperienced
in the ways of Amor, and so cannot describe its joys "for lacke
of like experience" (on which, we feel, he really congratulates
himself). Therefore his view of love is utilitarian and ironic;
for instance, he feels that one might as well use a single love
poem over and over merely by changing the names in it (415).
And satiety is as good a reason for breaking off a love affair
as disloyalty: "they founde [Elinor] lying on hir bed, whether
gauled with any griefe, or weary of the thing (which you
woote of) I know not, but there she lay" (448).

His attitude toward Elinor and the code she uses is, therefore, a mixture of shrewd amusement and disgust (as we saw
in his presentation of the consummation scene and the bedchamber combat). He reserves his wholehearted admiration
for Frances, and takes a peculiarly objective stance toward
his hero—a much more objective stance, by the way, than had

[15] *A Hundred Sundrie Flowers*, ed. Prouty, p. 49.
[16] See Adams, "Gascoigne's 'Master F. J.' as Original Fiction," p.
318.

G. T. in the original version.[17] His main means of keeping a distance between himself and Ferdinando is to operate as literary critic, for he breaks in after every poem to analyze and judge it, to praise, to express puzzlement, to excuse faults: "this is but a rough meeter, and reason, for it was devised in great disquiet of minde, and written in rage" (401), or to condemn: "Of this Sonet, were it not a lyttle to muche prayse (as the Italians do most commonly offend in the superlative) I could the more commend it. . . . *Ferdinando* did compile very many verses according to sundrye occasions proffred, and they were for the most parte sauced with a taste of glory" (416).

In his brilliant article on the narrator, Robert P. Adams has shown how this intrusive companion, who always insists on breaking into the story to tell his own tales, to give us his opinions literary and otherwise, to shatter our illusions by snide indications of the reality of a case, performs the comic function of distancing us from the action by means of his own unsympathetic attitude toward it.[18] This the clowning narrator does most conspicuously at the turning point of the action, which he withholds from us in a most infuriating manner. He starts with a clumsy commentary on Ferdinando's brag, "Beautie shut up thy shop," pointing out the hero's hybris: "By this challenge I gesse, that eyther he was then in an extasie, or else, sure I am nowe in a lunacie, for it is a prowde challenge made to *Beautie* hir selfe" (415). He proceeds to a discussion of its real subject with tongue-in-cheek pedantry, breaking off with the offhand conclusion, "Wel by whome he wrote it I know not," in order to take up a new sonnet, which he condemns for hyperbole. He then teases us with bits of plot interrupted by a long allegory of Suspicion and other matters, before finally turning to Ferdinando's reversal. He is here at his greatest distance from a high concept of love and

[17] See Leicester Bradner, "Point of View in George Gascoigne's Fiction," *Studies in Short Fiction*, III (1965), 21.

[18] Adams, "Gascoigne's 'Master F. J.' as Original Fiction."

from Ferdinando himself, whom he treats as a madman; and his diction now becomes robust and colloquial: "never a barrell of good herring betweene them both," "not unlike to a Poticares pot," "an old saying is . . . ," and so forth. As the narrator grows clumsier and more earthy, the tone of the book becomes progressively coarser (embracing as it does slapstick diction and sexual puns), in keeping with the plot's bathetic decay.

The reader's experience of Gascoigne's book, then, becomes this: the spectacle of a homely, down-to-earth narrator looking at "highfalutin" lust with irony and disgust. We must accept his base view of things (just as we cannot ignore Falstaff's) no matter how sly and clumsy he is, for the narrator is the comic realist. It is he who is the guardian of the story which demonstrates that the fine theories of the courtiers amount, as often as not, to glamorous masks for the neural itch. Whereas the *Libro del Cortegiano* ended in transcendence, the experienced *Adventures* follow a curve downward to this conclusion: "thus we see that where wicked lust doeth beare the name of love, it doth not onelye infecte the lyght minded, but it maye also become confusion to others which are vowed to constancie. And to that ende I have recyted this Fable which maye serve as ensample to warne the youthfull reader from attempting the lyke worthles enterprise" (453).

⟨ II ⟩

John Lyly's *Euphues. The Anatomy of Wit* has a plot similar in outline to that of Gascoigne's *Adventures*—a prodigal son story of the downward path to wisdom—but it is presented much more deliberately. For Lyly was the most self-conscious literary artist in Renaissance England, the formulator of a style that has become a byword for deliberate artifice. Two regions of this self-consciousness worth exploring are Lyly's use of ideas and his vivid histrionic sense. Indeed, we might say that Lyly was so acutely conscious of the distinctness and even polarity of traditional ideas as to make any contact with them as histrionic an activity as the assumption of a disguise in pastoral romance.

Lyly's very family background forced upon him an acute sense of the stance he was taking at any time regarding any given ideas or traditions. His grandfather was William Lyly, the distinguished Hellenist and grammarian, a friend of Erasmus and Colet. His father, Peter Lyly, prebendary and registrar at Canterbury, was the contemporary of second-generation Humanists like Elyot and Ascham, in whom we see the educational goals of Humanism taking precedence over the first generation's emphasis on the presentation of ideals. By the time of John Lyly's own generation, "the Humanist ideal shrunk to that of 'the courtier' who was required, within a certain elegant and disdainful playfulness of manner (what Castiglione calls *sprezzatura*), to have some knowledge of classical authors. But the courtier was to use his learning as decoration, not as part of his belief."[19] The combination of this Humanist heritage and his personal situation as a court entertainer produced in Lyly a curious attitude toward Humanist ideals such as wit, honor, love, and friendship. On the one hand, he was obviously fascinated by concepts, as both the intellectual formulations introduced into his narrative and the treatises on women, education, and religion (out of Ovid, Plutarch, and others) that he appended to *The Anatomy of Wit* amply demonstrate. Lyly's works display far more learning than do any other examples of Elizabethan fiction. On the other hand, though he dealt with ideas so much more explicitly than Gascoigne or others, he tended to play with ideas rather than to promulgate them, to present them from a variety of viewpoints in order to show a spectrum of possible attitudes.

Unlike Gascoigne, Lyly begins by providing an ideational framework by which the actions of his plot may be judged throughout. The hero and situation of *Euphues. The Anatomy of Wit* (1578) arise directly from Roger Ascham's *The*

[19] Hunter, p. 31.

Scholemaster, begun in 1563 and published in 1570. Of the seven qualities in the child fit for education which Ascham drew from Book VII of Plato's *Republic,* the first is aptness of wit: "Εὐφνής is he, that is apte by goodnes of witte, and appliable by readines of will, to learning, having all other qualities of the minde and partes of the bodie, that must an other day serve learning, not trobled, mangled, and halfed, but sounde, whole, full, & hable to do their office"[20]—the "other qualities" being command of language, a good voice, a comely countenance, a well-knit body, and so forth. Ascham went on to define the proper goal of such an ideal of grace and wit, and at the same time to issue a warning:

> And, even as a faire stone requireth to be sette in the finest gold, with the best workmanshyp, or else it leseth moch of the Grace and price, even so, excellencye in learning, and namely Divinitie, joyned with a cumlie personage, is a mervelous Jewell in the world. And how can a cumlie bodie be better employed, than to serve the fairest exercise of Goddes greatest gifte, and that is learning. But commonlie, the fairest bodies, ar bestowed on the foulest purposes. I would it were not so: and with examples herein I will not medle. . . .[21]

It is precisely Lyly's purpose to meddle with examples, to put this moral concept into the firm context of experienced reality in order to see what happens when the *euphues* does take a foul direction, how he recovers, and so on. In the work that results, Ascham's precept will be a touchstone rather than an earnest imperative, and nothing more; for this is the *anatomy* of wit, dissecting its strengths and weaknesses as they present themselves to the play of many minds within the book.

The major vehicle for wit and playfulness in the book is, of course, the style that Lyly welded for himself. Euphuistic form insists on pairing qualities and enforcing balance and

[20] Roger Ascham, *English Works,* ed. William Aldis Wright (Cambridge, 1904), p. 194.
[21] *Ibid.*

antithesis by *isocolon, pairson,* and *paramoion*; Euphistic ornament insists on projecting antitheses into the general by *sententiae,* exempla, and *similia.* Both Albert Feuillerat and Jonas Barish agree that the one distinguishing characteristic of such a style is antithesis.[22] Feuillerat goes so far as to claim that the entire book *"n'est en somme qu'une antithèse longuement prolongée,"* and we can see this principle operating in the plot structure, where Euphues' reply contradicts Eubulus' opening expostulation, where the two contrasting visits of Euphues to Lucilla frame their two contrasting laments, where Philautus' letter to Euphues is capped by the latter's reply, and so forth. Within the period, Lyly's characteristic procedure is to polarize opposite qualities and then to project this polarization outward by illustrative *similia* or exempla, as in the following passage:

> So likewise in the disposition of the minde, either vertue is overshadowed with some vice, or vice overcast with some vertue. *Alexander* valiaunt in warre, yet gyven to wine. *Tullie* eloquent in his gloses, yet vayneglorious: *Salomon* wyse, yet to too wanton: *David* holye but yet an homicide: none more wittie then *Euphues,* yet at the first none more wicked. The freshest colours soonest fade, the teenest Rasor soonest tourneth his edge, the finest cloathe is soonest eaten with Moathes, and the Cambricke sooner stained then the course Canvas: whiche appeared well in this *Euphues,* . . . who preferring fancy before friends, & his present humor, before honour to come, laid reason in water being to salt for his tast, and followed unbrideled affection, most pleasant for his tooth. (184–85)[23]

Extreme is set against extreme—virtue against vice, wisdom against wantonness, wit against wickedness, humor against

[22] Albert Feuillerat, *John Lyly* (Cambridge, 1910), p. 412; Jonas A. Barish, "The Prose Style of John Lyly," *English Literary History,* XXIII (1956), 17.
[23] Parenthetical references are to *The Complete Works of John Lyly,* ed. Bond, Vol. I.

honor, reason against affection—to prove that these opposites
are not merely alternatives but are irreconcilable. If two qualities are opposed, Lyly sharpens their opposition so that they
appear to be products of totally different systems of value and
possessed of totally opposed consequences. Faced with single-
ness, he is at pains to show that it contains within itself not
only duality but self-contradiction: "in the greenest grasse is
the greatest Serpent" (202). As Barish writes, "the more
absolute of its kind a thing may appear to be, the more certain
it is that somewhere within it lies its own antithesis, its anti-
self."[24] Such a style—with its constant insistence on doubleness,
the ambivalence of choices, the fissure between appearance
and reality—conveys an image of the world as infinitely incon-
sistent and an image of the mind as perpetually ambiguous.[25]

This style is in itself self-consciously histrionic, and the
extremes it imposes on characters who perforce believe in the
world it renders make them acutely aware of the necessity of
role-playing in the world. Antithesis implies choice, and when
two terms are so presented as to be absolutely destructive of
one another, choice becomes a crucial act. Therefore, when
this style is projected into the speeches that form practically
the entire plot of the book, the two characters in a dialogue
must present irreconcilable views, and the mind of a man in
soliloquy must be torn by contrary passions—as in the opening, where the two warring parts of Euphues, his good nature
and bad nurture, cause a war in Eubulus' own mind between
love and hate. As a consequence of this dichotomizing, any
moment of choice is presented as an oscillation between two
directly opposed courses of action which presuppose totally
different sets of values and even different versions of the choos-
er's character. As a result character is conceived as dual, composed of both the hero's present nature (which we assume is
his normal one) and a possible future one, which he envisions
as a dramatic role he is to play henceforth.

[24] Barish, p. 22.
[25] See Barish, pp. 23-24.

The plot of *The Anatomy of Wit* begins with Euphues' rejection of the traditional role of the good man because it seems to him unwitty. Old Eubulus is the voice of Ascham: he exhorts young Euphues to moderation and caution, lest his "tender wit" and good nature dwindle to foul purposes without the props of nurture, which Eubulus considers to be the cumulative advice of the aged. But this is a tiresome if a good old man. Though Eubulus is no Polonius, there is a touch of satire in the presentation of this purveyor of conventional wisdom, and it comes out in his style, which Euphues scorns as "aged & overworn eloquence." In his formal oration Eubulus masses *similia* and exempla (sometimes as many as seven of them in a row) analyzed and reworked around every repetitious point. Euphues' impromptu reply in defense of unaided nature shows wit instead of the studied eloquence of wisdom; in a discourse stripped (for once) of the baggage of *similia*, couched in direct and often curt statements, Euphues snipes at Eubulus' position, often turning his own eloquence back upon him ("The similytude you rehearse of the waxe, argueth your waxinge and melting brayne") and ending with this quip, mocking Eubulus' style with sexual puns: "The Birde *Taurus* hath a great voyce, but a small body, the thunder a greate clappe, yet but a lyttle stone, the emptie vessell giveth a greater sownd, then the full barrell. I meane not to apply it, but looke into your selfe and you shall certeinley finde it, and thus I leave you seekinge it, but were it not that my company stay my comming, I would surely helpe you to looke it, but I am called hence by my acquaintance" (194).

Since the conventional wisdom embodying the ethical mean has been proved unworthy of a witty man, Euphues attempts to circumvent it by erecting his own ethically independent code of action. The code that wit contructs is a personalist one; it is friendship, wherein good and evil are defined by loyalty or disloyalty to a single man rather than by conformity to an absolute precept. Instead of relating the lower to the higher (witty youth to wise old age, or things as they are to an ideal of things as they should be), it relates like to like. The implications of self-love involved in binding yourself to a friend as much like you as possible are brought out both by the friend's name, Philautus ("Self-love") and by the arguments Euphues uses in constructing his code: the friend as preserver of the self, as "an other I," as the mirror wherein one sees and loves his own "lively Image" (197).

And the fragility of this bond becomes apparent almost immediately: Philautus introduces Euphues to his fiancée Lucilla, and a new force, passion, breaks open the ritual of friendship Euphues has constructed with such care. He must give up the code of friendship for the actions proper to a lover. Euphues is caught in the standard Renaissance conflict of friendship and love, but Lyly's version of the conflict derives a peculiar power from its clarity and generality. For Euphues is not merely wronging Philautus or transferring the code of loyalty from friend to mistress; rather, he is giving up friendship for love, and almost becoming another person in the process. Such is the dichotomizing pressure of the Euphuistic form that the conflict immediately rises from the personal to the general, and Euphues leaves one whole sphere of values for another—altruism for selfishness, candor for deceit (deceit in general, victimizing not only Philautus but Ferardo and Livia as well), a code near the center of everyday morality for one definitely beyond the pale. Therefore his decision is achieved with maximum clarity: to "deceive Philautus to receive Lucilla," for "to love and to lyve well, is not graunted to *Jupiter*." And he attempts to accustom himself to his new course of action by proposing exempla to follow, traditionally negative exempla which he revaluates by stripping them of their normal connotations:

Did not *Paris* though he were a welcome guest to *Menelaus* serve his hoste a slippery prancke? If *Philautus* had loved *Lucilla,* he woulde never have suffered *Euphues* to have seene hir. Is it not the praye that entiseth the theefe to ryfle? (210)

Hadde *Tarquinius* used his love with coulours of continu-
aunce, *Lucretia* woulde eyther wyth some pitie have aun-
swered hys desyre, or with some perswasion have stayed
hir death. It was the heate of hys lust, that made hyr hast
to ende hir lyfe, wherefore love in neyther respecte is to bee
condempned, but hee of rashnesse to attempte a Ladye fu-
riouslye, and shee of rygor to punishe hys follye in hir owne
fleshe, a fact (in myne opinion) more worthy the name of
crueltie then chastitie, and fitter for a Monster in the
desartes than a Matrone of *Rome*. (211)

In short, Euphues' decision amounts to an assumption of a
new role, that of the passionate lover who plays fast and
loose with the rules, and the action of *The Anatomy of Wit*
consists of his playing that role to the full. His first action
is to deceive Philautus by using Livia as a stalking-horse;
then, in his compact with Lucilla, he enters on full promis-
cuous deceit. Philautus' letter of remonstrance only hardens
the hero in his role:

Love knoweth no lawes: Did not *Jupiter* transforme himselfe into the shape of *Amphitrio* to imbrace *Alcmena*? Into
the forme of a Swan to enjoye *Laeda*? Into a Bull to be-
guyle *Io*? Into a showre of golde to winne *Danae*? Did not
Neptune chaunge himselfe into a Heyfer, a Ramme, a
Floude, a *Dolphin,* onelye for the love of those he lusted
after? Did not *Apollo* converte himselfe into a Shepheard,
into a Birde, into a Lyon, for the desire he had to heale hys
disease? If the Gods thoughte no scorne to become beastes,
to obtayne their best beloved, shall *Euphues* be so nyce in
chaunging his coppie to gayne his Lady? No, no: he that
cannot dissemble in love, is not worthy to live. . . . As *Lucilla*
was caught by frawde so shall she be kept by force. (236)

The emphasis on leaving one's proper self is unmistakable: Euphues has *made* himself into a bounder, and what of it? The only thing that can shake him out of his new persona is something other than ethical self-awareness, and that is achieved when he discovers the irony of his course of action reflected in the behavior of Lucilla, who, having first cast him aside for Curio and having then outfaced him, shows the faithlessness he himself had exhibited enlarged into complete treachery. He recoils, drops the masks of lover and friend, and returns to his former life of scholarship at Athens.

Euphues and Lucilla present contrasting examples of the influence of will on wit, or of nurture on nature. While he discovers who he really is by playing out what he is not, she finds out her real nature by exploring it mimetically. Therefore, we see how the role she adopts and her realization of her true nature in that role both *grow* in the process of the action. Her first moment of decision is not as clearly envisioned as Euphues' is; she knows that she is giving up the role of obedient daughter and faithful fiancée, but she does not yet realize the significance of the role she is entering upon. At first, she conceives of it generally as a yielding to passion: "What a doubtfull fight dost thou feele betwixt faith and fancie? hope & fear? conscience and concupiscence?" But she shields herself from its full implications: "Let my father use what speaches he lyst, I will follow mine own lust. Lust *Lucilla,* what sayst thou? No, no, mine owne love I should have sayd, for I am as farre from lust, as I am from reason, and as neere to love as I am to folly. Then sticke to thy determination, & shew thy selfe, what love can doe, what love dares doe. . ." (207). The real nature of her choice is to risk becoming what she really is, to tread, like Beatrice-Joanna and the Duchess of Malfi, the dream forest of "will" or "lust." She discovers this gradually, in the course of playing out the part to see "what love can doe." Thus, after indulging her desires deceitfully with Euphues, she has acquired enough self-knowledge to face her father Ferardo with a frank admis-

sion in these terms: "You neede not muse that I shoulde so
sodeinely bee intangled, love gives no reason of choice, neither
will it suffer anye repulse. *Mirha* was enamoured of hir natu-
rall Father, *Biblis* of hir brother, *Phaedra* of hir sonne in lawe:
If nature can no way resist the fury of affection, howe should
it be stayed by wisdome?" (231). But it is only after her un-
leashed desires have led her from Euphues to the base Curio
that she realizes what her role really is: she is led by lust, not
love, and she is not merely a high-spirited girl but a fickle
whore who will break her father's heart. Thus, with an iron
face, she reveals herself to Euphues—and perhaps to herself—
in these clear terms:

> I have chosen one (I must needs confesse) neither to be
> compared to *Philautus* in wealth, nor to thee in wit, neither
> in birth to the worst of you both, I thinck God gave it me
> for a just plague, for renouncing *Philautus*, & choosing thee,
> and sithens I am an ensample to all women of lightnesse, I
> am lyke also to be a myrrour to them all of unhappinesse,
> which ill lucke I must take by so much the more patiently,
> by howe much the more I acknowledge my selfe to have
> deserved it worthely. (238–39)

She has broken out of her own dream to find it real, and her
realization shatters Euphues' own amoral role. For the first
time, Euphues pushes aside the trick of logic by which both
of them have revised negative exempla, and sees their real
moral import. Picking up her words, he says: "Shall the
lewdenesse of others animate thee in thy lightnesse? why
then dost thou not haunt the stewes bicause *Lais* frequented
them? why doest thou not love a Bull seeing *Pasiphae* loved
one? why art thou not enamoured of thy father knowing that
Mirha was so incensed?" (240).

   As Euphues awakens from his amoral dream, the consciously assumed role has been played out, and the possibilities of love have been fully tasted. The mimetic test of love
forms, in turn, a test of Ascham's ideal; for we evaluate

Eubulus' precepts by observing Euphues' adoption and experience of their opposites. Hunter presents the plot as a five-act drama of abstractions: "(1) wit rejects wisdom, (2) wit meets friendship and love, (3) wit chooses love, (4) wit loses friendship, (5) betrayed by love, wit repents its wilfulness and so recovers friendship."[26] But it might be simpler to say that the plot begins with precept, proceeds through experience, and ends with precept. After the revelation of Lucilla, Euphues laments his rejection of Eubulus and announces himself in complete phase with Ascham's *euphues*:

> I will so frame my selfe as al youth heereafter shal rather rejoice to se mine amendement then be animated to follow my former lyfe. Philosophie, Physicke, Divinitie, shal be my studie. . . . If witte be employed in the honest study of learning what thing so pretious as witte? if in the idle trade of love what thing more pestilent then witte? The proofe of late hath bene verefied in me, whome nature hath endued with a lyttle witte, which I have abused with an obstinate will. (241)

The Anatomy of Wit is a book celebrating experience. As G. K. Hunter puts it, " 'Wit' or good endowment is only turned into wisdom when experience breaks the mind that would not bend to precept."[27] In order to taste experience fully, Euphues must take up various unconventional or even immoral roles and force them to the ultimate test before dropping them in disillusionment.

The various treatises and letters appended to *The Anatomy of Wit* display the fruits of the experiences recorded in the narrative; in Wallace Stevens' terms, they show the whole mind sitting in judgment on the ideas of value which part of the mind has acted out previously. Here we see, in an alternation between renunciation of past folly and acceptance of better versions of life, the development of full moral aware-

---

[26] Hunter, p. 55.
[27] *Ibid.*, p. 52.

ness in the hero. "A Cooling Carde for Philautus and all fond lovers" is a bitter rejection of love and women, in which Euphues, having achieved the state of experienced man, submits a wry renunciation of folly as evidence of his wisdom. "Euphues and his Ephoebus" is more positive in approach, for there Euphues as it were rewrites *The Anatomy of Wit* as it should have been, by constructing, in the Humanist manner, the image of a good scholar: "the whole effect shall be to sette downe a young man so absolute as that nothing may be added to his further perfection" (260). He shows himself fully in agreement with Eubulus here by reproducing Eubulus' early speech to himself as his speech to Ephoebus.[28] In "Euphues and Atheos" Euphues has arrived at a state of contempt of the world, and it is from this high moral plane that he then, with decreased bitterness, renounces love, the courtly life, and even the life of this world in a series of letters.

The persona of the experienced man that Euphues assumes as his right in these appendices is especially important in showing how experience brings ideas to life, so that what before he had heard he now knows. While Euphues returns to Eubulus' position, it is now an earned position endued with the strength of life, instead of being merely words mouthed by a good but dull man. Euphues is often self-conscious about his position, but he uses it to enforce his authority, as when he writes Philautus, "Thou wilt muse *Philautus,* to here *Euphues* to preach, who of late had more minde to serve his Ladye then to worshippe his Lorde" (306). Experience, he insists, is the better way—indeed, the only way—to wisdom: "It is commonly sayd, yet doe I thinke it a common lye, that Experience is the Mistresse of fooles, for in my opinion they be most fooles that want it. . . . I was heereof a studente of great wealth, of some wit, of no smal acquayntance, yet have I learned that by Experience, that I shoulde hardly have seene by learning" (260). Yet, though it is the better way, it is certainly not an

[28] Compare *Works*, I, 189-90 and 286.

unmitigated good. There is, as Euphues writes, no way to wisdom without wounds: "the minde once mangled or maymed with love, though it be never so well cured with reason, or cooled by wisedome, yet there will appeare a scar by the which one may gesse the minde hath bene pierced, and a blemish whereby one maye judge the hearte hathe bene stayned" (284).

Lyly's tone is not simple, for he stresses not only the painfulness of experience along with the necessity of undergoing it, but also the residue of bitter memory, the scars, along with the wisdom it produces. Here lies the value of *The Anatomy of Wit,* for it refreshes the reader's sense of the wisdom of conventional wisdom (just as does Alan Sillitoe's modern novel, *Saturday Night and Sunday Morning,* a book which, upon examination, is seen to bear a striking resemblance to Lyly's work) in demonstrating both the necessity of accepting such wisdom and the mixed attitude with which a man of wit does so.

⟨ III ⟩

Lyly's interest in the movement of the mind suffering under the onslaught of experience was so great that he consistently subordinated narration to dialogue or soliloquy; at times it might be more accurate to say that he buried narrative beneath dialogue. In one passage, for example, he disposes of a whole series of contretemps (whereby Lucilla casts off both Euphues and Philautus for Curio while her father is away) in a single sentence (237), in order to set up a four-page dialogue. It is not surprising that the imitators of a model whose interest centers in putting ideas into action by means of dialectic should cultivate dialectic alone—should imitate the appendices of *The Anatomy of Wit* rather than its story, as it were—and produce works that belong as much to the history of rhetoric as to that of prose fiction. Indeed, this fact has caused C. S. Lewis to create a third category of fiction besides the "realistic" and "romantic," that of "the rhetorical *genre,*" in order to account for the work of such imitators of Lyly as Gosson, Munday, Saker, Melbancke, Riche, and Greene.[29]

The purest exemplar of the rhetorical mode is Stephen Gosson's *The Ephemerides of Phialo* (1579), which consists entirely of dialogues, since it is "devided into three Bookes. The first, A method which he ought to follow that desireth to rebuke his freend, when he seeth him swarve: without kindling his choler, or hurting himselfe. The second, A Canvazado to Courtiers in foure pointes. The third, The defence of a Curtezan overthrowen." Also relatively pure in its rhetorical orientation is *The Golden Aphroditis: A pleasant discourse* (1577), the work of Lyly's predecessor John Grange. Basically a manual of amorous approaches, it buries its rather strange semi-autobiographical account of a successful courtship among inserted poems, letters, incidental tales, conversations, and other rhetorical elements.

Anthony Munday's *Zelauto. The Fountaine of Fame* (1580) is somewhat of a borderline case. It does contain some narrative, but of a fragmentary nature and subordinated to discourse. The first of its three parts is given over to the character of a charitable hostess, Ursula, and a description of the English court; the second part contains among its lengthy dialogues and orations slight accounts of a trial by combat and an escape from prison. It is only in the third part that narrative develops, and then in a novella (an analogue to *The Merchant of Venice*) that Zelauto reads while his host prepares dinner.[30]

But three followers of Lyly (besides Robert Greene, whose tension between ideas and action we shall explore in the next chapter) showed more than perfunctory interest in plot: Austen Saker, Brian Melbancke, and Barnabe Riche.

Saker's *Narbonus. The Laberynth of Libertie* (in two parts,

[29] C. S. Lewis, *English Literature in the Sixteenth Century*, pp. 418-21.

[30] See Jack Stillinger's edition of *Zelauto* (Carbondale, Ill., 1963), pp. xviii-xxi.

1580) is in many respects closer to Lyly's work than are any of the other imitations, for it is composed largely of dialogue and hinges on the themes of love, friendship, wisdom, and prodigality. But while the style and framing story are Euphuistic, the book develops in new narrative directions by adding adventures in travel and an Italian novella, and moves toward realism by including conny-catching episodes and an extended realistic portrait of the soldier's life—its jests and brawls, the absurdities of war, and the stench of the battlefield. The book therefore insists on the necessity and validity of experience: "though *Narbonus* were in his youth allured to many wanton lustes, yet once having felt the force of Fortune, was seduced to an honest lyfe. . . . this youth would not be reformed untyll he sawe his owne follyes before his face, nor be reclaimed tyll he had tasted some purging Pilles for his mad maladyes" (first part, sig. A3). His fortunes as he tastes experience follow a rhythm of rise and fall: having first wasted his patrimony in prodigality, he then forms a friendship with Phemocles (an untroubled friendship, unlike that of Euphues and Philautus) and plights his troth with Fidelia. It is fortune that breaks off these Euphuistic relationships. Narbonus is pressed into military service in Spain; upon returning home to Vienna he finds Phemocles gone and himself rejected by Fidelia, and tries a year at court—with disappointing results. So great is the book's insistence on experience that it almost catapults its hero out of the universe of ideational conflict: when he returns from the horrors of war, he has become so insensitive that "his desire towardes *Phemocles* was nothing so deepe as before, nor his love to *Fidelia* nothing so great as before his going" (second part, sig. F2v). But Narbonus, like Lyly's hero, recovers and ends in a firm life of scholarly friendship with Phemocles.

Melbancke's *Philotimus. The Warre betwixt Nature and Fortune* (1583) is a derivative book, owing as it does heavy debts both to Lyly and to Tottel's *Miscellany, The Paradise of Dainty Devices,* and other collections, which supplied Melbancke with several lyrics to insert bodily into his prose.[31] It stands on the line between courtly fiction and the purely rhetorical mode, stuffed as it is with speeches, letters, and even an entire pamphlet. Yet Rollins asserts that it has a more interesting plot than *The Anatomy of Wit*;[32] and while this may be an overstatement, it does have a very clear and elaborately schematic plot line.

As the story begins, Philotimus' father is expounding the myth of the Judgment of Paris to his fledgling son in order to hold out to him three possible courses of life: that of the scholar dedicated to Pallas, that of the man of honor and wealth following Juno, or that of the courtier vowed to Venus. The myth defines the ensuing plot, for Philotimus is to try all three courses of life in turn; in doing so, he is really attempting to find a proper role for himself to play. His first choice, the role of philosopher, is abortive, for his budding career at the university is cut short by family disaster. He then shifts his allegiance to Venus and tries the role of courtier. This action constitutes the bulk of the book and makes it, like *F. J.*, a critique of courtly love, but a critique carried out basically from an economic point of view. His father had been careful to point out the dangers of Venus, for the life of the courtier painted in such glamorous colors by Castiglione may turn out to be a trap for the unwary, especially when it is placed in a concrete socio-economic context. The precepts of the aged turn out to be validated by experience: once Philotimus has spent his entire patrimony on his mistress, aptly named Aurelia, she casts him aside for "one *Cornelius* a stale hacking Courtier" (sig. Q3), but wealthy withall. In an extensive series of letters between the cast-off lover and his sometime mistress the veil of appearances gradually falls away, and

[31] See Hyder E. Rollins, "Notes on Brian Melbancke's *Philotimus*," *Studies in Philology*, Extra Series I (1929), 40-57, and "Notes on the Sources of Melbancke's Philotimus," *Harvard Studies and Notes in Philology and Literature*, XVIII (1935), 177-98.

[32] Rollins, "Notes on Brian Melbancke's *Philotimus*," p. 44.

such things as entertainment, service, and *congé* are seen as merely the payments and rewards of a whore in high place.

This disillusionment spreads so far as to envelop almost all of life. His courtly companion Aemilius fails him too, and his response is to set down his rich experience of human falsehood at Venice in a repentance pamphlet. Philotimus' subsequent path leads downward: penniless, he wanders through the countryside of Greece lamenting, seeking in vain for shelter from the wind and rain. When a band of pirates solicits his membership, he almost joins them. But his refusal to sink to their level brings insight. When, destitute and sick, he reviews his life, he sees that the role of courtly lover has made him into a beast. He sees himself as Io, the victim of violent love: "now when shee looked in the streame and saw her horned head, she was agast and from herselfe would all in hast have fled, and when she thought to lift her handes unto her head for helpe, she saw she had no handes at all . . . even such, and much alike was the life of *Philotimus*" (sig. Dd4).

Insight, crystallized in an emblem of the courtly life, leads to regeneration as the book enters the pastoral mode. Philotimus, half-dead of starvation, stumbles into an archetypal pastoral circle with its traditional symbols of plenitude: a wall of trees shutting out the outside world, in the center "a livelye springe with christall streame" (sig. Dd4v) surrounded by greenery. Here the shepherd Laurus receives Philotimus and restores him to life, and in the course of his recovery tells him his own story of amorous disappointment in bourgeois life. "Thou and I have bene birdes of one feather," he says, and his story, with its several parallels to and variations of Philotimus' own adventures, serves to generalize the hero's experience. When judgment is given, therefore, it is given in general terms and from a point of view totally outside Philotimus' own bitter perspective: it is that love, and most of the active life based on love, is vanity. But though this verdict is allowed to stand, as in *The Anatomy of Wit*, it is too simple to represent the final stance of the book. For Philotimus refuses to share the contemplative life of Laurus, and goes off instead to try his fortunes in the service of a nobleman. This he conceives of as a new, regenerate role, and deliberately adopts a costume for it: "all yclad in grene, semblable to his griefs which were ever fresh and grene" (sig. Ff2). It is, of course, the final role, that of the seeker of honor under Juno. Philotimus has finally discovered his proper role, and one equivalent to his true identity, for this is the role to which his name ("lover of honor," the *philotimon* or auxiliary of the state in Plato's *Republic*)[33] has destined him from the beginning.

Though Barnabe Riche was not an imitator of the Euphuistic style like Melbancke and the others, his relationships to Lyly are many and various. *The Adventures of Brusanus, Prince of Hungaria* (1592), Riche's most uneven book, starts out by following *The Anatomy of Wit* in its use of the prodigal son motif as the basis of the plot. Somewhere in the middle of Book I, however, its hero turns virtuous (we are never actually told that he does, or why, but he does), and the book shifts, first to a plot revolving around love and friendship (with many direct debts to Pyrocles and Musidorus in *Arcadia*, but very few to Lyly) in Book II, then to standard chivalric romance (with no relation to Lyly at all) in Book III. On the other hand, a tale like "Of Gonsales and his vertuous wife Agatha," the sixth in *Riche his Farewell to Militarie Profession* (1581), while totally uninfluenced by Lyly (it is an adaptation from Cinthio)[34] presents a plot based on the testing of ideas or wishes by experience that is quite as fully developed as Lyly's.

The relationship is most direct in *The Second Tome of the Travailes and Adventures of Don Simonides* (1584), where the hero, after hearing a debate at Rome and then undergoing a strange adventure in a desert before arriving at Naples, sets

[33] *Republic*, 580-81.
[34] G. B. Giraldi Cinthio, *Gli Hecatommithi* (1565), Decade III, Novel 5; see Thomas Mabry Cranfill's edition of *Rich's Farewell to Military Profession* (Austin, 1959), pp. xxii-xxxvi.

sail for Athens with a letter of introduction to Euphues himself.
Not only do Simonides and Euphues meet and talk at length,
but at this point Lyly is allowed to direct Riche's plot: Simonides is described as one who has "tried such like path waies
as once did *Euphues* of *Athens*" (sig. I4), and when Euphues
fails to convince him of the folly of loving, he sets sail for
England and meets Philautus and the rest of the cast of characters from *Euphues and his England.*

The first tome, *The Straunge and Wonderfull Adventures
of Don Simonides* (1581), is the best of Riche's extended
fictions, and is, moreover, a unique kind of book for its age.
It is really a sixteenth-century *Sentimental Journey,* resembling
Sterne's novel not only in its plot, in which an afflicted traveler
meets a series of people whose situations shed some light on
his own, but in its heavily sentimental atmosphere. Riche
occasionally even adumbrates Sterne's trick of shifting tones
rapidly, so that an episode which seemed serious all along
turns out to be silly, either at its conclusion or when it is
juxtaposed with a subsequent episode.

Its hero is an especially dogged Euphues who never accepts
the position that love is folly, and who consequently pursues
the role of melancholy lover to the full, exploring all its possibilities. The other lovers he meets alter his sense of himself
and our sense of him continually, so that the whole book
records the developing implications of his role, which gradually is revealed as a cloak of folly.

Disappointed in love, Don Simonides exalts that love to a
religion by adopting a disguise and entering into an amorous
pilgrimage: "being of opynion, that the chaunge of soyle,
and protration of time, would weare out the remembraunce
of his conceived sorrow, and the rather, that his deedes, might
aunswer his determynation: he invested himselfe into the
order of traveyling Pilgrimes, to the perfourmance of which,
hee made hym an new habit, and being apareled with it, . . .
he secretlye . . . by nyght betooke himselfe to his vowed Pil-
grymage" (sig. C2). The first person he meets on his pil-

grimage corresponds to his disguise, for it is the holy hermit
Aristo, who sits atop a hill in "a second *Elisium*" (sig. C2)
meditating on the world below, which he has abandoned,
and contemplating the world above, which he desires to enter.
Aristo's story at first seems to be a happy contrast to that of
Simonides, for Aristo married his beloved; but upon learning
that she then died after eight months of marriage, Simonides
considers "that in comparing of *Aristo,* his mishappes with
his: his calamytie might seeme happynesse" (sig. C4). His
response to this counter-image is interesting, for he makes up
his mind to imitate him. After finding an isolated valley, he
decides that he has come to rest: "Truely, *Simonides,* thou art
happie, by arryval heere, the onely place, whiche the Goddes
have appointed for thy penance, where shakyng off thy worldly
conceiptes, thou mayst be partaker of thy Unckle *Aristo* his
Contemplation" (sig. D3).

But his attempt to set up for a hermit is interrupted by the
huntress Porcia, who tells him the story of her happy life with
Hernando and of her tragic life after his death. Having
related her tale (darker than Aristo's) and compared it to
Simonides'—she calls his "a Counter verse, in my uncomfort-
lesse and tragicall Orysons" (sig. E1v)—she dies in his arms.

Simonides' next adventure forms a deliberate contrast to
the first two, for its setting is the city of Venice and its substance that of an Italian novella (a very free adaptation of
Bandello, *Novelle* IV, 17) full of realistic dialogue and bawdy
detail. It is a comic tale of a tricked husband: finding his
wife in bed with her lover, he sends for a friar to shrive them
before he kills them; the lover changes clothes with the friar
(really a bawd in his service) and then, as friar, reveals to
the husband's consternation that his wife is really only in bed
with another woman (the bawd). The manner of its telling
adds to the irony, for it results from a comic misunderstanding.
The lady Lamia, seeing Simonides in his pilgrim's clothes
praying at a shrine in Venice, takes him for a priest and asks
him to hear her confession. His prurient interest aroused, he

plays along: "Our *Simonides,* tickeled with this unacquainted talke, and seeing that necessitie inforced hym to this occasion, makes his wordes sutable to his Coate" (sig. H4). He answers her in priestly jargon, and she recounts her tale from the strict point of view of an old lady looking back on her sins. The tone that results is curious, for bawdy detail is always overlaid by antagonistic diction: "our Moone-shine (naie, rather mornefull) banquet, where servyng the appetite of our vile fleshe, we ministred discomfort to our soules" (sig. L3).

The effect on Simonides' disguise is interesting too, for it calls up questions of identity. Originally intended as an expression of his sadness of heart, the disguise became the badge of his vow to become a hermit; and now, when people take him for what he seems—a religious dévot—misprision results, and even (later) accusations of fraud. Now the action illustrates the lack of relation between man and man, and the presence of misunderstandings as well as sympathetic connections.

The next episode shows the interplay of rejection and sympathy between men. When Simonides observes the strange ritual penance of the shepherd Titerus—constantly tempted to love by the nymph Aglara, who cruelly retreats whenever he advances—he attempts to gain Titerus' confidence and comfort him. But Titerus steadfastly repulses him and refuses to tell his tale. Simonides pursues him, and finally gets him to recognize the bond between them by hiding behind a rock and acting as echo to Titerus' lament. The story is couched in terms of glamorous mythology. At a rustic wedding attended by the gods, Cupid's nymph Daphne fell in love with Titerus, and became ill with grief when he repulsed her. An angry Venus sent Aglara to inflict revenge by enticing Titerus to love her and then relentlessly refusing him. This is an education by turnabout: as Titerus scorned Daphne, so Aglara scorns him, and he consequently is enabled to feel what Daphne felt. Simonides helps him complete his education and leads him to Daphne's cabin, where they revive the nymph

and subsequently hold a second wedding blessed by the attend-
ing gods.

Riche has run a gamut in these episodes: two tales of tragic
renunciation; and two tales of success in love, one low and
bawdy, the other high and idealistic. The three final episodes
are essentially dialogues rather than stories, and, in the light of
the traditional wisdom they convey, Simonides appears increasingly more foolish. At Genoa the good soldier Andruchio tries
to get Simonides to "conquer your corrupt nature" (sig. Q2),
and tells him an exemplary tale of his own escape from the
clutches of a courtesan in order to persuade him. When
Simonides refuses, he is treated as a fool.

He proceeds toward Rome in his "religious Habite to cover
an ungodly purpose" (sig. Q4) and along the way meets the
old farmer Thomerchus. "*Simonides* tolde him of his Countrie, of his Love, and the rest you knowe how foolishe" (sig.
Q4), and Thomerchus too tries to dissuade him from loving.
But Simonides merely refuses to listen to his long tirade, and
beats a quick retreat in order to join a more promising companion, also a pilgrim to Rome. Irony develops to the full in
this last episode. Anthonio in his pilgrim's weeds seems at first
a mirror to Simonides, but turns out to be his opposite: he is
fleeing from a love match, and the two are really in their
respective melancholy and happiness "two mates of unequall
disposition" (sig. R2v). When they argue the pros and cons of
love, the debate grows so heated as to issue in a complete
forensic impasse. Each calls the other fool, and advises the
other to cast off his ridiculous costume and return home.
Finally the lover in his rage shouts, "Farewell too precise
Puritan" and flings off; but the unruffled victor Anthonio
follows "easilie on, laughing verie hartely, to see the follie of
our Spanishe Lover" (sig. T2).

The book ends at Rome with Simonides "growne so obsti-
nat, and his harte so indurat, hym self so malancholy, [that he]
can utter nothyng" (sig. T3). It is at this point, and with this
attitude, that *The Second Tome* takes up the tale again:

He was counsailed by the advice of aged *Aristo,* yet refused it. He was admonished by the fall of *Porcia,* yet he continued unconstant. What women were, *Lamia* taught hym. What Love was, *Titerus* made triall: and neither the perswasion of a gallant Soldiour, nor the advise of an auncient Father, neither yet the sharpe invectives of his travailing companion *Anthonio,* were ever able to withhold hym, but he would needes prosecute his follie to the ende.[35]

The new moral tone of *The Second Tome,* its several new attempts to dissuade Simonides from his course, and his final meeting with the reformed characters out of Lyly's books all make clear his connection with Lyly: Simonides is a Euphues who never learns, who, by pursuing so doggedly the role of lover, becomes the complete melancholy fool. By the end, Simonides has united himself to a small and special world of sentimental lovers, but has done so (like the hero of Joyce's "Araby") at the expense of cutting himself off entirely from the world of wisdom and reality.

While Riche and the Euphuists were developing the possibilities of the paradigm set up in *The Anatomy of Wit,* Lyly himself was developing in a different direction. *Euphues and his England* (1580) is in many ways a complete departure from the book to which it forms a sequel. As Lyly himself says of it and *The Anatomy of Wit,* "Twinnes they are not, but yet Brothers, the one nothing resemblyng the other" (5).[36] The style of the sequel is more relaxed, chiefly in that strings of *exempla* and *similia* are less frequent than in its predecessor. Narrative takes precedent over dialogue here: people tend to tell stories to each other instead of conducting general arguments, and we have multiple plots instead of a single, slow-moving plot. Perhaps as a consequence of this new emphasis on storytelling, the book exerts less ethical pressure upon action. While the result may not be, as some critics claim, a

[35] *The Second Tome,* sigs. A4-A4v.
[36] Parenthetical references are to Lyly's *Works,* ed. Bond, Vol. II.

completely amoral book, it is at least true that the narrator directs the responses of his audience less and less overtly as the book proceeds. The role of the narrator, in fact, changes from one of ethically interpreting the action for the audience to one of questioning the audience. Compare, for example, the narrative tone of "Heere Gentlemen you maye see . . ." (109), an aside near the middle of the book, with that of this aside, found near the end: "Nowe Gentlewomen in this matter I woulde I knewe your mindes" (160).[37] Most importantly, the new narrative emphasis brings the action of experience to the fore more luminously than was the case in *The Anatomy of Wit.*

In *Euphues and his England* the relation between ideas and experience becomes more complex than in the other works we have examined, and is, moreover, made the central topic of both discourse and plot. Experience is figured concretely as exploring the unfamiliar in travel, and the territory explored is in turn dichotomized into the realms of fortune, among the elements, and of wisdom, among men (13,15); Lyly (unlike Robert Greene) chooses to dwell exclusively on the latter. The interesting fact about the ideas in this book is that they are not presented directly, as precepts, but only indirectly, as embodied in exemplary stories, so that theory is shown to be really only abstracted experience. The two therefore continually interact, as a passage like this one shows: "I finde too late yet at length that in age there is a certeine foresight, which youth can-not search, and a kinde of experience, unto which unripened yeares cannot come" (29). The relationship between abstracted and raw experience is examined by means of a nest of analogous and interacting stories.

The book opens with Euphues (who is now the young Eubulus we saw in the appendices of *The Anatomy of Wit*) warning Philautus against heedless prodigality in travel. He does so by telling the story of young Callimachus, who wasted his patrimony in travel, returning home penniless and diseased.

[37] See Hunter, pp. 64, 67.

When Callimachus started out, he had been warned against prodigality by his uncle, the hermit Cassander, who told him how *he* had ruined himself by waste and travel, and so forth. Thus Philautus, about to set out on his travels, is put into the position of Callimachus, who has already been ruined—a very interesting set of interlocking situations. Box within box, the stories offer analogous versions of the single action of experience confirming precept, and becoming in turn part of the collected wisdom.

The penetration of the audience into the story becomes rather comic. For instance, Euphues tells how Callimachus became "Sea sicke, (as thou beginnest to be *Philautus*)" (29), and Philautus warns Euphues gently but ironically at the start, "I knowe not howe it commeth to passe, that my eyes are eyther heavy against foule weather, or my head so drowsie against some ill newes, that this tale shall come in good time to bring me a sleepe, and then shall I get no harme by the Hermit, though I get no good" (14). At the same time, Euphues' preconceived ideas of what the England of 1579 is like—derived from Caesar's *De Bello Gallico*—are hilariously inept. In this book it becomes doubtful that precept will affect experience; and it is ironic but right that this should be so, for only if precept does fail to control experience will the traditional story be continued into act and therein be modified by time until it itself becomes part of the traditional wisdom.

What happens is that when the young men touch British soil, Philautus begins to act out the story of Callimachus in a new modality. They first meet old Fidus, who, like Cassander, has retreated to the life of a contemplative hermit after his unhappy experiences.[38] The tale of his life is an exemplum condemning courtly love: at the court of Henry VIII he fell in love with Iffida and pursued her through the usual courtly pastimes, receiving rebuff after rebuff until he discovered that she had previously pledged her faith to Thirsus. At that point he became her confidant, and remained so until the tragic

[38] Compare *Works*, II, 46 and 20.

end of her love caused him to retreat into the country in despair. Once Philautus-Callimachus reaches the court, he goes through the same experience that Fidus-Cassander did: he fixes his eye upon the fair Camilla, is rebuffed in his more sophisticated Elizabethan (or Italian) approaches to her, and at length finds that this is due to her previous love for Surius, the paragon of courtly grace. Thus his experience is an acting out of the experience-as-precept which Fidus had offered him, and the whole British plot becomes a repetition of the Callimachus plot, this time in terms of courtly love among men rather than of prodigality in a world controlled by fortune. Just as Philautus threatened to fall asleep during Euphues' story, so here the story of Fidus has had no effect on him. For instead of becoming Camilla's honorable confidant and servant, or even accepting defeat graciously, Philautus persists in his purpose in spite of plain unalterable fact, seeking first to win Camilla by sorcery and then to persuade her by epistolary argument.

Here the plot takes a surprising turn, for instead of completing the analogies and coming into phase with *The Anatomy of Wit* (and, for that matter, with *Philotimus* and *Don Simonides*) by showing Philautus ruined once again by love, *Euphues and his England* becomes revisionary. Euphues himself has come to see the limitations of precept, and tells Philautus, "Well *Philautus* to set downe precepts against thy love, will nothing prevaile, to perswade thee to go forward, were very perillous, for I know in the one love will regarde no lawes, and in the other perswasions can purchase no libertie" (156). Euphues himself has seen his naïve clichés about England overturned by the facts, and the virtuous English ladies have changed his opinions of women and love; therefore, instead of dissuading Philautus from love as the precepts require, Euphues attempts to divert his love to another woman, the witty Frances. At this point there also occurs a shift in emphasis from courtly love to successful marriage, and the whole latter segment of the book following Philautus' failure tends to view the unalterable fact of love and its lawless nature sympathetically, as both natural and right. Before Euphues had decided that his friend's love could not be altered by moral advice, Philautus himself had found Camilla's will unshakable, and had been mocked by the wise Psellus, in an interchange satirizing natural magic, to this effect: "Doe you thinke Gentleman that the minde being created of God, can be ruled by man, or that anye one can move the heart, but he that made the heart?" (114). The human arts, be they magic, sophistic, or accumulated moral advice, have little or no control over the nature from which they stem.

Therefore, the attitude toward Philautus' passion is complex: on the one hand, he and Cupid are condemned in the usual moral terms for adopting villainous means in their rage (109); but on the other, it is allowed that the cruel mistress is also at fault for driving him to such desperate shifts (120). The force of these new realizations is to leave the various discussions with which the plot ends unresolved; and so the questions of whether the true end of love should be enjoyment or Platonic contemplation, or of whether time, reason, favor, or virtue are preeminent in "true and vertuous love" are left open in the humility of the experienced.

The plot of *Euphues and his England* presents an interesting revision of the usual relation between idea and reality as offered by *The Anatomy of Wit*. For it implies that the conventional theoretical wisdom must be overridden if it is to live and grow. Thus the plot proceeds from ideas of reality (themselves presented as stories showing the truth of prudent ideas in operation) to actions which totally override them, and ends with the revaluation of the original ideas, producing a new, more pragmatic and humane wisdom, the wisdom of human nature.

⟨ IV ⟩

If we compare the courtly fiction of Gascoigne, Lyly, and the Euphuists with the pastoral romances which we examined in the previous chapter, many similarities and differences stand out—similarities of aim, differences of means. Both kinds of fiction are of course devoted to the testing of ideas of order by experience, but the ideas they inspect differ slightly. Those scrutinized by pastoral romance are general and traditional notions of man's possible ennoblement by love, contemplation, or humility; those dealt with by courtly fiction are the specific and often Humanistic concepts of the value of courtly or Platonic love, or ethical imperatives such as self-control, prudence, education, or the Aristotelian mean—"the merry meane" as Saker calls it.[39] Consequently, while pastoral romance operates indirectly, in order merely to exhibit or perhaps modify its basic premise, the fiction of Gascoigne, Lyly, and their followers attacks the specific ideas it contains directly and fiercely, in order to destroy or at least damage them.

Both types of fiction test their ideas by forcing their heroes into roles which both dramatize the ideas and pull these ideas into the orbit of experience. Pastoral disguise is an explicit and extreme form of role-playing; but at the same time, the hero of courtly fiction must have a more heightened sense of conscious histrionics in everyday life than his pastoral counterpart. The courtly hero is the fool of ideas who deliberately adopts a role that is the converse of the ideal, and therefore tests the ideal in a very complex way by a histrionic indulgence in its opposite. He becomes the passionate man in order to test, for his author, the values dictated by reason, as in *The Anatomy of Wit* and *Don Simonides*. When, having forced his part to its ultimate test, he drops it in disenchantment, the result is a plot of significant failure, a veering toward satire rather than romance. The issue of this mode of action in both romance and satire is the adjustment of the relation between ideas and reality; at the end, the full mind judges the single desire which a part of the mind has acted out in its search for value. But romance fulfills Sidney's concept of poetry as an act of speculation directly by expanding through its plot the

[39] *Narbonus*, first part, sig. Crv.

range of possibilities. Social fiction works conversely (as do satire and comedy in the *Defence*), denying possibilities and imposing limits on life; but it does, at the least, raise existence into contact with an ethical norm. In the fiction of Gascoigne, Lyly, and their followers, reality criticizes the idea, destroying it if it suggests a circumvention of normal morality (as in *F. J.* or *Philotimus*), but more often accepting it ruefully if it enforces the mean (as in *The Anatomy of Wit*). In the romance, reality turns out to fulfill the idea, but does so with modifications—as in *Rosalynde,* where one may actually experience his true ideal nature, though only momentarily, or in *Arcadia*, where love leads to stability rather than to transcendent vision. In either case, the central concern is, as always, to show reality acting on ideas, and the effect is to focus our minds on the area of interaction.

CHAPTER 5

Robert Greene and Greek Romance

The most prolific writer of Elizabethan fiction began his career
as the staunchest of the young Euphuists, but by the end of it
he had rejected everything Lyly stood for. In *Menaphon,* his
last romance, he subjected the Euphuistic style to mockery;
he had progressed, by the time of his death, from courtly fiction to recording the very unromantic deeds of the London
underworld. Having begun in the Lylyan mode of fiction as
experience's comment on precepts, he ended by totally divorc-
ing ideas and action, and rejecting the very grounds of fiction
in the process. Since Robert Greene's output was so large and
continuous, we can trace these various processes closely and
with considerable exactness.

In his painstaking study *Robert Greene et ses romans,*[1]
René Pruvost divides the products of Greene's pen, usually
year by year, into eleven periods: 1. in the footsteps of Lyly
(*Mamillia,* Parts I and II); 2. toward the romance of adventure (*Gwydonius*); 3. toward the Italian novella (*Morando,*
Part I, *Arbasto,* and *Planetomachia*); 4. exempla addressed
to women (*Morando,* Part II, and *Penelopes Web*); 5. from
the exemplum to pastoral romance (*Euphues his Censure to
Philautus, Perimides the Blacke-Smith,* and *Pandosto*); 6. the
reputation of women (*Alcida* and *Greenes Orpharion*); 7.
return to romance (*Ciceronis Amor* and *Menaphon*); 8. con-
trition (*Greenes Never too Late, Greenes Mourning Garment,
Greenes Vision,* and *Greenes Farewell to Follie*); 9. the revelation of criminal practices (the three conny-catching pamphlets); 10. in pursuit of the realistic novel (*A Disputation
Betweene a Hee Conny-catcher, and a Shee Conny-catcher*

[1] René Pruvost, *Robert Greene et ses romans (1558-1592), Contribu-
tion à l'Histoire de la Renaissance en Angleterre,* Publications de la
Faculté des lettres D'Alger, II, ix (Paris, 1938).

and *The Blacke Bookes Messenger*); and 11. *Ultima verba* (*Greens Groats-worth of Wit* and *The Repentance of Robert Greene*). Such an account well illustrates the variety of this man. But if we attend to dates of composition (rather than dates of publication, as Pruvost does) and generalize a bit, we can simplify Pruvost's diagram to four main periods: experiments in the Euphuistic mode (1580–84); collections of short tales or novelle (1585–88); pastoral romances strongly influenced by Greek romance (1588–89); and pamphlets of repentance and roguery, in the main nonfictional (1590–92). Through these four periods we can trace Greene's lingering farewell to John Lyly.

Greene's first book, *Mamillia. A Mirrour or looking-glasse for the ladies of Englande,* Part I (1580),[2] is, after Saker's *Narbonus,* the most slavish of the imitations of *The Anatomy of Wit.* Totally Euphuistic in its style and in its use of the narrative technique of paired soliloquies and dialogues, it derives its plot by means of a simple inversion of Lyly's. Its hero, Pharicles, is a male Lucilla who first courts Mamillia, then jilts her for Publia, and finally leaves them both in disgrace. Its title page links it with the literature of experience, reflecting the influence of both Gascoigne and Lyly: "Wherein is deciphered, howe Gentlemen under the perfect substaunce of pure love, are oft inveigled with the shadowe of lewde luste: and their firme faith, brought asleepe by fading fancie: until wit joyned with wisdome, doth awake it by the helpe of reason" (II, 3).[3] Moreover, both hero and heroine conceive of experience as a test of inner qualities. Mamillia considers the act of loving Pharicles a test of his faith, a refining act separating his shadow or reputation from his substance: "the linnen never shrinkes, till it comes to the wetting," she assures herself (28). Pharicles, similarly, thinks of his act of jilting

---

[2] Registered 3 October 1580, but perhaps not published until 1583.

[3] Parenthetical references to Greene's works throughout this chapter are to volume and page in *The Life and Complete Works in Prose and Verse of Robert Greene,* ed. Grosart.

Mamillia for Publia as testing to the full his hitherto carefree attitude toward women, and copies Euphues' trick of proposing the dislogistic exempla of Paris, Theseus, and Jupiter in order to strengthen his amoral resolve (92). Like Lyly's hero, he fails; unlike him, he has no intellectual position to which to retreat in the end, and, when his deceits have been uncovered, can only flee in disgrace from Italy.

The differences between *Mamillia* and *The Anatomy of Wit,* though in themselves slight, are significant as indicators of Greene's future development. In *Mamillia* there is no conflict between love and friendship or between love and wisdom (as in *Narbonus*), but merely the single conflict between the firm faith of woman and the fickleness of man. Greene is, in general, less interested in concepts than is Lyly. Experience tests people, not ideas, and what the plot reveals here is the movements of a variable mind, rather than an exploration of the precepts which that mind accepts or rejects. As a result of this focus the book has somewhat of a seesaw structure, as opposed to Lyly's clear dialectic progression downward. And what is always in the foreground, in keeping with this structure, is fortune, fate, the ungovernable force of love (even chaste love, not merely lust as in *Euphues*);[4] for it is these, not reasoned choices, that govern the world and the mind.

Pruvost's verdict, "Imitateur de Lyly dans son premier roman, Greene introduit pourtant dans celui-ci une peinture idéalisée de la femme, et des aventures romanesques, dont son aîné ne lui offrait guère le modèle,"[5] applies less to Part I than to Part II. In *Mamillia The second part of the triumph of Pallas* (1583),[6] there is more romantic intrigue than in Part I, more action in the sense of changes in fortune; therefore the wayward forces of fortune and passion that were evoked in

---

[4] See, e.g., *Works,* II, 55-56 and 78.

[5] Pruvost, p. 139.

[6] Registered 6 September 1583; the only surviving edition, however, is that of 1593.

Part I can be seen in action here. Yet this action involves little play of mind, because hero and heroine have become simply exemplary: Pharicles reforms early in the book, and Mamillia has progressed from the simple, faithful maid of Part I to an absolute paragon of constancy like the patient Griselda. Hence the action does not test character or ideals, but merely subjects the ideal hero and heroine to a few shrewd turns before they are at last united.

Chief among the new elements of intrigue in Part II is the employment of disguise. Mamillia's intervention at the trial "richly attired and straungely disguised" (II, 244) expresses little more than her nobility and leads to a *coup de théâtre;* but Pharicles' disguise presents a more complex case. At first the disguise of palmer that he adopts in Sicily is treated, like the costume of Riche's Don Simonides, as an intensification of his natural deceitfulness: "*Pharicles* . . . dealt so clarkely in his calling, and behaved himselfe so demurely, as his pretensed kinde of life gave occasion to no man to suspect his fained profession: for his Palmers weed was worne with such a gravitie in his countenance, and such a modestie in his maners, as all men thought the man to be halfe mortified" (181). But his acting out of the life appropriate to the disguise as a solitary hermit is presented as an actual purgation rather than a feigned one, and after a period of giving full rein to remorse he emerges as in fact what he had pretended to be: a humble and modest young man worthy of Mamillia's fidelity.

Such a use of disguise becomes very important in Greene's next book, *Gwydonius. The Carde of Fancie* (1584).[7] The elements of Euphuism are as strong here as they were in *Mamillia* (indeed, they were to remain strong throughout most of Greene's career), the style being even more schematic than in *Mamillia,* the narrative technique still mainly one of paired speeches, and the plot derived from the prodigal-son model of Lyly. But at the same time, action in the form of

[7] Registered 11 April 1584.

changes of fortune is much more apparent here than in Part II of *Mamillia*, especially in the last fourth of the book.[8]

Here the action exerts a force on character denied it in *Mamillia,* for this romance records the transformation of a wastrel into the perfect hero, under the tutelage of experience. Gwydonius begins as a headstrong and desperate profligate and ends as the knight of love, who in a single stroke quells his father's barbarity, serves his adopted king, helps his friend, and wins his mistress. The "fancie" of the title is dual in its reference, standing both for the "frantike fancie" or willfulness of rash youth and for the calmer fancy of love;[9] the latter turns out to be the cure for the former. King Clerophontes of Mitelyne, disgusted at the depravity of his son Gwydonius, sends him away to travel. Gwydonius responds by giving his fancy such full sway that he becomes "a verie patterne of witlesse prodigalitie" at Barutta (IV, 24) and ends in bankruptcy and prison. The first phase of Gwydonius' education is hence the "haplesse experience" of the position of willfulness he had assumed; he has already exceeded his father's expectation that "travell" (the exploration of unfamiliar reality) "chaungeth vanitie to vertue, staylesse wit to stayed wisedome, fonde fantasies to firme affections" (19).

Gwydonius' response to experience is to adopt a disguise: presenting himself as penniless and baseborn, he offers himself as a servant to King Orlanio of Alexandria. His disguise, be it noted, is the diametrical opposite of the character he had chosen and played to the full at Barutta, for he is now the loyal and humble servant of the king rather than the proud and rebellious prince. And in playing out his second role he soon becomes so wise, courteous, and modest that he is accepted as

---

[8] See Pruvost, p. 178: "Après une introduction relativement brève où se marque encore l'influence de la prédication de Lyly, *Gwydonius* se contente dans toute sa seconde partie, qui est de beaucoup la plus développée, d'être tout simplement un roman."

[9] By and large, "fancie" in Mitelyne and Barutta means willfulness (e.g., *Works*, IV, 14, 19), while in Alexandria it refers to love (e.g., IV, 55, 58).

the friend of the king's son, Thersandro. But the role demands more of Gwydonius; it demands the final subjection which always brings about "an alteration of minde" (64). He falls in love with Castania, the king's daughter, who must in turn scorn him because of the low birth he has claimed as part of his disguise; thereupon follows the double humiliation of subjecting himself to another in love and of suffering continued repulse. Castania submits Gwydonius to a long and deliberate trial to assure herself that his protestations are "no signes of fleeting fancie, but of a firme affection" (120). The irony of it is that by the time she consents to love him, he must suffer the further trial of being accused of treason and forced to flee the country.

For close upon Castania's submission to love comes Clerophontes' invasion of Alexandria, and as a result Gwydonius' role holds him paralyzed between loyalty to his father (in his real identity) on the one side and love and loyalty to his adopted king (in his assumed identity) on the other. His true identity as the enemy's son having been revealed, he flees; and when he returns at the climax, it is in a third disguise that solves the problems of the other two roles. He tells Thersandro, "I will, resembling thy person, and disguised in thy armour, enter combat with my Father *Clerophontes*" (189). When he does so, he must exhibit all his acquired poise and restraint in the difficult feat of winning by retreating, but his success unites kingdoms, lovers, families, and the two sides of his own identity. Humiliation and suffering have ministered to Gwydonius, for his reappearance in armor (like Edgar in *King Lear*) shows him to be resplendent with heroic virtue. The demands of the various roles have been severe, but they have perfected Gwydonius.

Both *The Carde of Fancie* and *Arbasto, The Anatomie of Fortune* (1584)[10] are, like *The Anatomy of Wit*, celebrations of the power of experience. Expressions of the necessity for

[10] Registered 13 August 1584.

experience, such as the declaration "I speake by proofe and experience" (IV, 183) in *The Carde of Fancie,* are present in *Arbasto* as well: "I speake this by experience, which I pray the gods thou never trie by proofe" (III, 184). But as these paired quotations indicate, the nature of experience is rendered quite differently in each. In *The Carde of Fancie* experience consists mainly of "a cruell, Combate between Nature and Necessitie" (IV, 3), an area wherein human nature and the external pressures of existence meet and contend for the government of life. Experience is educative, it brings out the hero's true virtue by forcing roles upon him; and fortune, the chief external pressure, can bring out both the good and the bad in an individual. *Arbasto,* on the other hand, is "The Anatomie of Fortune" alone, and there experience is not a combat between human and cosmic forces but only an exhibition of the pressures of bad luck and other external forces upon the personality. Fortune is figured as chaotic, the bringer of evil only, and as a result experience destroys rather than educating.

Actually, *Arbasto* is as much the anatomy of love as of fortune,[11] the point of contact between the two being that both are chaotic and irrational. Love is presented from the first as lawless passion which overthrows reason, "a frantick frenzie which so infecteth the mindes of men, as under the taste of Nectar, they are poysoned with the water of *Styx*" (III, 201).[12] And this idea of love is acted out in the realm of experience, which is itself conceived of as the realm of the goddess Fortune, who raises men only that she may throw them down (184). The nature of action in a world governed by fortune is not one of pure chance or accident, as in the Greek romances, but rather one of irony, of the constant falsification of expectations and overturn of intentions. Experience does not so much test ideas here, as demonstrate that life, dominated as it is by passion and luck, is really absurd. Concepts

---

[11] See Pruvost, pp. 191, 198.
[12] See also *Works,* III, 197, 213.

of the normal and reasonable, the probable, are constantly overturned by the pervasive irony and reversals of bad luck.[13] The only possible response to life so conceived is to withdraw from it, and that is what Arbasto does after his series of tragic denouements. We find him, and we leave him, in a little cell alternately weeping over and laughing at an emblem of Fortune.

Philomela. The Lady Fitzwaters Nightingale (ca. 1584–88),[14] the last of Greene's four major endeavors within the mode of fiction set up by John Lyly, manages to give more form to experience by so controlling it as to make it into a laboratory experiment. When Count Philippo Medici decides to test the chastity of his exquisite wife, "the Venetian Philomela," he does so not because of a sudden rush of madness (as does Anselmo in Cervantes' tale of "The Curious Impertinent," which so closely resembles Greene's tale), but because of a relatively settled world view which presupposes that

. . . every outward appearaunce is not an authenticall instance, women have chaste eies when they have wanton thoughts, and modest lookes when they harbour lascivious wishes . . . the Salamander is most warme when hee lieth furthest from the fire, and then are women most hart hollowe when they are most lip-holie, and by these premisses,

---

[13] Compare Dinesen, *Last Tales*, p. 25.

[14] It was actually registered 1 July 1592 and published that year; but Greene writes in his dedicatory epistle that he had written it "long since & kept charily, being pend at the request of a Countesse in this land to approve wemens chastitie" and that "assone as I had red it over and reduced it into forme, lickinge it a lytle as the beares doe their whelpes," he presented it to the Lady Fitzwater (*Works*, XI, 109-10). John Clark Jordan dates it either 1584-87 or 1588-89 because of "its striking likeness to some of the earlier work" (*Robert Greene* [New York, 1915], p. 172), while Pruvost places it at about 1588 because of its style (p. 473); but Greene's explicit statement (above) that he revised it renders Pruvost's argument from style invalid. The book it most resembles is *Penelopes Web* (1587), and "a Countesse in this land" might be either the Countess of Cumberland or the Countess of Warwick, since *Penelopes Web* was dedicated to both.

Philippo argue of thy wives precisenesse, for though she
seeme chast, yet maye she secretly delight in chaunge. (XI,
119)

Philippo's convictions amount to a casually Machiavellian
view of human motives which reduces them to self-interest
under the cover of apparent virtue. And he puts this idea of
reality to an explicit test—by Machiavellian means, of course
—by persuading his friend Lutesio to attempt the corruption
of Philomela.

Lutesio's approach to Philomela ironically proves the letter
of Philippo's premise that things are not always what they
seem. For when he comes upon Philomela singing a song
celebrating the kiss of lovers as the meeting of souls (123–
24), he takes it as an invitation to lust. She, however, repulses
him with a diatribe against adultery and in praise of honest
physical love between husband and wife, and ends the scene
with a counter-song against lawless love (133–35). The scene
illustrates the converse of Philippo's premise, proving that a
bad appearance may hide a good reality as well as vice versa;
and the two songs that frame the episode offer a sophistication
of that premise: that life is not always a matter of one extreme
hiding another, but may be a pursuit of the mean, of honest
love as the mean between lust and insensitivity—just as Philomela herself is "modest without sullennesse, . . . chast, and yet
not coy" (116). Lutesio, convinced, falls to admiration of her,
and later feels so fully in fact the love he has dissimulated
that his honor forces him to refuse further testing. But Philippo's mind is too coarse to recognize distinctions. As his premise
grows into an *idée fixe,* he refuses to recognize factual evidence, a belief spills over into a mad obsession, and the tests
and roles he has created become, for him, reality.

Such is his faith in his own obsessive image of the real that
he pushes it to the limit in the face of experience by bribing
two Genoese slaves to testify to Philomela's adultery with
Lutesio, procuring thereby an annulment and the banishment

of the supposed lovers. Philippo has become a madman who projects his own image upon reality and wrests it to his purposes; and after Philomela's trial the outside world accepts his reality as fact:

> The rumours of this spread through al Venice, of the lascivious life of *Philomela*: some said all was not gould that glistered: that the fairest faces, have oft times the falsest harts: & the smoothest looks, the most treacherous thoughts . . . others said, it might bee a compacted matter, by the Earle to be rid of his wife: some said, that the matter might be mistaken, and made worse then it was. Thus dyverslye they did descant. (170-71)

Philippo has committed a rape upon reality (as did Tereus in the myth to which this story alludes throughout), and his hybris in so doing is finally punished when Philomela's father demands a retrial, in which Philomela is proved chaste and Philippo is revealed as a villain and is banished.

The denouement occurs in a world as thickly cloaked in appearances as Philippo in his rage had imagined it to be. Philippo has come in despair to Palermo (where, unbeknown to him, Philomela now lives). There he witnesses the murder of Arnoldo Strozzo (actually, of Arnoldo's servant dressed in his master's clothes), and, in order to rid himself of the burden he has made of his life, himself confesses to the deed. He is saved from his innocent lie when Philomela for once tells a falsehood and claims that she is the murderer. When matters are finally straightened out, Philippo, the hero of the idea, dies of joy and grief. *Philomela* subjects the whole concept of submitting ideas to the test of experience to intense scrutiny: while trial purifies the heroine, it destroys the man who set up the trial. One may not be able to see any further into reality than he is willing to, and conversely, reality may turn out to be, in quite an ironic way, just what one imagines it to be but wishes it were not.

The three books Greene produced after his apprenticeship

in *Mamillia* show him exploring in detail several of the various avenues opened to fiction by John Lyly: the possibilities of education through playing a role in the realm of experience in *Gwydonius,* the sometimes tragic nature of experience itself in *Arbasto,* and the consequences of testing ideas by action in *Philomela.* As he proceeded, the world of action that he rendered grew darker, tragedy supplanted education as the main result of the experience of such a world, and his final effort cast doubt both on the advisability of bringing ideas to bear on experience and on human educability in general.

In the period between 1585 and 1588 Greene turned away from extended fiction in order to devote his attention to collections of novelle from Italian and other sources. Pruvost finds in the series of six such collections a gradual movement away from the exemplary tale toward the purely romantic, "à un renforcement graduel du romanesque et à un affaiblissement parallèle de l'élément didactique."[15] In them, exemplary ideals and the actions of the world start to revolve in separate and distinctive spheres, and through them, Greene began his separation from Lyly's view of reality.

Though *Morando, The Tritameron of Love* (1584) suggests by its title a comparison with Boccaccio's *Decameron,* it really contains no tales but only three debates on questions of love.[16] It did, however, set up the framework of debate into which stories were inserted in the collections that followed. The first of these collections was *Planetomachia* (1585), which pulls three separate tragic novelle into a debate among the planets.[17] The stories are not of themselves exemplary, being as they are—after the manner of Bandello—full of chance, passion, treason, and bloody action, and each culminating in multiple revenge;[18] but they are linked to the realm of ideas by their

[15] Pruvost, p. 263.

[16] *The Second part of the Tritameron of Love* (1587) contains an account of a love affair between two of the disputants.

[17] Grosart prints an imperfect text containing only two tragedies; Pruvost prints the third from the British Museum copy as Appendix III (pp. 586-98).

[18] On its resemblances to Italian novelle, see Pruvost, p. 200.

remorseless determinism. *Penelopes Web* (1587) is a far more harmonious collection, since each of its three tales illustrates one of the female virtues, and each is resolved (after the manner of Cinthio)[19] by having the heroine's exhibition of that virtue convert the hero to similar virtue. The first tale of Barmenissa has a plot quite similar to that of "Saturnes Tragedie" in *Planetomachia,* where a king, to the consternation of his heir and his people, sets a strumpet beside him on the throne. But Penelope's tale is told from the deposed queen Barmenissa's point of view, and therefore stresses less the folly of the king than the exemplary obedience of the wife who finally brings him back to his senses.

The most completely exemplary of these collections is *Euphues his Censure to Philautus* (1587), a masculine counterpart to *Penelopes Web* which announces at the outset its relation to early Tudor constructivist fiction like *Utopia:* "wherein under the shadow of a philosophicall combat betweene Hector and Achilles, imitating Tullies orator, Platoes common wealth, and Baldessars courtier, he [Euphues] aymeth at the exquisite portraiture of a perfect martialist" (VI, 152). Once love is dismissed in a preliminary tragedy, the collection becomes heavily schematic: Helenus, Hector, and Achilles each offer a discourse on the virtues of wisdom, fortitude, and liberality, respectively, and then illustrate their points with exemplary tales preceded by appropriate Latin mottoes (the tales seem to have been drawn from rhetoricians' collections of exempla). Each exemplum includes the other two: Helenus' tale of wisdom, for example, first shows the failures of brave and generous soldiers before exhibiting the success of the wise one. Furthermore, the order in which the exempla are presented is important, for Priam at the end links them together as steps toward perfection: wisdom is necessary to conceive strategy, fortitude then puts wisdom into practice, and liberality to one's troops insures the continuation of the military

---

[19] See, e.g., *Gli Hecatommithi* (1565), II, 6; III, 5; and VI, 3.

gains achieved by wisdom and fortitude (283–84). In this way, three exemplary tales are placed together to form the ideal image of a soldier.

Alcida Greenes Metamorphosis, produced a year later,[20] continues, in the main, the exemplary concerns of *Euphues his Censure,* since it offers three tales illustrating the female faults of pride, fickleness, and blabbing. But several considerations show how much less purely exemplary it is than were its predecessors. For one thing, its heroines are not flat exemplars of good or evil, but flawed human beings such as the witty but fickle Eriphila. For another, the morality resides more in the framework than in the tales themselves, which if they were lifted from the framework would read more like *The Anatomy of Wit* than like the absolute exempla of *Penelopes Web.* The framework is quite schematic: the beauty of Fiordespine (a devotee of Venus) is flawed by pride, the defect of love; the wit of Eriphila (a devotee of Pallas) is flawed by fickleness, the excess of love; Marpesia represents the *tertium quid* (and thus for once claims some significance for the triad we find Greene using so often in his novelle). As the scheme shows, the third tale is especially distant from the exemplary: Marpesia is a good woman who, warned by the examples of her sisters, seeks the mean. She loves a commoner (thus denying pride) and loves him with constancy (thus denying fickleness), but she is betrayed in the end by the totally human fault of gossiping. Marpesia is not an example of a bad or even a flawed woman, but merely of an imperfect one; consequently her metamorphosis, unlike that of her sisters, comes about not through divine revenge only but also "to ease her of her sorrow" (IX, 112). Not only is there a general absence of moral commentary in these tales,[21] but Alcida the narrator thinks of them as "delightfull" to the listener (though not to the narrator) and as satisfying the

[20] Registered 9 December 1588; the earliest surviving edition is that of 1617.

[21] See Pruvost, p. 313.

desire for "novelties" (54)—in other words, as fiction pure of moral aims.

The title of the last of the collections, *Greenes Orpharion* (ca. 1588),[22] derived as it is from a lute-like instrument, leads the reader to expect a book full of music, and so this is. The bulk of the book concerns a dream of a banquet of the gods, at which two famed singers, Orpheus and Arion, are present. Each first sings a song, then gives his opinion of women, and proceeds to tell a tale. Orpheus, the tragic singer, thinks of women as being either too easy of access or too hard, and goes on to give an example of the latter extreme in Lidia, a cruel princess who requites the humble submission of her lover, Acestes the general, by starving him to death. Arion, the happy singer, thinks of women as transcendently good, and tells of the constant Argentina, who agrees to lie with the lustful conqueror Marcion if he will fast for three days and refuse to touch meat before he lies with her on the fourth. The two tales have several obvious cross-references: both combine arms and love (Mars and Venus) in the conquering general who expects to be rewarded with the fair meed, the conqueror conquered; and in each, starvation leads to the climax—in one case, the terrible death of Acestes, who is reduced to gnawing the flesh of his own arms, and in the other the action of Marcion, who, upon his release after his ritual fasting, pushes the lovely Argentina aside to gobble up a plate of food. Such cross-reference is the main design of the book and the most important aspect of its musicality, as the subtitle implies: "Wherein is discovered a musicall concorde of pleasant Histories, many sweet moodes graced with such harmonious discords, as agreeing in a delightfull closse, they sound both pleasure and profit to the eare" (XII, 3).

The book's total design is imitative of harmony, that phenomenon in which two different notes, when sounded simul-

---

[22] It was registered 9 February 1590 but probably written in 1588, since Greene announces it as ready for the press "the next tearme" in the epistle to *Perimides the Blacke-Smith* (1588); see *Works*, VII, 9.

taneously, produce the effect of a single note. Such is the total effect of the book, for after Orpheus has sounded the lowest note and Arion the highest, Mercury offers this final judgment: "*Arions* tale paints out a paragon, a matchles mirrour, as wel for constancy, as the other for cruelty: these extremes therfore infer no certain conclusions, for they leave a mean betweene both, wherein I think the nature of women doo consist, neither so cruel but they wil grant, nor so constant but they will yeeld" (93).[23]

It will be noticed that the structure—two extremes and a mean—is the same as that of *Alcida,* but here the mean is not given in a third story but merely evoked by the cross-references of the two extremes. The two stories are exemplary, each deliberately designed to illustrate a point; but just as deliberately they cancel each other out and leave the reader on neutral ground—thereby abdicating their power as exempla. A neutral tone pervades this book about the mean: for example, the story in praise of women ends with the lascivious villain's comic realization that hunger is more important than lust, meat than women—and this realization induced by a woman. So it is, too, with the frame, which consists of the narrator's entrance into Erecenus suffering the wounds of love and his exit after the dream, when he finds that "either I had lost love, or love lost me: for my passions were eased" (94). Perhaps he had come to see love, like women, in a larger perspective, as parts or aspects of life rather than its whole.

The watershed between the totally exemplary tales of *Penelopes Web* and *Euphues his Censure* on the one hand, and the modified exemplary effects of *Alcida* and *Greenes Orpharion* on the other, can be found in *Perimides the Blacke-Smith* (1588), whose date of composition falls between the two sets.[24]

---

[23] It should be noted that in this context the musical meaning of "mean" as the middle voice between bass and treble parts is important to the book's total meaning.

[24] *Perimides* was registered 12 March 1588, between *Euphues his Censure* (18 September 1587) and *Alcida* (9 December 1588).

Its title page is especially interesting, in that it uses the syntax proper to an exemplary collection to carry the content of pure, honest mirth:

> Perimides the Blacke-Smith, A golden methode, how to use the minde in pleasant and profitable exercise. Wherein is contained speciall principles fit for the highest to imitate, and the meanest to put in practise, how best to spend the wearie winters nights, or the longest summers Evenings, in honest and delightfull recreation. Wherein we may learne to avoide idlenesse and wanton scurrilitie, which divers appoint as the end of their pastimes. (VII, 3)

Elements of the didactic and mere delightful storytelling have a curiously separate existence in this book, as Greene indicates when he promises "diverse precepts interlaced with delight-full histories" (6). For instance, the framework consists of three evening conversations between Perimides and his wife Delia on good health, gambling, and the values of content; but the three stories they tell are not meant to exemplify any of their moral precepts, nor are any of them, as Pruvost points out, exemplary tales at all.[25] Similarly, Perimides' first tale is pure romance, but Greene has inserted in its margins moral *sententiae* (such as "Friends & countrey deare to a man" or "Patience the best salve against fortune") that one may, indeed, draw from the story if he wishes. But since they are neither embedded in the action nor even announced by one of its characters, they are not at all germane to it.[26]

The third and last of the tales comes closest to the purely exemplary, for it shows how Bradamant brings about a happy conclusion for himself and his beloved through his virtue. But its characterization and narrative technique are totally differ-ent from those of the other two. The heroes of the other two tales form direct contrasts to Bradamant, the hero of the sec-

[25] Pruvost, p. 275.
[26] Compare the similar technique of W. C.'s *The Adventures of Ladie Egeria* (1584), discussed at the beginning of Chap. 6, below.

ond tale being a pirate, that of the first a generally good man who smirches his image by the unedifying deed of begetting a child on a noblewoman out of wedlock. The third tale is conducted in Greene's usual Euphuistic manner, which employs paired laments and dialogues to slowly pull hero and heroine together in love; the other two proceed in a style of rapid narration and exhibit what might be termed "pure" action, in that their characters are required to do nothing but move, to go somewhere where they either leave or meet somebody. The first tale, in particular, is governed entirely by fortune, so that the plot proceeds by a rhythm of chance separations and unions.

The fall of Tyre separates Mariana and her two sons (one as yet unborn) from her husband Prestines. "Fortune who ment to make hir a mirrour of hir inconstancie" (23) causes a storm to put her ship aground at Decapolis, where she gives birth to her second son. By chance, pirates attack while she is absent and carry away her two sons, Castrior and Infortunio, to Japhet, where they sell them as slaves to the governor Lamoraq; similarly, the Despot of Decapolis comes upon Mariana "by chaunce" (27), and takes her into his household. Husband, wife, and children have thus been completely severed from one another, and have each formed new and separate liaisons; the work of reuniting them is now left to fortune. This part of the action begins with another separation: Castrior (disguised as Procidor) leaves his brother and travels to Decapolis, where he falls in love with Marcella, the Despot's daughter, and gets her with child. He is saved from execution by her wrathful father when he reveals that he is no slave, but a prince, and from this revelation of his true identity all the reunions flow: Castrior marries Marcella, he is reunited with his mother, they send for the other son, Infortunio, and all four then go back to Tyre to be reunited with Prestines, who (after spending fourteen years in prison) has been restored to power.

The operation of fortune in this tale is totally different from that in *Arbasto, The Anatomie of Fortune,* produced four years earlier. "Fortune" in *Arbasto* was really bad luck, the thwarting of one set of human purposes by another, of Arbasto's love of Doralicia by her hatred of him, for instance. In *Perimides,* as we have seen, fortune is something totally distinct from human purposes, mere accident or chance that governs the events of human action no matter what a character's intentions. "Though men determine the Gods doo dispose" (81), asserts Perimides, and this we can see in the first two tales, where it is seemingly only chance that brings people together or pushes them apart in a wide expanse of space and time. This view of life as governed totally by accident explains in part the curious disjunction between the didactic conversations of Perimides and his wife and the tales they tell; for they think of their tales as illustrating a kind of life in the great world which they have avoided by embracing pastoral seclusion.[27] One can, it seems, retreat from the world, sit by the fireside, and talk of morality; or one can go out and experience the vicissitudes of fortune in a world where moral values make no difference.

The novella, which probably had its origins in biographical anecdote, had usually maintained an air of factuality whose main attributes were realistic detail and a remorseless detachment from ideals. Of course, there were exemplary novelle like Boccaccio's Titus and Gisippus, and some writers, notably Cinthio, had infused their tales with romantic idealism. But the characteristic trait of the genre as a whole was "a picture of life in which men are motivated by desire, not by reason, and their lives by chance, not by Providence: it is the world of Machiavelli."[28] The novella usually presents love from the fabliau's point of view, and it presents tragedy in a world unrelieved by divine grace. Greene's conduct (it would be misleading to call it progress) in handling the novella

[27] See the opposition of virtue and fortune, *Works,* VII, 61.
[28] See *The Palace of Pleasure, An Anthology of the Novella,* ed. Harry Levtow and Maurice Valency (New York, 1960), p. 7.

veered away from the exemplary toward the ethically neutral. *Penelopes Web* and *Euphues his Censure* present totally exemplary novelle; *Alcida* and the *Orpharion* modify their exemplary tales; *Planetomachia* catches some of the tragic tone of Bandello, and *Perimides the Blacke-Smith* manages to elude moralistic pressure totally in the telling of stories pure and simple.

Many years ago, Samuel Lee Wolff demonstrated that the first two tales in *Perimides* are adaptations of Boccaccio, from *Decameron,* II, 6 and V, 2, respectively.[29] But he went on to insist not only that Boccaccio had probably derived these tales from lost Greek romances, but also that Greene saw them as miniature Greek romances; and he adduced as evidence for his assertion the fact that Greene had changed Boccaccio's Italian setting in the first tale to the Mediterranean setting of Tyre, Sidon, and Decapolis typical of the Greek romances. After examining another adaptation of Boccaccio in *Ciceronis Amor,* Wolff concluded, "Greene has thus chosen from the *Decameron* only Greek Romance material, and has used it almost exactly as he found it. Indeed, his talent in general has a distinct affinity to Greek Romance."[30] For Greene the novella was, then, the channel for Greek romance, which was to exert so great a force on his last romances. And if, in his intensive exploration of the novella form, he showed a tendency to abandon the purely exemplary tale, he found its antithesis in Greek romance, with its action of losing and finding in a world governed by time and fortune.

⟨ II ⟩

That it should have been Boccaccio who brought Greek romance to Greene is not surprising, in view of the diffusion of that subgenre. For even though editions and translations of the three major specimens—Heliodorus' *Aethiopica,* Lon-

[29] Samuel Lee Wolff, *The Greek Romances in Elizabethan Prose Fiction* (New York, 1912), pp. 370-73.

[30] *Ibid.,* pp. 374-75.

gus' *Daphnis and Chloe,* and Achilles Tatius' *Clitophon and Leucippe*—did not appear until the middle of the sixteenth century (the first English translations appeared in 1569, 1587, and 1597, respectively),[31] Greek romance had exerted a continued though oblique influence on fiction since the Middle Ages. A Latin version of a lost Greek romance, *Apollonius of Tyre,* had been popular throughout the Middle Ages and had been translated by John Gower, from whom Shakespeare received it for his *Pericles*; many saints' legends, notably those of St. Eustace and St. Placidus, had adapted Greek romantic themes; and, as we have seen, Greek romance entered the novella tradition early, perhaps via lost Greek originals, in Boccaccio—as in the tales of Lady Beritola (*Decameron,* II, 6) and Alatiel (II, 7).

The fact of such a diffusion of influence can be brought home by a look at an example of Elizabethan neo-Greek romance. Barnabe Riche's "Sappho Duke of Mantona," the first tale in *Riche his Farewell to Militarie Profession* (1581), has, along with the second, fourth, and seventh tales, been justly cited by critics as the first appearance of true Greek romance in English.[32] Yet in a careful study of its sources, D. T. Starnes discovered that Riche took as the basis of his plot the legend of St. Eustace, that he took its love element from Bandello's novella of the Duchess of Malfi as translated in Painter's *Palace of Pleasure,* and that only its ending comes directly from Greek romance, from the conclusion of the *Aethiopica.*[33]

The main direct (as distinguished from the oblique) influence of the Greek romances when they appeared in translation occurred in two realms. This influence exerted a pressure

[31] See *ibid.,* pp. 8-10.

[32] See, e.g., Wallace A. Bacon's edition of William Warner's *Syrinx or A Sevenfold History,* Northwestern University Studies, Humanities Series, No. 26 (Evanston, 1950), pp. xvi-xvii.

[33] D. T. Starnes, "Barnabe Rich's 'Sappho Duke of Mantona': A Study in Elizabethan Story-Making," *Studies in Philology,* XXX (1933), 455-72.

in both of these realms toward weaning Elizabethan fiction away from Lyly's mode of fiction, which centered on conflicts within characters conveyed by the technique of paired speeches, and directing it toward a mode that concentrated on action and narrative alone; for as Wolff asserts, "the Greek Romances give to *plot*—the mere happening of things—a place much more important than they give to character."[34] First, the romances provided "a methodology for producing heightened intricacy in the plot,"[35] chiefly for producing suspense by such devices as beginning *in mediis rebus* and narrating previous matter later, dropping and then picking up separate strands of plot at crucial moments, and introducing an oracle or other obscure mode of prediction near the beginning to show its clear fulfillment at the end. Second, it reinforced interest in a vision of the world governed purely by chance, time, and fortune, a medieval vision to which it brought new intensity and a new direction. For fortune in the Greek romances is not adequately expressed by the medieval emblem of Fortune's wheel, with its socio-economic emphasis on rise and fall in place, but is rather a vision of man fighting for survival in a hostile universe. Hence its typical motifs of life and death: the reappearance of children captured or left to die of exposure; storms, shipwrecks, and other typical sea accidents; the separation and union of lovers; the finding of the lost. The narrative techniques of Greek romance were really absorbed by only three books, Sidney's *Arcadia*, Greene's *Menaphon*,[36] and William Warner's *Pan his Syrinx* (1584), though they did have some influence on Elizabethan chivalric romance, as we shall see. But the late Greek view of life exerted a strong pull on Elizabethan fiction, started to dominate the scene with Riche, Warner, and Greene in the 1580s, and continued to be influential long thereafter.

The major elements of such a world view, most of them

[34] Wolff, p. 137.
[35] Schlauch, *Antecedents of the English Novel*, p. 175.
[36] For *Arcadia*, see Wolff, pp. 307-66, and for *Menaphon*, pp. 444-45.

identical with those we saw in the first tale Greene borrowed from Boccaccio, in *Perimides,* are adequately exhibited by Riche's "Sappho Duke of Mantona." Among the features that strike the reader who comes to this tale fresh from Lyly or the early Greene are relatively immense expanses of space and time—enough space (stretching from Macedonia to Egypt) to allow the various members of a group to become separated and lead much of their lives in isolation from one another, enough time (fifteen years) for children to grow and parents to age enough so as to be unrecognizable to one another. Within all this time and space is contained enough action to fill *The Anatomy of Wit* five times over, and this action in the great world is produced not by men making decisions but by accident and chance in nature. Especially striking is a structural and thematic difference: instead of the symmetry of paired speeches and scenes, we have a rhythm of separations and reunions, as in *Perimides.*

By adapting his plot to the rhythm of separation and reunion, Riche threw his emphasis on movement rather than character. Location in space becomes more important than human purpose; it is not a question of who you are and what you want, but only of where you are and what means will be used by fortune to get you somewhere else. Nor are the places one leaves or enters symbolic of values, as they are in pastoral; they are merely spaces occupied by people. In the great world of time and space, people move like figures on a chessboard, passively, for as Sappho says, "all my enterprises bee quite pluckte backe, and my purposes tourned cleane topse torve"[37] by fortune or chance, which governs this world.

Wolff has admirably characterized the totally "unclassic" Alexandrian view of life conveyed by such romances as based on the premise that the normal links of causation have collapsed in a world of fragments. In such a world events are no longer calculable, one is constantly being shocked by "the

---

[37] *Rich's Farewell to Military Profession*, ed. Cranfill, p. 31.

queerness of the turns things take,"[38] and the human element is all but negligible. For not only is human character powerless to affect human destiny, but character itself becomes as a result an empty concept. Character in the Aristotelian sense is absent from these romances, for their people neither have moral purposes nor make choices, but only take what comes to them.[39] And so sentiment issues in no action, and the mental and physical components of the person become as fragmented as the elements of the world in which he dwells.[40]

These facts suggest that, to an Elizabethan raised on the Christian view of providential world order and on the rhetorical tradition that gave to human choice the determination of human destiny, the Greek romances seemed to present life in the world as almost pure chaos (even though to the Greeks themselves the happy ending was an assurance of some vague sort of order in the universe). For example, when Greene surveyed a world governed entirely by fortune, he viewed it with none of the Boethian sense, common to Chaucer and Spenser, that fortune was the hidden hand of providence. Rather, as "Peratio his discourse upon Fortune" in *Morando* well shows (III, 128-39), he saw fortune as mere accident, mutability without reason, order, or meaning. Such a world of chance, in which human purposes are both powerless and irrelevant and action is void of ethical meaning, comes very close to what we moderns call "the absurd."

Hence William Warner, in the main example of a full-blown Greek romance in English, and one that influenced Greene considerably,[41] evoked such a world only to reject it with complete abhorrence. *Pan his Syrinx, or Pipe, Compact of seven Reedes: including in one, seven Tragical and Comicall Arguments. . . . Whereby, in effect, of all thinges is touched, in few, something of the vayne, wanton, proud, and inconstant*

---

[38] Wolff, p. 5.
[39] *Ibid.*, p. 143.
[40] *Ibid.*, p. 4.
[41] See *Syrinx*, ed. Bacon, pp. lxxiii-lxxviii.

course of the World (1584; revised in 1597) is, as its title implies, a successful venture at uniting the diverse by quite accidental means. In a sense it is structured by accident. The first tale of Arbaces and Sorares, split into two parts placed at the beginning and the end of the book, embraces six other quite diverse tales that range from tragedy through love story and quasi-pastoral romance to satire. Inter-relationships among them are accidental, since some of the six framed stories are episodes in the search of Atys and Abyndos for their father Sorares, others are merely told to them by people they meet by chance (the second, for example), and still others are tales told to other characters while Atys and Abyndos are absent (the third). As tale succeeds tale, no overall view of world order emerges, only a welter of diverse fortunes.

The world of this book has its bright spots, but by and large it is a brutal and horrible place where even the state of nature has its bestial side (170)[42] and a woman can be forced to eat the flesh of her lover (34-35). Reason is ineffectual in this world: a courtly debate is interrupted by a passionate man who imprisons three of the disputants and kills one of them (129), and the reasoned oration of Chebron leads not to persuasion but to his murder and finally to mass suicide (26-27). Ineffectual, too, is all human endeavor, for it is only ignorant groping in a world of chance, as the ending well shows. There the goddess Fortune overturns all purposes and the motive power of the main plot with the revelation that Sorares the Assyrian is really the long-lost son of his supposed enemy Arbaces the Mede. Within such a frame of reference, it is only natural that outcries against the absurdity of Fortune are rife: "Fortune is only constant in inconstancy . . . the flattering pleasures of this world cannot promise one hour's certainty" (99).[43] Life is only a meaningless play contrived for

[42] Text and parenthetical references are to Bacon's edition of *Syrinx*; it should be noted that Bacon uses the revised edition of 1597 for his copy-text.

[43] See also *ibid.*, pp. 18, 184.

passive humans by Fortune (151), and it is best not even to inquire into her reasons or those of providence: "let us be thankful to the gods that are the givers, and wholly to their significant and secret wills refer all our actions, lest, by being over-curious, from the moon we fall into the mire" (62).

As this last quotation indicates, there is a strong tendency toward withdrawal from the world of chance and pain in *Pan his Syrinx*. Experience, celebrated as the only bringer of wisdom by Lyly and his school, is termed here "the philosophy of fools" (172),[44] and people are constantly being exhorted to leave a world where one learns only such a philosophy:

> If . . . adversity would offer unto other the opportunity to contemplate and consider of the world as was and is allotted to me, beauty would seem vanity, the loss of riches the recovery of quietness, a ransom from Fortune, and a discovery of ourselves should appear to ourselves no other than examples of weakness, spoils of time, the game of Fortune, patterns of inconstancy, receptacles of misery, marks for envy—in conception loathsome, in birth helpless, in youth witless, in age wretched, of life uncertain, of death sure. Therefore should we behave ourselves here not as though we live only for our bodies, but as though we could not live without bodies; neither should we so follow the world that we also fall with the world. (184)

An appeal to the Christian *contemptus mundi* catapults Warner's characters out of the absurd world of Greek romance. Therefore, at the end, when all the lost have been found, the reunited family, "tired with the world" (188), retire together into the closed circle of the isolated island.

Pan his Syrinx is the only major example of Greek romance in English outside of Greene's work. Two others, Nicholas Breton's mechanical *The Strange Fortunes of Two Excellent*

---

[44] For Lyly's explicit contradiction of this statement, see *Works*, ed. Bond, I, 260.

Princes (1600)[45] and George Wilkins' *The Painfull Adventures of Pericles Prince of Tyre. Being the True History of the Play of Pericles* (1608),[46] a romance that he adapted from both Gower's translation of *Apollonius of Tyre* and a play of *Pericles* (possibly Shakespeare's), are of minor importance; and there has survived only half of a rather interesting third example, *The Second Part of the Historie, called The Nature of a Woman: Containyng the end of the strife betwixt Perseus and Theseus*, by "C. M." (1596). But Greek romance did infuse some of its character into romances like Lodge's *A Margarite of America* and Chettle's *Piers Plainnes* (which we shall discuss in the following chapter), and its influence is especially evident in the late chivalric romances of Emanuel Forde, where it atrophied. Only one of Forde's romances, *Ornatus and Artesia* (1598?),[47] with its equal emphasis on love and chivalry, its motifs of fortune, storms, and pirates, and its plot based on the separation and reunion of lovers through the vicissitudes of chance, "owes more to the Greek tradition of Heliodorus" than to the *Amadis de Gaula* cycle.[48] But the influence of Greek romance can be seen in the other romances as well, chiefly in a greater density of action and emphasis on chance than is found in the *Amadis* cycle, but also in structural method, as Schlauch claims:

> In one respect Forde showed a certain advance over his predecessors, namely in the complications of his plot structure. Whereas the previous neo-chivalric tales had depended

[45] Schlauch's negative verdict on this romance (pp. 195-96) is entirely justified.

[46] See the edition by Kenneth Muir, Liverpool Reprints, No. 8 (Liverpool, 1953), pp. iv-xv. The original romance of *Apollonius* had itself been translated earlier as *The Patterne of painefull Adventures* by Laurence Twine (ca. 1594, 2nd edn. 1607).

[47] The earliest surviving edition is dated 1607, but Meres mentions it in *Palladis Tamia* of 1598 (see *Elizabethan Critical Essays*, ed. G. Gregory Smith [2 vols.; Oxford, 1907], II, 309).

[48] Philip Henderson, ed., *Shorter Novels, Jacobean and Restoration* (London: Everyman's Library, 1930), p. xi.

mostly on the intertwining of two simple, forward-moving themes ("Now leave we Sir X and return to Sir Y"), Forde likes to introduce a baffling situation suddenly, to leave it in partial suspense, and to reserve development and explanations for a much later point in the story. This means taking care of retrospective action chiefly in the form of enframed autobiographies. The technique brings Forde close to the imitators of Greek romance . . . but despite this and other affinities he is not to be identified with their school.[49]

Schlauch illustrates her contention by an analysis of the interweavings of plot in the first seven chapters of *Parismus* (1598).

Forde goes beyond the Greek romancers in cultivating action almost to the exclusion of ideas. Action in the Aristotelian sense of deeds showing moral states disappears entirely, and mere activity takes its place. This explains much of the dissatisfaction that critics have always expressed regarding Forde. Baker found him "mechanical," and Victorian critics like Jusserand found him licentious,[50] since adultery is frequently depicted in his romances with narrative approval and even, sometimes, with amusement.[51] But it is not merely a matter of immorality or amorality in Forde, it is the complete absence of care for mental states at all. Q. D. Leavis, who expresses qualified admiration for his work, must do so by negatives: "It is not unhealthy, it satisfies no morbid cravings, offers nothing in the way of wish-fulfilment or opportunities for emotional orgies, the story is the opposite of exciting, the characterisation is so unpronounced and abstract as to give no scope for day-dreaming."[52] What separates his

---

[49] Schlauch, p. 172.

[50] Ernest A. Baker, *The History of the English Novel* (10 vols.; London, 1924-39), II, 123; J. J. Jusserand, *The English Novel in the Time of Shakespeare*, trans. Elizabeth Lee (London, 1903), p. 198.

[51] See, e.g., the fabliau treatment given the affair of Parismus and Violetta in *Parismus* (1598), sigs. M2-M3.

[52] Q. D. Leavis, *Fiction and the Reading Public* (London, 1932), p. 89. The last part of Mrs. Leavis' statement is historically inaccurate, for the reader can see in the margin of the Folger copy of the 1640

romances from those of Sidney, Warner, Riche, or Greene is this empty or negative quality: his wooden heroes never fail, are never even embarrassed, external action replaces any psychological analysis (even in the love scenes), and dialogue expressing ideas or principles of choice is entirely excluded.

When Forde's coworkers in Elizabethan chivalric romance wish to give their action some human depth, so restrictive is their commitment to action separated from character that they must do so by external moralizing. Henry Robarts, for example, is much given to extolling virtue by the narrative voice alone and to ethical comment on the actions of fortune, the latter practice inherited from Greek romance. Thus when a storm drives Andrugio's ship off course Robarts comments, "see howe this cruell enemie fortune envying the towardnesse of this brave Gentleman" thwarts him; and then when Andrugio is rescued, Robarts cries out in joy, "loe there, behold how sweete a comfort," and ushers in providence to counteract fortune.[53] When Forde himself wants to give some depth to his usually flat action, he remains loyal to his premise and accomplishes this by action or structure alone. In *Montelyon*,[54] the most interesting of the romances, he gives his action depth for once through the use of parallel plots: for example, at the moment when Persicles and Constantia are conceiving Montelyon, the villain Helyon is lying with Selia under the impression that she is Constantia; the latter episode is treated

---

edition of *Montelyon* (sig. K3v) a childish scrawl of a sword and a spear with "Montelyons sword/ speare" written above them. Apparently the very abstractness of the characters could allow daydreaming children to identify with them; Marshall McLuhan would call chivalric romance a "cool" medium which like the comic strips invites a high degree of audience participation (see *Understanding Media: The Extensions of Man* [2nd edn.; New York, 1964], Chap. 2).

[53] Henry Robarts, *A Defiance to Fortune* (1590), sigs. E4v and F4v.

[54] The earliest surviving edition of *Montelyon* is dated 1633, but of course it must have been written before Forde's death in 1607. It was written after *Parismus* (1598) and *Parismenos* (1599), as the epistle, which calls those two romances "my elder off spring" (edition of 1640, sig. A3v), makes clear.

as "a merry Jest," the former as a pastoral idyll, complete with an epithalamion sung by the forest birds.[55]

As Leavis says so well, "Forde and his kind can be trusted never to exploit an emotional or even a pathetic scene; they coolly proceed with the business of getting on with the plot (the intricate meaningless web that Sidney popularised)"[56]— or the meaningless web that Greek romance suggested. In Forde's romances we can see the inevitable consequences of the late Greek presentation of action divorced from character or ideas, of action over which states of mind have no control. Warner presented such an absurd world, but showed men suffering in it and eventually retreating from it; Forde accepted absurdity as the way of the world, and consequently his absurdities became meaningless.

To put the matter perhaps too simply, the writers of prose fiction in the 1580s, faced with the opposed models of the Euphuistic mode and Greek romance, were essentially confronted with a choice between dialogue expressive of character and ideas but devoid of action, and action devoid of meaning. But Robert Greene made just such a simple and radical choice in *Pandosto,* and by so doing integrated several diverse strains in his work.

Separate elements from Greek romance had been with Greene almost from the beginning, since 1584. The setting and some of the names in *Gwydonius,* for example, had been Greek (Mitelyne, Alexandria, "Lewcippa"), and the final battle scene had owed something to Heliodorus. The frame of *Arbasto* had probably come from Achilles Tatius, as had many of its complaints against fortune.[57] But these details had garnished tales whose plots were of the Euphuistic type. Likewise, the Greek themes of fortune and time had dominated *Arbasto* and *Philomela,* respectively; but these themes were

---

[55] Chaps. IV and V (edition of 1640, sigs. D4v-E4); see the explicit comment on the relationship of the two scenes, sig. G2.

[56] Leavis, p. 90.

[57] See Wolff, pp. 393-98.

detached from the action, for *Arbasto* illustrates human purposes working against each other rather than a life governed by chance, and in *Philomela* truth is discovered by the human intellect rather than by the excavations of time. Greene was never able to weld these themes and plot elements together until he accepted from Boccaccio the Greek romantic vision of a world governed not by the precepts of human reason but by the absurdities of chance. Then he produced some of the most impressive pure narrative fiction to come from the sixteenth century, in *Pandosto* and *Menaphon*.

⟨ III ⟩

With its rash of Heliodoran motifs such as infant exposure, shipwreck, and a trial, its pastoral interlude heavily indebted to *Daphnis and Chloe,* and its plot unfolded in a world full of passion, violence, and accident, *Pandosto. The Triumph of Time* (1588) exhibits "with the greatest fulness the influences of the Greek Romances upon Greene."[58] One mark of such influence is the relative absence of the didactic element, for the title page promises, instead of edification, the delight proper to tragicomedy: "Wherein is discovered by a pleasant Historie, that although by the meanes of sinister fortune, Truth may be concealed yet by Time in spight of fortune it is most manifestly revealed. Pleasant for age to avoyde drowsie thoughtes, profitable for youth to eschue other wanton pastimes, and bringing to both a desired content" (IV, 227). In point of fact, Greene's story is much less edifying than the play Shakespeare drew from it. For example, whereas Shakespeare allowed his Leontes to repent and rewarded him with a "reborn" Hermione, Greene allows no such ethical reversals: his Bellaria dies for good, and his unrepentant Pandosto's last action is to pursue with lust his long-lost daughter Fawnia and then (when he discovers that his lust has been incestuous) to kill himself out of despair.

[58] *Ibid.*, p. 376.

Greene's is a crueler and more illogical world than Shakespeare's, and than the world of most of his own earlier work as well. His motto for this book, *Temporis filia Veritas* ("Truth is the daughter of time"), had appeared in *Penelopes Web* (1587) and had pervaded *Philomela,* as when in the latter Philippo says, "Now doo I prove that true by experience, which earst I held onelye for a bare proverbe, that trueth is the daughter of tyme" (XI, 189).[59] But this motto was inappropriate to *Philomela,* for there truth did not appear at long last by accident (as when we discover that the youth raised as a shepherd is really a prince), but by the revelation of a lie, a revelation given full human motivation when the consciences of the two Genoese slaves force them to reveal the truth. Such is not the case in *Pandosto*; there, partly because the questions submitted for trial by truth are questions of identity more often than of guilt or innocence, truth is discovered not by the human intellect but by external means: an oracle of the gods must tell Pandosto the truth about his wife, mute tokens of a gold chain and jewels must tell us who Fawnia is.

Similarly (as in *Perimides*), chance, rather than the human will, governs the action of losing and finding. "Fortune minding to be wanton" (IV, 264) decrees that the boat in which the infant Fawnia has been exposed be driven by a storm to the coast of Sicilia. "It fortuned" (264) that the shepherd Porrus finds her there and raises her. It is by chance that Fawnia meets Egistus' son Dorastus, that old Porrus meets the courtier who conveys him onto the ship in which the lovers are to flee, that a storm finally drives them to Bohemia, where Fawnia finds her father and her true identity. The degree to which chance governs Greene's plot can be seen by noting two small changes made by Shakespeare, who tried to introduce as much human motivation into his plot as he could: in *The Winters Tale* it is Antigonus who takes the infant to Bohemia (Greene's Sicilia), not a storm; and simi-

[59] See also *Works,* XI, 158, 165, 168, 197, and 201.

larly, the return journey is accomplished not by chance but through the sage advice of Camillo.[60]

The title page of *Pandosto* indicates that the tale records the conflict of time and fortune, with no interference by human action; and such is the case in the plot, where time replaces the intellect and moral sense as the instrument for the discovery of truth, and fortune replaces willed action as the instigator of events that make this discovery so difficult. This must be so because Pandosto, the man in power, has abdicated his right to be called a reasonable human being, as we see within the compass of the first few pages. The result of his swift decline into villainy is a trial where Pandosto's "reason" is nothing but rationalization, its issue a complete perversion of justice. Pandosto's decline is irreversible, for at the moment when the oracle reveals the truth to this man his son dies and Bellaria dies of grief; and he continues to the end a passionate and even incestuous villain. In such a dark world, where human nature is seen as motivated only by mad desires, time is the only possible revealer of truth, and the operations of fortune, no matter how fickle, appear as actually benevolent.

As in *Perimides,* the Greek influence issues for Greene in a split world, with action, time, and fortune on one side and the human mind and its virtues on the other. Theoretically, the pastoral circle of Sicilia is the realm untouched by fortune, for Fawnia as shepherdess can claim there that "we shepheards are not borne to honor, nor beholding unto beautie: the lesse care we have to feare fame or fortune" (282). And there, for once, we can see human purposes operating effectively in the beautiful dialectical process (repeated by Ferdinand and Miranda in *The Tempest,* III, i) by which Dorastus descends from his pride of place, Fawnia gives up a little of humility's security, and they both reach the middle ground of content where each is the other's servant.[61] But it is fortune

---

[60] See Wolff, pp. 452-53.
[61] See above, Chap. 3, pp. 78-79.

that frames this episode and even initiates its action, for "it fortuned" (274) that Dorastus met Fawnia while on his way home from hawking in the first place. In Chapter 3 we found Greene's pastoral idealism rather empty; this is so because the humane values cultivated in the pastoral world have no influence beyond its confines. When Dorastus and Fawnia emerge from Sicilia into Bohemia they meet the negation of their love in fortune, and instead of effecting any changes in the dark country, they become its victims.

In *Pandosto* Greene presents his readers with a book which is to excite their desire to see tragedy eventuate in a happy ending. To achieve this, he freed his fiction not only from the presentation of ideals for the reader's edification but from all ideational content as well. For beneath the split between people and the events of their lives in *Pandosto* lies the almost cynical or Calvinistic assumption of the inconsequentiality of human purposes—not only of their ineffectuality in determining the ends of life but also of their essential irrelevance in the face of time's relentless flow. Here Greene's concept of the workings of time approaches that of much modern fiction, for which "the largest discrepancy between idea and reality is time, the issue of time as duration."[62]

Ciceronis Amor. Tullies Love (1589) is the only one of the three last romances to be untouched by Greek romance. Based on Roman legend (and containing the interesting pastoral episode we discussed in Chapter 3), it records the cross-relations between three sets of lovers. What it does share with the other two romances is narrative detachment, for, as Pruvost writes, Greene stoutly resists moralizing on love and friendship here: "C'est qu'en effet l'auteur vise surtout à se divertir, et ses lecteurs avec lui, au spectacle des plaisantes complications engendrées par la nature capricieuse de l'amour."[63] Its main departure is stylistic, since it contains a variety of

[62] Georg Lukacs, *Die Theorie des Romans*, quoted by Albert Cook, *The Meaning of Fiction* (Detroit, 1960), p. 302.

[63] Pruvost, p. 343.

styles English and Latin: a Latin letter, Latin elegiacs translated into English blank verse, Greene's usual style of relaxed
Euphuism, and attempts at the Ciceronian style. About this
last Greene offers several disclaimers, stating in several places
that his own "rude and barbarous english" cannot hope to
reproduce Cicero's "sweete and musicall cadence" (VII, 153,
149); though in one place he denies attempting to imitate
Cicero (100), in another he apologizes for "coveting to counter-
fait Tullies phrase" (102). What we find in the speeches
Greene composed for Cicero is an occasional abandon-
ment of the Euphuistic seesaw of antitheses for a well-con-
structed periodic sentence with subordinate clause leading to
predication, the application of the Ciceronian proportion of
commata to *cola* in clauses of equivalent length, and even
occasional rhythmic cadence, as in the following: "If then it
be requisite in friendshippe to abandon suspitious secrecie, I
cannot but take it unkindly that *Tullie* is not made partaker
of *Lentulus* passions. For as the Carbuncle is not hid in the
darke, nor the fire shut up in strawe, so sorrowes cannot so
covertly be concealed but the countenance will purtray out the
cause by the effectes" (143). But even here the imagery is
Euphuistic, and we find Cicero lapsing into plain Euphuism
a few lines later; Greene was not to free himself from Lyly
until his next book, *Menaphon*.

Menaphon Camillas Alarum to Slumbering Euphues (1589)
is Greene's masterpiece. He creates interest in the plot by
beginning *in mediis rebus,* by spacing elements for suspense,
and by framing the whole with an obscure oracle announced
at the beginning and fulfilled at the end. For once the narrator is unobtrusive, refuses moralizing comment, and lets actions and characters speak for themselves. And *Menaphon* is
filled with verse—it contains more verse than any of the other
romances—and that of high quality. The influence of Greek
romance, acquired through or combined with that of Sidney's
Arcadia (as its running title, "Arcadia, the Reports of the
Shepheardes," and its verse suggest), is in part responsible for

its excellence, for in it we see imitation of the narrative technique as well as the themes of Heliorodus.[64]

Especially interesting is its continuation of stylistic experiment from *Ciceronis Amor*. Apparently Greene had been rankling since the spring of 1588 from attacks on the baseness of his style, for he had written then in the epistle to *Perimides*: "I keepe my old course, to palter up some thing in Prose, using mine old poesie still, *Omne tulit punctum,* although latelye two Gentlemen Poets, made two mad men of Rome beate it out of their paper bucklers: & had it in derision, for that I could not make my verses jet upon the stage in tragicall buskins, everie worde filling the mouth like the faburden of Bo-Bell, daring God out of heaven with that Atheist *Tamburlan*" (VII, 7-8). *Menaphon*, prepared in the summer of 1589 (it was registered on 23 August), formed Greene's answer to his critics. The commendatory verses of Thomas Brabine issue the challenge (VI, 31):

> Come foorth you witts that vaunt the pompe of speach,
>   And strive to thunder from a Stage-mans throate:
> View *Menaphon* a note beyond your reach;

and Thomas Nashe's famous preface directly attacks "the servile imitation of vainglorious tragoedians, who contend not so seriouslie to excell in action, as to embowell the clowdes in a speach of comparison; thinking themselves more than initiated in poets immortalitie, if they but once get *Boreas* by the beard, and the heavenlie bull by the deaw-lap" (9-10),[65] while praising "thy *Arcadian Menaphon*; whose attire though not so statelie, yet comelie, doth entitle thee above all other, to that *temperatum dicendi genus,* which *Tullie* in his *Orator* tearmeth true eloquence." Greene did in fact conceive of his

---

[64] See Wolff, pp. 444-45.

[65] It is interesting to note that Nashe took these two comparisons from the mouth of one of the silly shepherds in *Menaphon*, who describes Samela as a lost sheep "whose fleece was as white as the haires that grow on father *Boreas* chinne, or as the dangling deawlap of the silver Bull" (VI, 119).

style here as the middle style which can either rise to metaphor or fall to the plain statement of fact. The reader, he wrote, will "finde my stile either *magis humile* in some place, or more *sublime* in another" (7). It is chiefly in the verse that fills so much of the book (and which the running title emphasizes: "the Reports [i.e., echoes] of the Shepheards") that the style rises; but even there, as in the prose, the keynote is the variety the epistle promises, as when "plaine *Doron,* as plaine as a packstaffe" (68) first sings a highly metaphorical description of Samela (65) and then follows it by a plain country jig (69).

Variety of style is always kept foremost in the reader's mind in *Menaphon,* chiefly because its characters are always so much concerned with style, constantly discover things through style, and so frequently comment on each other's style. For example, when the shepherd Melicertus (really the disguised Maximius, Sephistia's long-lost husband) sings a song in the high style, "*Samela,* perceived by his description, that either some better Poet than himselfe had made it, or else that his former phrase was dissembled" (84). The first meeting of Melicertus and Samela results in an interesting cross-criticism through styles of speech, with confusion ensuing. Melicertus approaches Samela in the usual Euphuistic style: "I was by a strange attractive force drawne, as the adamant draweth the yron, or the jeat the straw, to visite your sweete selfe in the shade" (81). She finds this funny, and "thought to bee pleasant with her shepheard" by replying in the same fancy mode, concentrating on schemes of word repetition instead of on metaphor: "welcome, and so welcome, as we vouchsafe of your service, admitte of your companie, as of him that is the grace of al companies." This explicit mockery, Greene's final gesture of freedom from John Lyly, presents Euphuism as a pretentious style, the sort of thing a shepherd or shopkeeper trying to act fine would use; and its effect is to cloud over reality with appearances: "*Samela* made this replie, because she heard him so superfine, as if *Ephaebus* had learnd him to refine his mother tongue, wherefore thought he had done it of an inkhorne desire to be eloquent; and *Melicertus* thinking that *Samela* had learnd with *Lucilla* in *Athens* to anatomize wit, and speake none but *Similes*, imagined she smoothed her talke to be thought like *Sapho, Phaos* Paramour."[66]

Style is of considerable importance in this book. It is, for one thing, the vehicle of the social distinctions which are so uniquely emphasized here. For example, the comic lovers Doron and Carmela sing an eclogue in which she praises him as being white as his mother's calf, and he declares in return:

> Thy lippes resemble two Cowcumbers faire,
> Thy teeth like to the tuskes of fattest swine. . . . (138)

The narrator (in his single obtrusion into the story) comments, "if it be stufft with prettie Similies and farre fetcht Metaphores; thinke the poore Countrey Lovers knewe no further comparisons then came within compasse of their Countrey Logicke" (139).[67] The high style is emblematic of high estate, the low style of the lower classes. This fact is frequently reflected in the verbal texture, as in the aforementioned case of Melicertus' song, whose high style and pervasive imagery of rising reflects "the height of my thoughts soaring too high" (85) in expressing his love of the supposedly noble Samela, and initiates in Samela the suspicion that he may be noble too. Nobility is of the utmost importance in love and war—thus young Pleusidippus reacts hotly when his mistress questions his birth (110) and mocks the shepherds turned soldiers in devastating mock-epic style (130)—and since style is the sign of status, it becomes so important that it contributes to the book's denouement in a novel manner. The catastrophe is set in motion by Pleusidippus' kidnapping of Samela. When the shepherds raise an expeditionary force to rescue

---

[66] The allusions are to *Euphues his Ephoebus, The Anatomy of Wit*, and Lyly's play *Sapho and Phao*.

[67] Perhaps a satirical allusion to Abraham Fraunce's manuscript treatise *The Shepheardes Logike* or *The Arcadian Rhetorike* (1588).

her, they decide to choose their leader by the unique method
of a singing contest between the two main contenders. Menaphon, who apologizes for his "homely" lay, merely lists each
of Samela's physical attributes, applying conceits to them
stanza by stanza. Melicertus scorns Menaphon's conceits as
earthy and "stale," mocks the Petrarchan mode of conceits
itself—"What neede compare where sweete exceedes compare?" (125)—and tries for the sublime style of invention
by inspiration. The result is an evocative song in which each
of Samela's features is drawn into a myth of creation:

> Those eyes, faire eyes, too faire to be describde,
> Were those that earst the Chaos did reforme:
> To whom the heaven their beauties have ascribde,
> That fashion life in man, in beast, in worme.

Of course Melicertus wins: the man with the best style is
fittest to lead an army and redeem the beloved.

When different social levels with their distinctive styles
meet and interact, it is natural that an exploration of different
levels of awareness results. For example, when the shepherd
Menaphon courts Samela, his terms are so homely "that
Samela could scarce keepe her from smiling, yet she covered
her conceipt with a sorrowful countenance" (58-59). A series
of contretemps results: Menaphon, taking her countenance
as a true measure of her mood, sings a song to cheer her up;
but the song is about the rapprochement of the lofty eagle and
the lowly fly—a thinly veiled appeal for love—and when she
refuses to see the point, he is put to confusion. Similarly, in
the Euphuistic meeting of Melicertus and Samela discussed
above, each takes up a false style to which he or she assumes
the other will respond, with just the opposite effect of complete
confusion, since instead each thinks the other affected—a
confusion that can be cleared up only when Melicertus sings
a song in his proper high style. A comic instance of differing
levels of awareness is the arrival of young Pleusidippus in the
garden of Agenor and Eriphila at Thessaly. The scene he

interrupts might have found a place in the most refined medieval courtly romance: the atmosphere is one of rarefied, almost decadent sentiment, as Agenor and his wife moralize on the marigold for almost two pages of exquisite dialogue. Their response to Pleusidippus is delicately aesthetic. Agenor cries out in his ecstasy, "Had sea-borne *Pontia* then an appliable eare in our idlenesse, that to testifie hir eternall deitie, she should send us a second *Adonis* to delude our senses?" But the boy's response to them undercuts all this talk. As they stand fixed in amazement, "the faire childe *Pleusidippus* not used to such hyperbolical spectators, broke off the silence by calling for his victualls, as one whose emptie stomack since his comming from sea, was not overcloyed with delicates" (97). Plain hunger erupts into the refinements of feeling again when they turn to question him and he "cut off all their further interrogatories by calling, after his childish manner, againe for his dinner."

This last example shows that when different levels of awareness and social status meet, they frequently criticize one another. The ironic diction of "not overcloyed with delicates" makes the demands of the body mock a style of life full of delicate feeling and cloying expressions. But basic needs are not of themselves absolute; values are, in fact, variable in *Menaphon*. Near the beginning, Menaphon utters the usual pastoral *sententiae* about content, naturalness, and humility (37-38); these ideals are allowed to stand, but so too is their absolute rejection by Samela, who is never condemned for having preferred any misfortune to lowering her eyes to "the face and feature of so lowe a peasant" as virtuous Menaphon (58). Action frequently undercuts sentiment, as in Pleusidippus' response to Agenor, or in the episode where Menaphon, who has filled the air with protestations of his disinterested love of Samela, hears that she will not love him, and unceremoniously kicks her out of his house (101).

The title page promised "sundrie conceipted passions (figured in a continuate Historie)"—several songs expressing the passions linked together by narrative prose, after the model of Sannazaro's *Arcadia*—but instead of the promised relation between passion and action, we find just the opposite in the text itself. There is no contact at all between values and reality, the mind and action. In *Pandosto* Fawnia had asserted that "the body is subject to victories, but the minde not to be subdued by conquest" (IV, 310); this is all too true of *Menaphon,* where mind and body are virtually without contact. The sense of the vanity of intellection in a world governed by chance that pervaded *Pandosto* exists here as well, and is often directly expressed. King Democles, asserting "that the interpreters of *Apollos* secretes, were not the conceipts of humane reason, but the successe of long expected events" (VI, 35), forbids by edict the interpretation of an oracle lest it breed civil discontent; and by the end events have become so clouded that a prophetess has to step in and tell everyone what has been going on.

So little do the mind's intents influence reality that human action frequently becomes absurd, and seemingly willed action an illusion covering what is really happening. Melicertus, for example, spends many suspenseful years in the diligent wooing of a woman who is really, all along, his lawfully wedded wife. The climax is a web of illusions: Pleusidippus (who is really Sephistia's son) and Democles (who is her father and Pleusidippus' grandfather) are both consumed by lust for Samela (really Sephistia), and they kidnap her with the intent of committing rape if necessary; to her rescue comes Melicertus (who thinks he is Samela's lover, but who is really Maximius, Sephistia's husband and Pleusidippus' father); in the spectacular conclusion, husband fights son for the favors of the mother until the grandfather steps in, has them imprisoned, and then tries to seduce his daughter for himself!

Not only is there a complete lack of contact between mental decisions and the actions that ensue, but people are actually only going through motions when they think they are accomplishing a purpose. Pleusidippus may think that the final cause of his lust for Samela is sexual enjoyment and act on that premise; but the final cause, in this book with its two separate levels of action, is actually the will of the gods, and he and Democles are deemed innocent of evil by the narrator in a way denied to the incestuous Pandosto. Moral states are irrelevant. For the entire action of *Menaphon* consists of a variety of people playing out roles within a scenario written by the gods. In an oracle couched in such obscure metaphors that it takes a prophetess to discern at the end of the book how time has unraveled it, the gods announce that only after such events as father fighting son, only when "Dead men shall warre, and unborne babes shall frowne" (34) and many other such absurd events, shall peace and plenty come to Arcadia again. And the human actors, in their complete web of ignorance and confusion, dutifully go through the motions that will turn out to bring their salvation. The world of *Menaphon* is truly a world where certitude is impossible and, in Arnold's phrase, "Where ignorant armies clash by night."

Menaphon is a highly sophisticated rendering of a rather unsophisticated view of life much like the modern "absurd." In it, there is a complete cleavage between intention and result, character and action, apparent fact and real fact, values and reality. Action is spastic and meaningless, moral states of mind—and, in fact, any form of intellection—completely irrelevant. Every action is drenched in irony, for no one really knows anything, least of all what he is doing or who people really are. One style of life clashes with another and destroys its validity, but its own validity is destroyed in turn; style can either reveal character or conceal it by an impenetrable web of appearances. So full of life's unresolved contradictions is this romance that at times it becomes anti-romance.

⟨ IV ⟩

Menaphon is the last of Greene's works to fall unequivocally within the boundaries of prose fiction. His next book, *Greenes Never too Late,* appeared in two parts, both published in

1590. The first bore the Horatian motto that he had used since 1584, *Omne tulit punctum qui miscuit utile dulci* ("He wins all the prizes who mingles the useful with the pleasant"), the second an entirely new motto, *Sero, sed serio* ("Late but sincere"), related to the Latin proverb from which he had drawn his title (*Nunquam sera est ad bonos mores via*).[68] The two mottoes sum up admirably the shift in emphasis between the two parts—though it must be insisted that it is a shift in emphasis, not a radical change.

Part I records the progress of a prodigal husband. It is a moral tale, not without didactic asides to the gentlemen readers, but at the same time Francesco's love and his wooing of his bride Isabel are given the same amount of space and attention as are his fall and repentance. Part II records Francesco's repentance and regeneration, as he repulses the advances of his strumpet and finally rejoins his faithful wife. Together the two parts form a plot consisting of the fall and repentance of a fickle lover, much like that of Greene's very first work, *Mamillia*; but several differences in the way the plot is handled separate it completely from that work, chief among them heavy moralizing and an attempt at verisimilitude. The subtitle of the first part promised the reader "a true English historie" (VIII, 3), but did not fulfill this promise very well, since the England presented therein is that of the distant or mythical past, its setting Caerbrancke and Troynovant under the reign of King Palmerin. But in the second part the "truth" of the English history starts to seep through, for there Francesco (like his author) becomes a successful playwright in Troynovant (London).

As the second part becomes thinly veiled autobiography, so its manner of presentation changes slightly. In his epistle Greene promises "no great adventures, but you may see plotted down many passions full of repentant sorrowes" (VIII, 118); and in keeping with this promise, most of the book

---

[68] In 1591 he changed his motto again, this time to *Nascimur pro patria* ("I was born for my country").

consists of moral discourses (clearly labeled as such by sub-titles like "Bernardos discourse to Isabel" and "Isabels reply to Bernardo"), which keep the focus on concepts and passions rather than action. Adventure in this second part is severely and deliberately separated from the main concerns of the story. It consists, in fact, mainly of a single inset tale of pastoral love told at an inn to Francesco and Isabel. What is interesting about this inset tale is not only that it bears no relation to the main plot, but also that it contains no ethical meaning. Its sole end is delectation, and at its close "*Francesco, Isabel,* and all the rest of the guests applauded this discourse of the pleasant Host" and went to bed, where we leave them (220). The author who changed his motto to *Sero sed serio* has managed here to separate the *dulce* and the *utile* quite com-pletely: the *utile* consists in moral discourse and repentant passions, the *dulce* in narrative which has no relation to moral-ity.

The fictional time established for *Greenes Vision* (1593) locates its action between that of the first and second parts of *Never too Late,*[69] and therefore it explains quite explicitly what happened between *Omne tulit punctum* and *Sero sed serio*. It is a deliberately archaic work, belonging as it does to the medieval genre of dream vision and containing as its main characters the ghosts of Chaucer and Gower. Its purpose is to define what an exemplary tale ought to be, for in it Chaucer and Gower each tell a tale demonstrating the dangers of jealousy: Chaucer's is a fabliau about a jealous fool who gets his just deserts by being cuckolded in fact,[70] Gower's a sententious tale about the conversion of a jealous man by his chaste wife. Greene rejects Chaucer as a trifler, and sides with Gower and his method; with such a choice goes the implicit

[69] Near the end he tells Gower that "I must end my *Nunquam sera est,*" but promises that after it he will write no romances, but instead his *Mourning Garment* (*Works*, XII, 274).

[70] It comes from Boccaccio, *Decameron*, III, 8.

rejection of two critical positions which underlay much of what we have seen in Elizabethan fiction.

First, it is implicitly denied that comedy has a moral function: the appearance of the jealous man as fool may indeed make it "impossible that any beholder can be content to be such a one,"[71] as Sidney maintained, but it may go on to persuade us to follow the opposite example of the successful cuckolder. This position casts severe doubt on the ethical integrity of such works as *Don Simonides* and *The Adventures of Master F. J.*, and calls into question that of many another. Greene seems to be assuming that the successful hero is always a model to be imitated, and that if the witty rogue comes out on top, the reader will want to imitate him. Beneath the denial of oblique methods in comedy lies a much more sweeping denial of any obliquity in literary method, of any ethical effect in literature except that gained by the most direct and bald means. This Greene makes explicit: when Chaucer announces that men "will sooner bee perswaded by a fable, than an Oration" (XII, 270), just as Sidney had argued, Gower responds, "the more pittie." This is simply a denial of the validity of fiction. Here we see in theory what *Never too Late* presented in practice: a clean rift between moral persuasion and fiction, and between usefulness and delight.

The narrative technique of *Greenes Mourning Garment* (1590) is practically identical with that of its immediate predecessor, Part II of *Never too Late*. It is conducted for the most part in clearly labeled discourses, and narrative is again confined to a single inserted tale of pastoral love. But there is a new historicity to it, for the mourning garment that Greene offers his readers is a very old cloak indeed. What he has done, as he says, is "onely with humanity, moralized a divine Historie" (IX, 125): he has taken the parable of the prodigal son from Luke 15, kept its Biblical setting (even attempting Biblical imagery in the first few pages), and altered it only

---

[71] Sidney, *The Defence of Poesie*, in *Prose Works*, ed. Feuillerat, III, 23.

by expansions into discourse that keep its moral applications to the fore. His distrust of oblique methods has led him to the only ethical validated form of fiction, parable. When he confesses in the dedicatory epistle to earlier acts of "publishing sundry wanton Pamphlets, and setting forth Axiomes of amorous Philosophy" (119), he has chosen to allow no distinction between subject matter and stance, and accuses himself of having done in *Mamillia* and other works that of which Ascham accused Malory: recommending "open manslaughter and bold bawdry" merely by writing about them. To such a severe view of fiction, typical of the early Tudor Humanists and continued into Greene's time by Gosson and other "Puritanical" enemies of poetry, fiction must be exemplary if it is to exist at all; and Greene has accepted this view.

Therefore it comes as no surprise that the next book, *Greenes Farewell to Follie* (1591), is also Greene's farewell to fiction. In the dedicatory epistle he again laments his love stories, which he terms his "follies," not only for their subject matter but for what he now thinks of as the utter incompatibility of the delightful and the useful in romantic fiction: "Follies I tearme them, because their subjects have bene superficiall, and their intents amorous, yet mixed with such morrall principles, that the precepts of vertue seemed to crave pardon for all those vaine opinions love set downe in hir periods" (IX, 227). His book represents a ritual act of farewell to the follies of his fiction in two senses: it represents the thing given up, for it is the last time Greene's readers will see fiction from his pen; and it changes the thing given up, by restricting fiction to pure exemplum. The book itself attempts to define folly by analyzing it, containing (after the manner of *Morando*)[72] three discourses, each with its exemplary tale, on the three vices of pride, love, and intemperance.

[72] In some respects it is a return, with renewed fervor, to the manner of *Penelopes Web* and *Euphues his Censure*; what was probably an earlier version of the *Farewell* had been registered on 11 June 1587, but apparently not published then.

During the last year of his life, Greene dedicated himself exclusively to the literature of fact. The admonitory pamphlets against conny-catchers, all five of them, are full of assertions that "no one untrueth is in the notes, but everie one credible, and to be justified if neede serve" (X, 145) and that a story he records is "not a fiction, but a truth of one that yet lives" (X, 201). *Greens Groats-worth of Wit* (1592) breaks off its fictional beginning to announce that "Heere (Gentlemen) breake I off *Robertos* speech; whose life in most parts agreeing with mine, found one selfe punishment as I have doone" (XII, 137), and ends with an application of the fable of the ant and the grasshopper. The last work of his pen, *The Repentance of Robert Greene* (1592), is totally autobiographical.

Greene presented the conflict of his last years to his readers as one between love and divinity, or between the pleasant and the useful, or between fiction and fact. But what we see when we subject his factual pamphlets to scrutiny is rather some deeper tension, an exacerbation of the split we observed in *Menaphon* between thought and action, the former rational and ethical, the latter absurd and meaningless.

There are two distinct voices in *A Notable Discovery of Coosnage* (1591), the first and best of the conny-catching pamphlets. Consider, for instance, this continuous passage:

> Thus have the filthie felows their subtle fetches to draw on poor men to fal into their cosening practises: thus like consuming moths of the common welth, they pray upon the ignorance of such plain soules, as measure al by their own honesty, not regarding either conscience, or the fatal revenge thats thretened for such idle & licentious persons, but do imploy all their wits to overthrow such as with their handy-thrifte satisfie their harty thirst: they preferring cosenage before labor, and chusing an idle practise before any honest form of good living. Wel, to the method again of taking up their conies. If the poore countreyman smoake them still, and will not stoupe unto either of their lures:

then one, either the verser, or the setter, or some of their crue, for there is a general fraternity betwixt them, steppeth before the Cony as he goeth, and letteth drop twelve pence in the high way, that of force the cony must see it. The countreyman spying the shilling, maketh not daintie, for *quis nisi mentis inops oblatum respuit aurum,* but stoupeth very mannerlie and taketh it up: then one of the cony catchers behind, crieth halfe part, and so chalengeth halfe of his finding. The countriman content, offreth to change the money. Nay faith frend, saith the verser, tis ill luck to keepe found mony, wele go spend it in a pottle of wine, or in a breake-fast, dinner or supper, as the time of day requires: If the conye say he wil not, then answeres the verser, spende my part: if stil the cony refuse, he taketh halfe and away. (X, 18-19)

The abrupt break in style that occurs with "Wel, to the method again" is so striking as to be shocking, as Greene leaves the balanced periodic style with its Euphuistic touches ("handy-thrifte" and "harty thirst," for example) for a flexible paratactical style full of movement ("and will not . . . then . . . steppeth . . . and letteth . . . then . . . and so"), with a lively and almost exclusive stress on verbs. These two styles, the periodic moralizing style and the paratactical narrative style, run side by side constantly, as in this passage:

See Gentlemen what great logicians these cony-catchers be, that have such rethoricall perswasions to induce the poor countrie man to his confusion, and what varietie of villany they have to strip the poore farmer of his mony. Wel, imagine the connie is in the tavern: then sits down the verser, and saith to the setter, what sirrha, wilt thou geve mee a quart of wine, or shall I geve thee one? wele drink a pint saith the setter, & play a game at cards for it, respecting more the sport then the losse. (20-21)

Greene dodges in and out of his two styles all through the pamphlet. And, of course, the different styles are each emblematic of different voices and different values. One of the voices is that of a sage and serious conventional moralist, the other that of an amoral and delighted observer of quick action; one is static and formal, the other dramatic and slangy; one relates things as seen through the Conny's eyes, the other comments on the minds of those whoreson mad knaves the Setter, the Verser, and the Barnacle. Therefore it is not surprising that the two voices even make different judgments on the Conny: to the moralist, he is "some honest, simple, & ignorant" man, "the poore countreyman," the pitiable farmer, serving man, or prentice; to the lover of technique (who, in the last analysis, has a more vivid sense of moral realism), he is simply "the conny," often the victim of his own greed— "Thus the simple cony closeth up smoothly to take the versers part, only for greediness" (23)—and ultimately, of course, "the foole" (17). The commentary says one thing and the narrative shows something quite the opposite. In the one, cheating is evil and the man who does not cheat is automatically good, while in the other, any man who allows greed or lust to lead him on deserves anything he gets, and the sky is the limit. The realm of traditional moral evaluations and the realm in which the actions of the world actually occur have become separate, full, and self-sufficient kingdoms; each has become, for Greene, a highly developed and totally distinct system of values.

Here we see the rift exhibited by *Menaphon* carried to its logical conclusion: values or moral states have no contact with reality, human action has of itself no ethical dimension, but only an amoral code. Values are announced and action is narrated, but the two never meet. They occur separately, in separate styles, and with separate narrative voices—in the voices of two men, or of two sides of the strangely divided mind of Robert Greene. Some of the tension between these two aspects of Greene's mind is relaxed in the sequels *The Second part of Conny-catching* (1591) and *The Thirde and last Part of Conny-catching* (1592), but this comes about only because the balance has been heavily tipped away from pure moralizing toward pure action, especially in the third part, where moral disapproval practically disappears in the face of the narrator's delight in fast action.[73] The epitome of this movement is reached in the last of the criminal pamphlets, *The Blacke Bookes Messenger. Laying Open the Life and Death of Ned Browne* (1592). Purporting to be a repentance pamphlet, it is in reality a biographical jest book containing such things as "A Pleasant Tale how Ned Browne crossebit a Maltman" or "A merrie tale how Ned Browne used a Priest." What was latent before now lies on the surface: the victims are lecherous, avaricious, and proud, while the criminal himself and his crimes perforce seem just. And its tone is for once single, as is its voice, since its slangy and vivacious narrator (whose voice will reappear in Thomas Nashe's *The Unfortunate Traveller*) is Ned Browne himself, and his motive is to make us laugh, "discoursing to you all merrely, the manner and methode of my knaveries, which if you hear without laughing, then after my death call me base knave, and never have me in remembrance" (XI, 9).

The fiction we examined in the previous chapters operated from the basic assumption that concepts of the real or the valuable and experience of the real worked in some kind of loving converse, that not only did concept obviously cause action, but also action led to the clarification, modification, or even the rejection of some concepts. Such a relation Robert Greene seems never to have been able or willing to achieve, as appears with increasing clarity after his early Euphuistic imitations. His collections of novelle waver between tales that merely illustrate a point and pointless tales, his late romances present action as untouched by human motives, and his final pamphlets show a complete cleavage between precepts asso-

---

[73] One exception to the amorality of this late work must be recorded: the supposedly factual report of a repentant prostitute in *A Disputation Betweene a Hee Conny-catcher, and a Shee Conny-catcher* (1592); see *Works*, X, 237-76.

ciated with the divine and the pointless amorality of human affairs. Literary influences such as Italian novelle and Greek romances seem to have been the channels rather than the causes of such a view of life, which is probably to be ascribed most judiciously—though with a sense of futility—to the dim reaches of the mind of a man whose actions constantly belied his convictions of right and wrong, and who perhaps conceived of a deity (as it appears in *The Repentance*)[74] to whom human efforts to attain virtue form a fantastic joke.

Whatever the causes, Robert Greene's obsessive repentance completed a whole series of destructive acts whereby he severed himself first from the previous tradition of fiction and finally from fiction itself. He had bidden farewell to the Euphuistic style and its necessary association of ideas and actions in 1589. He then drove a wedge between the useful and the pleasant (whose relation, if not their identity, had always been a basic assumption of fiction), and rejected the latter. He rejected love, the traditional subject of all Renaissance fiction and the chief agency by which it had shown change of character, for divinity. He located the pleasant exclusively in action and the useful in ethical principles, and elected thenceforth to deal only with the latter. And, of course, he finally gave up fiction altogether.

But in such matters destruction is often fruitful. If Greene rejected from his writings love, which had dominated the fictional scene for centuries, his rejection had the effect of opening up new possibilities for the subject matter of fiction. The realms of satire and economics, for instance, were explored by his successors, Thomas Nashe and Thomas Deloney. Similarly, if he gave up fiction for such matters of "fact" as biography, autobiography, criminal practices, and historical jests, his successors were free to reach out and pull such matters back into the fictional world, thus increasing its scope

[74] See, e.g., *Works*, XII, 180 for Greene's sense of God's inscrutability, and XII, 169 for his evocation of the doctrines of election and predestination.

considerably. Greene's reactions against fiction had the paradoxical effect of opening up new areas to it, and these areas would demand, in their turn, new and various adjustments between ideas and actions.

CHAPTER 6

Thomas Nashe
and the Elizabethan "Realists"

There is only one work of prose fiction produced before 1590 that relates to Greene's radical dissociation of ideas from actions, and it is a strange work indeed. It is *The Adventures of Ladie Egeria* by "W. C. Maister of Art" (ca. 1584).[1] Within the compass of its one hundred and forty pages, it proceeds through three quite different stages of development that parallel in little the entire career of Greene. The first section of the book is more deeply embedded in the rhetorical tradition than *Gorboduc* or *Euphues,* where the action "was often treated as a kind of rhetorical exemplum showing vice and virtue in action, while the long speeches which made up the greater part of the work elaborated in more general terms the moral doctrine illustrated in the action."[2] Action consists mainly of persuasive speeches and descriptions of their effects, as the sycophant Andronus convinces Lampanus that his wife Egeria is unchaste, Egeria convinces Lampanus that Andronus is wrong, and so forth; these are not Euphuistic debates within the self (the book shows an independence of Euphuism almost unique for its time), but formal speeches, epistles, and declarations. The action of the first segment is therefore insistently filtered through the interpretations and judgments of the characters, so much so that the narrative scarcely exists as anything more than the vehicle for some exemplary precept about flattery, mutability, and so forth. The narrative, in fact, begins as an exemplum of several general precepts: "Such is the uncertayne condition, of vayne livers in this worlde, [who] confusedly

---

[1] It was entered in The Stationers' Register on 15 December 1580, but apparently not published until 1584 or 1585.

[2] Lorna Challis, "The Use of Oratory in Sidney's *Arcadia*," *Studies in Philology*, LXII (1965), 561-62.

blinded thorow daungerous delights, stopped from the right course, pursue the marveiles of wandering vanitie, cloked under false felicity, deny the steps and right paths of honourable renowne. . . . All which approvedly is knowne to fall out, in the renowmed dayes of young *Duke Lampanus* of *Hetruria* . . ." (sigs. B1-B1v). But at the point of the book, where events turn wonderful with the birth of a son with a golden thumb and a daughter with a golden leg (sig. G2), the oratorical style is dropped in favor of rapid narration, and event piles rapidly and improbably upon event. The filter of individual judgment provided by the characters' speeches vanishes, and instead the author has inserted marginal glosses alongside the narrative at various points in order to make the ethics of the action clear: "Harlots procure effusion of blood," "Whooremongers dotage," "Voluptuousnes preventeth all impediments," "True friendship is a companion . . . in al extremities." Action and ethical meaning have become concurrent but unconnected in the middle of the book, and it is interesting that Lampanus' prophetic dream marks the separation: for the action of the dream itself is absurd, and it must suffer a complex allegorical interpretation in order to achieve human if horrifying meaning.

The last forty pages (sigs. O1 to S2) take the disjunction one step further, for there the most abhorrent events take place without evoking any but the most casual comment; even the marginal *sententiae* disappear. Lampanus, cast out of his kingdom, plays several nasty tricks as he wanders from place to place, but they are treated with the merriment proper to a jest book. Pantiper ravishes his mother Egeria but she, after a page of lamentation, turns to seek help for him later the same day "like a good mother." The denouement is even stranger: Lampanus' daughter Selewsa has regained her father's kingdom, but the crowd-pleasing Pleasmanus (who arouses the narrator's animosity) threatens her security. It falls to the part of Lampanus to rid the kingdom of Pleasmanus, but new security only acts to spur his lust, and he rapes his daughter. The rape scene is narrated with little moral commentary other than a strange and undefended evocation, in a single phrase, of what Hobbes was later to label "natural lust," and Selewsa's response to the divine punishment of Lampanus is the curious one of filial duty! The passage must be quoted in full to be believed:

> This *Pleasmanus* by subtilty convayed him selfe into the favoure of the common sort, wretchedly with shame and dishonour ended his life. Now *Lampanus* assuring the estate of his Dukedome from al tempestes unshaken, gave him selfe greatly to voluptuous desire, olde filthy lust incombring the high counsels of his understanding, desired incestuous concupiscence with fayre *Selewsa* his daughter. . . . *Lampanus* drowned in forgetfulnesse of former miseries, inforced vehemently the ravishment and deflouring of Ladye *Selewsaes* honourable chastitie, the which obtayned, as shamefully committed, was converted presently to a venemous filthy snake. *Lampanus* most odious to behold in the similitude of a snake, al which [was] to fayre *Selewsa* grevous vexation, heart sorrow and teares, *Selewsa* altogeather remembring the duety of a daughter to her Father, framed of pure wrought Gold a fayre casket to preserve *Lampanus* in, during the continuaunce of these plagues happened, fead him with the milke of a she Unicorne. (sigs. R2v-R3)

Not only are the standard judgments of good and evil suspended, but the two turn out to be inextricable in human affairs: the father rids the kingdom of evil before raping his daughter, the other incestuous rapist Pantiper becomes the savior of his country.

This strange book—how consciously one cannot tell—takes the reader from stifling rhetorical judgments upon action to conjunction of action and judgment, and finally, to a position where any judgments on the action seem curiously irrelevant to the human condition, and the narrator himself seems stunned by reality. On the one hand the book looks back toward the sermon and exemplum, on the other it looks forward to the unmitigated horrors of that baroque masterpiece, *Morindos* (1609).[3] Its major affinities are, in fact, with works produced later, in the Jacobean moral climate, its closest analogue being John Hynde's *Eliosto Libidinoso. . . Wherein their imminent dangers are declared, who guiding the course of their life by the compane of Affection. . .*(1606). The moral sense gradually deliquesces in Hynde's book, too, though much less radically than in W. C.'s. The extensive tirades of the author against love and lust in the early part of the book decrease as it proceeds, and when the act of love is finally committed by Eliosto and Cleodora, it is both celebrated as glamorous and lamented as incestuous. Moreover, a dual attitude presides over its final pages, for the incestuous lovers are justly executed (though by a lecherous king whose own sins go unpunished), but are then buried in a rich common mausoleum with public mourning.

The radical disjunction of moral value and real action in the fiction of Robert Greene and the rapid dissolution of rhetorical evaluation before the dazzling juxtapositions of observed reality in *The Adventures of Ladie Egeria* both reflect a change in the basic orientation of Elizabethan literature. They each begin by insisting on the relation of every particular event to accumulated generality, and on the ethical judgment of every event by means of such a relation. But they end with a bare recounting of events with no moral commentary, and with little expression of emotion—even of surprise—at the strange and brutal turns life takes. Such a progress betrays an unconscious sense of the irrelevance both of generalities and of the traditional rhetorical evaluations of life (despite what may be a conscious and abiding respect for them in themselves).

In the mid-1590's, English literature experienced one of its perennial turns toward a more "realistic" orientation. Involved were a rejection of the love poetry that had given high

---

[3] See Charles C. Mish, ed., *The Anchor Anthology of Short Fiction of the Seventeenth Century* (New York, 1963), p. 3.

Elizabethan literature much of its "golden" cast, and its replacement by new genres purporting to represent the daily city life that men could observe around them: epigram, satire, the informal verse epistle, and the frankly erotic elegy. In terms of style, we find prose turning from the periodic to the Senecan style (which supposedly conveyed the movement of the mind in the act of thinking),[4] verse turning from the middle style to the plain style of unadorned colloquial discourse, and, in both, a rejection of an oratorical and evocative mode of presentation for a more factual, discursive mode.[5] The intellectual developments reflected in these changes include what Hiram Haydn terms "the hand-in-the-wound school" of skepticism and radical empiricism, with a pronounced preference for the particular over the general, the brazen world of what is over the golden world of what should be, the actually observed over a romanticized or mythical exaltation of it.[6] This last is of the utmost importance for fiction: an antipathy to myth or even fiction as a distortion of "fact" rather than a true representation of its ultimate reality.[7]

In the field of prose fiction, we find the counterpart of these general movements in the work of three men closely associated with Robert Greene. They are Thomas Lodge (in his late work), whose *Euphues Shadow* (1592) Greene edited while the author was abroad, and who collaborated with Greene on

---

[4] See Morris W. Croll, "The Baroque Style in Prose," in *Style, Rhetoric, and Rhythm: Essays by Morris W. Croll*, ed. J. Max Patrick, Robert O. Evans, et al. (Princeton, 1966), p. 221.

[5] For the "rejection of the middle style," see Wesley Trimpi, *Ben Jonson's Poems: A Study of the Plain Style* (Stanford, 1962), Chap. 5. For a representative statement about the new "function of a *Poem*, to discourse," see Samuel Daniel, *Musophilus* (1598), l. 998.

[6] Hiram Haydn, *The Counter-Renaissance*, pp. 190-250. Representative statements by Bacon on these matters may be found in *Of the Advancement of Learning*, ed. Kitchin, pp. 83, 142, 165.

[7] See Maurice Evans, *English Poetry in the Sixteenth Century* (2nd ed.; New York, 1967), Chap. 8, esp. pp. 157-61; the entire first book of Joseph Hall's *Virgidemiae* (1597) is devoted to the rejection of the sonnet, tragedy, and other forms of fictional poetry opposed to the "Truth" of satire.

A Looking Glasse for London and England (ca. 1589); Henry Chettle, who edited the posthumous *Greens Groats-worth of Wit* (1592) and who, in *Kind-Harts Dreame* (1593), called upon Thomas Nashe to defend Greene's memory against Gabriel Harvey's slanders; and Nashe himself, who had written a long preface to *Menaphon* (1589) linking his own style to Greene's, and who responded to Chettle's call in a long series of attacks on Harvey. Their general debts to Greene are many, and include the banishment of love as the exclusive subject of fiction (*A Margarite of America,* the single love plot among Lodge's later works, and among the works of all three writers, treats love not from the romantic point of view but as the basis for a bloody tragedy after the manner of Bandello's tragic novelle), the introduction of low-life elements (whether from jest book or rogue pamphlet) and thus a new social dimension, and an insistence on verisimilitude. With these they combined elements of the new literary realism to produce work marked by both an air of factuality and a fully satirical world view. Finally, the insistence on the exclusive relevance of the particular in such a view tends to separate ideals from actions in their work. What we find, as a result, are various fictional worlds in which concepts of value and the motives by which men act have no connection.

⟨ II ⟩

Lodge was himself in the forefront of the new movement in verse, for *A Fig for Momus: Containing Pleasant Varietie, Included in Satyres, Eclogues, and Epistles* (1595) anticipated the professedly first English satires of Joseph Hall by two years, and introduced for the first time the epistle, "that kind, wherein no Englishman of our time hath publiquely written" (6-7).[8] He integrated the one "old" kind, the eclogue, with the two new ones by turning it into a form of occasional verse,

---

[8] Page references are to Lodge's *Works,* ed. Gosse, Vol. III; the individual works are separately paginated.

addressing eclogues, satires, and epistles alike to friends such as Digby, Spenser, Daniel, Bolton, and Drayton; and he gave unity to the volume as a whole by the plain style he applied to all three kinds:

> Who waites for words, may get him hence,
> For shepheards onely sing for sence. (19)

The main element of the new realism to enter Lodge's fiction after *Rosalynde* is historical verisimilitude—the concern for the appearance, if not the substance, of "fact" in fiction. Hall, in mocking the improbabilities of romance and rejecting many forms of poetry in favor of the "truth" of satire, came very close to doing what Marston accused him of: banishing fiction, "The soule of Poesies invention," from literature.[9] To this concern of the satirists in 1597-98 corresponds the appearance earlier in the decade of fiction based on real or legendary history (one might better term it a reappearance, since such fiction had shared the stage with chivalric romance in the first half of the century). The first of such works was Lodge's *The Famous, True and Historical Life of Robert Second Duke of Normandy* (a title that tells its own story), published in 1591; this was followed by Richard Johnson's *The Nine Worthies of London* in 1592, Lodge's *The Life and Death of William Long beard* in 1593, Johnson's *The Most Famous History of the Seaven Champions of Christendome* in 1596-97, and finally by Henry Robarts' *Honours Conquest, Wherein is Conteined the Famous Hystorie of Edward of Lancaster* in 1598. The rather nervous concern over historical accuracy common to all the examples of this minor fictional genre is conveyed in Robarts' preface:

> And if any will alleage, that in this Poeticall praising of him [Lancaster], there be many fictions (as, *Poetis et pictoribus permagna conceditur licentia*) let such learne to

---

[9] See Hall, *Virgidemiae*, I, iv, 5ff. and Marston, *The Metamorphosis of Pigmalions Image and Certaine Satyres*, Satyre 4, l. 88.

reade these manner of bookes, as Socrates wished women to
use their looking glasses; namely, faire women, to looke on
their glasses, to beware that their good maners may shine
as well as their beautie; and ill-favored women, to indevour
that their inward vertues might make gratious theyr outward deformities. (sigs. A4-A4v)

Similarly, Lodge was plagued by the problem of probability
and credibility in *Robert Duke of Normandy*. In the preface
he claims to have drawn his story from reliable sources, "the
old and ancient antiquaries, . . . wherein I stand out not so
much on the termes, as the trueth, publishing as much as I
have read, and not so much as they have written," and he concludes defensively, "yet many things have happened in times
past, incredible in our age, and in our age such things have
falne out, as had our fathers knowne they had mervailed: It
onely behoveth us to applie all things that tend to good, to
their end, which is vertue, and esteeme them" (4).[10] Despite
Lodge's assertions and gestures of critical skepticism, *Robert
Duke of Normandy* (largely derived from *The Lyfe of Robert
the Devyll* printed by Wynkyn de Worde near the turn of the
sixteenth century) is as improbable as any saint's legend has a
right to be. It is full of the marvels of romance, not the probabilities of history; and Lodge even added to the romance by
inserting a symbolic "wood of temptation" (43) to set in motion Robert's conversion, where in the same place Wynkyn de
Worde had only shown Robert's shocked recognition of the
horror he inspired in people. Actually, the plot of *Robert Duke
of Normandy* follows the same curve of decline followed by
regeneration that we find in the pastoral romances *Forbonius
and Prisceria* and *Rosalynde*. It is Lodge's attempt to present
romance as history.

Two years later, in *The Life and Death of William Long
beard,* Lodge achieved success in his self-appointed role of
fictional historiographer. He achieved the tone of genuine

---

[10] Page references are to *Works*, ed. Gosse, Vol. II.

history by breaking out of his fictional frame to cite authorities, as when he reports William's brother condemned "as some Writers suppose for coining" (6).[11] And he achieved verisimilitude by many specific references to dates, such as "in the yeare of our Lord 1197" (7), and places, as in the following: "William . . . at last incountred him bravelie, mounted on his foot cloth in Friday street, where taking him forceably from his horsse, he carried him into a Barbers shop, and caused both his beard and his head to be shaved close" (17). Finally, in order to underline the reality in his tale the more strongly, he treats the only romantic interlude in it satirically: William's love affair with Maudelin is presented as the wilfull creation of an illusion wherein he "pretended a new conceited love, and but pretending it at firste, at laste was enforced to practice it" (17). In order to exalt his unchaste mistress, William circulates sonnets to her beauty and dresses her in fine clothes, "sparing no cost to trick hir out in braverie, to the end he might by that meanes, give a foile and glasse to her beawtie. . . . wresting his wits to make an idoll of hir worth" (18). Lodge here treats William as Hall and the other satirists were later to treat the sonneteers.

History was frequently presented, as it was by Sidney, as a depiction of the world divorced from precept—as what *was,* instead of (and unrelated to) what could or should be. Such was not the view of Johnson and Robarts, who, sharing the more common sixteenth-century view of history as exemplary, consistently held up their heroes as models of virtue; but it is the view that pervades *The Life and Death of William Long beard.* Though this brief tale is structured like a tragedy in *A Mirrour for Magistrates* and William is presented throughout as a villain, the moral pressure never becomes so great as to make the tone one of simple condemnation. William's defense of the poor in the episode "How William . . . handled the cause of Peter Nowlay a Cobler" is handled with the zest proper to a jest book despite the narrator's reservations about

[11] Page references are to *Works,* ed. Gosse, Vol. II.

William's motives. Moreover, William is a passable versifier, and he dies well; even though the narrator mocks the superstitious folk who make William a martyr, he does end the book with three pious hymns that William composed before his execution. The subtitle of the tale itself betrays some of the duality of tone with which it is related: "the most famous and witty English Traitor." During the surprising process of change that Lodge underwent in his evolution from the pastoral mythographer of *Rosalynde* to the factual reporter of *William Long beard,* the assumption that life corresponds neatly to ethical norms (rather than to fortune, the realm of the absurd) became subject to doubt. Lodge therefore chose —as Robert Greene never did—to give up the confrontation of ideas of good and evil in order to present action in reality. If we seek to establish a continuity between the early and later Lodge, we may take *Euphues Shadow* (1592) as the watershed; for there, as we have seen, the action centers on the question (never finally resolved) of whether chance or reward for virtue determines the nature of human events. And *A Margarite of America* (1596), where the tragically absurd is finally embraced, presents us with its completion.

Lodge seems to have been at some pains to make *A Margarite of America* appear to be true history. In the dedicatory epistle to Lady Russell he avers that though the subject seems "historicall" his book yet shows diligence in presenting it, thus implying that he has merely clothed a plot he did not invent; and in the epistle to the readers he clarifies this implication by the following account: "Som foure yeres since being at sea with *M. Candish* (whose memorie if I repent not, I lament not) it was my chance in the librarie of the Jesuits in *Sanctum* to find this historie in the Spanish tong, which as I read delighted me, and delighting me, wonne me, and winning me, made me write it."(4)[12] Considering that the Spanish original has never been discovered and that writers from Chaucer to Gascoigne to Henry Robarts were often given to presenting

[12] Page references are to *Works,* ed. Gosse, Vol. III.

original works as translations, it is probable that Lodge is here deliberately distancing himself as narrator from the tale he has to tell, and that the tale is in fact an objective rendering of things as they are, the world viewed historically rather than romantically. C. S. Lewis writes of it: "If the book is not realistic, it is real; the compulsive imagination of a larger, brighter, bitterer, more dangerous world than ours. It is hard romance."[13] The main trait of the world as it is rendered so drily here is, as in Bandello, the imperviousness of evil in it.

Though the story begins with a gorgeous scene, plunging *in medias res* after the manner of Greek romance, it soon settles down to the more familiar Euphuistic model. The introduction of the hero-villain Arsadachus is accomplished in the familiar scene of the father admonishing his son, and with the usual schematic style: "for being well shaped by nature, there was not any man more estranged from nurture; so that it was to be feared, that he should sooner want matter to execute his dishonest mind upon, then a dishonest mind to execute any lewd matter" (19). But if we take this to be the introduction to a prodigal son plot, as the nature-nurture dichotomy seems to indicate, we are mistaken: Arsadachus is a Euphues hopelessly corrupt. He will not reform, nor will he be shocked out of his evil ways to become regenerate as Saladyne or Robert the Devil did. For the world as it is turns out, in Lodge's hard view here, to be almost Calvinistic in its stubborn corruption. As the poem "Humanae Miseriae discursus" by the book's wise man Arsinous puts it:

> An infant first from nurces teat he sucketh
> With nutriment corruption of his nature. (9)

People do not change here, and there is therefore no relief from suffering. Margaret Schlauch writes of *A Margarite,* "war and cruel violence play a greater part than in any other of the pseudo-Hellenic romances. Hating is stressed much more than loving. . . . This monstrous product is interesting

---

[13] Lewis, *English Literature in the Sixteenth Century*, p. 425.

to us chiefly as testimony to a prevalent sensationalism in literary taste."[14] There is, in fact, a pile of horrors, as Arsadachus' lust after Philenia causes him to kill her and her bridegroom Minecius, then his accomplices in the crime, then Margarite herself, and finally himself, after having delivered this dark verdict confirming Arsinous' view and standing as the book's final judgment on the actions within it: "True it is that *Plutarch* saith (quoth he) that life is a stage-play, which even unto the last act hath no decorum: life is replenished with al vices, and empoverished of all vertue" (91).

This dark view, equating as it does the formlessness of a life out of contact with ideals with pure meaningless horror, is the view of life that the author of *The Adventures of Ladie Egeria* showed fully but could not bring himself to express. This view, too, seems to be common in "realistic" stories centering on a suffering female. It is shared, for example, by John Dickenson's *Greene in Conceipt. New raised from his grave to write the Tragique Historie of faire Valeria of London* (1598), and especially by Nicholas Breton's *The Miseries of Mavillia* (1597), a book which, while making insistent demands on our supply of tears, pretends no moral save only that Mavillia is "the most unfortunate Ladie, that ever lived"—so unfortunate as to have her nose bitten off in the ultimate "Miserie." The book's insistently dark tone, as well as the unusual verisimilitude given to it by the first-person narrator, is adequately shown in its ending: "Let this suffice, hitherto I have written the tragicall discourse of my unhappy life. Now going to my husband, to see how he fares, [I saw] that he [was] left speechlesse, [and I am] so weake my selfe, as that mine eyes doo faile mee. In hope to goe to God, I bid you all fareweell."[15]

---

[14] Schlauch, *Antecedents of the English Novel*, pp. 198-99.

[15] *"A Mad World My Masters" and Other Prose Works by Nicholas Breton*, ed. Ursula Kentish-Wright (2 vols.; London, 1929), II, 166. On the resemblance, if not the indebtedness, of both *A Margarite* and *The Miseries of Mavillia* to Bandello, who was for the Elizabethans synonymous with remorseless tragedy, see René Pruvost, *Matteo Bandello and Elizabethan Fiction* (Paris, 1937), pp. 225-28.

The mythical fluidity of life as *Rosalynde* presented it has vanished in *A Margarite of America*. The world is uniform in its darkness, and personality remains forever fixed in its corruptness or its innocence. Hence, when someone seems to have changed, it is only a case of appearances covering reality. One of the old Euphuistic episodes that reappears in *A Margarite* is the court of love, in which Margarite, her supposedly ardent fiancé Arsadachus, and others debate which of the senses is paramount in love. That the reward goes to the eyes becomes ironic immediately after Arsadachus leaves, for he goes home to pen a poem about deceptive appearances:

> Judge not my thoughts, ne measure my desires,
>   By outward conduct of my searching eies,
> For starres resemble flames, yet are no fires. (57-58)

Arsadachus is an inveterate dissembler: while pretending love to Margarite, he proffers himself to her maid Philena, and when repulsed by her disguises himself and murders her and her new husband. His villainous deceptions mount until he has deposed his father and elevated the ambitious strumpet Diana to share his throne. In her he meets his counterpart: in reality the opposite of her chaste namesake, she first inveigles his eye in a masque about the goddesses, where she plays the part of Diana. His response to this dissembling is to heighten it into an enormous illusion; he marries her, and so indulges his lust as to cause Diana actually to be worshiped as a goddess, while he assumes the weeds of a shepherd who composes hymns in her praise and performs ceremonies of abasement and other mad pranks before her throne. This is the end result of his complex life of deception, his "Hiperbolical praise, shewing the right shape of his dissembling nature" (79), and complete madness soon follows.

Arsadachus and his Diana, be it noted, act out the same sort of play Rosader and Rosalynde did in *Rosalynde*; but in a fictional world divorced from attainable ideals of conduct, where personality never changes, such play-acting is merely

absurd. Lodge's handling of role-playing in each of his fictional
works is a convenient index of his progress from mythographer
to historiographer. In *Forbonius and Prisceria, Rosalynde,*
and *Euphues Shadow,* ideals are presented as available and
relevant to daily life, and role-playing in a prime imaginative
effort to attain mastery over life. In Lodge's later historical
fiction, role-playing reveals the separation rather than the rapprochement between face and mask, actual and ideal. In the
first of these later works, *Robert Duke of Normandy,* it is
presented as part of the distinction between *charitas* and *cupiditas*: while the converted Robert humbly worships his God,
the Souldan of Babylon constructs a temple to his beloved
Emine and worships her image in obvious idolatry. In *The
Life and Death of William Long beard* the role-playing of
William and Maudelin is shown, as we have seen, as comic
self-delusion. And finally, in *A Margarite of America,* what
had been a means of approaching the absolute is rendered as
a psychopathic fixation.

⟨ III ⟩

Henry Chettle and Thomas Nashe are bound together in
literary history not only as defenders of Robert Greene's ghost,
but as workers in similar literary veins as well. Both of Chettle's efforts in prose, *Kind-Harts Dreame, Conteining Five
Apparitions, with Their Invectives against Abuses Raigning,
Delivered by Severall Ghosts Unto Him to be Publisht, after
"Piers Penilesse" Post Had Refused the Carriage* (1593) and
Piers Plainnes Seaven Yeres Prentiship (1595), have an obvious dependence on Nashe's *Pierce Penilesse His Supplication
to the Divell* (1592). Both Chettle and Nashe gave some rather
shrewd turns to romance by means of satiric interpolations.
And finally, both were stylistic virtuosos.

Kind-Harts Dreame shows Chettle to be attempting from
the beginning the mastery of diverse juxtaposed styles. The
five apparitions mentioned in the subtitle are of five charac-

ters, each of whom ranges from his own occupation to satirize various abuses in contemporary London: Anthony Now-now, a musician who attacks lewd ballad-mongers; Doctor Burcot, a physician who satirizes quacks of all sorts (these two are also mentioned in Deloney's *The Gentle Craft,* Part II); Robert Greene, who defends himself against his detractors; Richard Tarlton, a clown who attacks the current stage and racking landlords; and finally William Cuckoe, a juggler whose occupation becomes a metaphor for all the "juggling" and cheating of lawyers, usurers, and their sort. This satire is also a stylistic showpiece, for Chettle gives to each of his characters a distinct and fitting style. Anthony Now-now's shows amusingly the traditional incoherence of the singer, for it is full of run-on sentences and obscure attempts at reasoning; Doctor Burcot's, on the other hand, is a clear oration based on the classical model, with bitingly satirical diction and short sentences for emphasis. Greene's style is an adequate imitation of that of his *Groats-worth of Wit,* combining Latinate learning with simple syntax, while Tarlton's is in the vein of Nashe, "extempore out of time tune, and temper."[16] Finally, Cuckoe's style, with its sense of spoken dialogue and its consequent abrupt shifts of attention, comes directly from Martin Marprelate: "Roome for a craftie knave, cries *William Cuckoe.* Knave, nay, it will neare hand beare an action: Bones a mee, my trickes are stale, and all my old companions turnd into Civill sutes. . . . Let me see, if I can see, beleeve mee theres nothing but jugling in every corner."[17]

Piers Plainnes shows a continued interest in juxtaposing different styles, but here the styles are reduced to two, and the contrast between them is radically sharpened (somewhat after the manner of Greene's conny-catching pamphlets, though the styles are not the same). The first is an exalted formal style,

---

[16] *Kind-Harts Dreame,* ed. together with *Kemps Nine Daies Wonder* by G. B. Harrison (London: The Bodley Head Quartos, IV, 1923), p. 42.

[17] *Ibid.,* p. 49.

rhetorical and Euphuistic, full of schemes, heroic comparisons, and periphrases, as typified by the opening: "The Sunne no sooner entred Gemini, but Natures plentie and Earths pride, gave the husbandman hope of gainefull Harvest, and the shepheard assurance of happie increase; the first cherished with the lively Spring of his deade sowne seede: The seconde cheared by the living presence of his late yeande Lambes" (122).[18] The second is its opposite, a relaxed extemporal style heavily influenced by the Marprelate tracts and Nashe; it usually merely gives the gist of an oration, and frequently lists actions in a string of verbs. It specializes in concrete adjectives and nouns conveying specific images, as in the following: "some in the long stocke and little ruffe like Brabanters, some with standing capes and slyced breeches like Danes, some with their beards cut *Alla Turquesa,* their hose hanging loose (like an emptie gut) after the Portugall manner" (144-45).[19] Most typically, its syntax is broken by statement and *correctio,* or by asides to the audience that convey the effect of recorded speech:

A new Master, a new, for thus Piers Plainnes hath parted with Prodigalitie, and meanes to learne thrift of Brokerie: a shrewd fall, from a Courtly waiter to be a Brokers booke-keeper. Well, what remedie? necessitie they say hath no law: and so it seemd by mee, for my neede drove mee to live without lawe, if I had said with an outlaw, I had kept within compasse: for besides my master, a number of his mysterie, did not onely deale unconscionably without law, but were indeed verie outlawes, banquerupts, what call ye them, or Brokers still let us call them, for a fitter name I have not for them.

I saw Menalcas smile even now, when I cald Brocage a mysterie: the terme was not much a misse, for there are more mysts used therein, than in anie Trade beside. (143-44)

The two styles are those of entirely different narrative voices, though both voices issue from the mouth of Piers Plainness. The formal style is that of a third-person narrator, reporting with comparative respect the things Piers has heard about high affairs of state. The extemporal style is that of a first-person narrator, satirically recreating the experiences Piers himself has gone through. Furthermore, the two styles and voices are used to convey the two quite separate plots that Chettle attempts to interweave in this strange book (combining, as it were, the two sides of Greene's late work): a Greek romance and a contemporary rogue biography.

The Greek romance, which forms the main strand of the book, begins with the successful conspiracy of Celydon, an ambitious nobleman, and Celinus, the evil son of King Hylenus of Thrace, to depose the king and exile him, together with his good son Aemilius and his daughter Rhodope. The three are driven by "the fortune of the wind" (130) to Crete, where they land separately. Aemilius arrives just in time to save Aeliana, queen of Crete, from incestuous rape by her uncle and regent Rhegius, who has disguised himself as a savage during a hunt. They fall in love and utter the usual Euphuistic *psychomachiae,* but are prevented by Rhegius. Meanwhile, things go from bad to worse in Thrace. Celinus is betrayed by Celydon and forced to flee for his life to Crete in a boat manned by Piers Plainness, while Celydon himself is killed. On Crete, Piers and Rhodope manage to free Aemilius from Rhegius' prison; Celinus reveals the lust of Rhegius (he has overheard his plans), Rhegius reforms by falling in love with Rhodope, and the story ends with a set of marriages and restorations, in which Piers is included.

Interspersed with the events of this romance are episodes from the life of Piers Plainness himself, after the manner of a rogue biography like *Lazarillo de Tormes,* and with a direct bearing on contemporary London life through references to fashions, the commodity swindle, dicing, and the like. Piers's progress, like that of Breton's *Grimellos Fortunes,* is the downward path of a courtier. "Wondring what brave life it was to bee a Courtier" (127), he becomes the servant of the threadbare braggart-soldier Thrasilio, a retainer of Flavius, one of the noblemen committed to Celinus' cause. When necessity forces Thrasilio to cast him off, Piers enters the service of Flavius himself; but Flavius is a prodigal, and the new luxury of Celinus' reign so reduces him as to expose him to bankruptcy. He becomes the victim of his own bailiff Petrusio, of a Broker, and of the usurer Ulpian. Piers is conveyed to the Broker with Flavius' lands; and with his new master Piers, transformed from a courtier to chattel, learns all the shifts of the underworld. When a capricious justice overtakes the Broker, Piers descends yet another step: "And now Piers having parted with Flatterie, Prodigalitie and Brokerie, is worshipfully entertained with Usurie. A service of good credite I assure ye" (146). With the usurer Ulpian and his daughter Ursula, whom Ulpian uses as a stale to draw prodigals, Piers suffers mistreatment and want; when he and Ursula betray Ulpian to the authorities for clipping of coins, the only result is to impel Piers to descend still lower as servant of Petrusio, a man compact of all vices. It is at the bottom of the ladder that Piers joins the main plot: the outcast Celinus forces him to convey him to Crete, where he joins in the denouement.

At one point in the book Piers pauses to defend the juxtaposition of opposites as the way the world wags: "Wonder not to heare, that riot should keepe house with wretchednes: for such is the pleasure of the heavens, that one iniquitie should consume another" (157). And so it is in Chettle's book as a whole, where the plot of the Greek romance, with its public character, its decorous third-person narrator, and its Euphuistic style, alternates with the private conny-catching affairs of Piers and his own racy style. Piers interrupts his romantic narrative four times to interject elements of his personal history; these interruptions mark four main divisions in the narrative, in which public and private plots achieve changing interrelationships.

In the first two segments, the public and private plots alternate rapidly and with narrative connection; for Piers is a minor actor in the deposition of Hylenus, and his main function is to show, from his stance, the underside of the main action. Thus, after the opening narration of the plan of Celydon and Celinus to overthrow Hylenus, Piers indulges in a brief description of his disordered household. His account centers in a character sketch of his master Thrasilio, a flattering braggart-soldier whose low-comedy lies underscore the baseness of deceit in high places. Then, after the tragic villainy of Celydon's capture and exile of Hylenus, Piers describes from his point of view Celinus' parallel capture of the capital, which is silly and confused. The braggart Thrasilio and his page Piers, rusty javelin in hand, join the ruffians on the scaffold beside Celinus: "Ill weapond though we were, welcome wee were, and among our fellow Cavaliers had the *Bien venuto*: for there everie cobler was a captaine, and he that had but a bat on his necke, thought himselfe a commander. O had you seene the miserie in those few houres of Insurrection, with what violence the giddie headed people were carried to ill, how easely disswaded from their alleagance, how willingly misled . . ." (131). Villainy in high places, though different in style, is in fact no different from the practices of the basest cutthroat.

In the third segment, the narrative occurs in large blocks, and elements of the two main plots diverge geographically. On the one hand, Crete (where the exiled royal family has landed) becomes a mythic realm where Aeliana plays Diana to Rhegius' savage; and events surge upward as Aemilius saves Aeliana and she takes both him and his father under her protection. On the other hand, in Thrace—to which Piers returns as narrator after a break for a drink—we witness the brutal decline of the state under Celydon and Celinus. Thrace in its contrary motion is an image of what Crete might become if Rhegius' plots were to succeed; as later Celinus says to Rhegius, "by like counsell and self conspiracie, am I cast downe from Princely dignitie unto this extremitie" (172). Furthermore, the vignettes from Piers's own history are presented as images of the general decline of Thrace. In "this frolicke Common-wealth" Piers passes from Thrasilio into the hands of Flavius; when Flavius is bankrupt by a Broker, he is beyond the help of his master Celinus, who has similarly come under the thumb of Celydon. Piers, exemplifying in the downward path of the courtier the decline of the court, passes from "Flatterie" under Thrasilio to "Prodigalitie" under Flavius to "Brokerie." By "Brokerie" he means a whole range of destructive acts—the breaking of law, the breaking up of estates, the breaking of men—and with the broker he enters the underworld that has come to dominate Thrace: "Not so few as a dozen Dice-makers had he at his reversion, that he would furnish in divers fashions. . . . and where ever they fell, they made manie light purses and heavye hearts. . . . Lackt ye a smooth tungd hypocrite to intrap young Gentlemen newly come from the Universitie? Hee was for ye" (144-45). When the Broker is himself broken, Piers passes from this Protean world of deceit toward the devil's center, "Usurie."

The final segment of the narrative accelerates the interweaving of plots, pulling them together first by parallel and then by interconnection, and draws Piers into the main romantic action. Toward the end, too, distinctions in style flatten out as Piers extends his narrative voice from satire into romance. The action at Crete, where Rhegius plots to satisfy his lust, is immediately intensified by that at Thrace: while Rhegius "covered his hatefull intention with a smoothed brow," in Thrace "all things (like an unmundified ulcer) festred inwardly, though outwardly there appeared a cloaked shaddow and painted show of civill and honest government" (156). The true character of the imposthumed state is sketched in Piers's fourth step down, when he descends to Ulpian the usurer and his strumpet daughter: avarice, deceit, lust, starvation. And Ursula's betrayal of her father prefigures Celydon's betrayal of Celinus, for "as in the Court were two Kings, so had wee two commaunders: videlicet Ulpian my miserable master, and Ursula my lascivious mistres" (157); and a state with two commanders must fall. When Ulpian and Celinus fall, Piers makes his final descent, this time to Petrusio, who combines the vices of "a Usurer, a Broker, a Farmer, and what not" (164), and moreover hides them under his high position; "to this," Piers asserts, "all my passed life was sanctimonie" (160). Here, at the low point of both plots, diverse actions converge, as the outcast Celinus forces Piers to take him to Crete, Rhodope and Piers free Aemilius from Rhegius' prison, and finally all is revealed and the plots resolved.

The total effect of *Piers Plainnes Seaven Yeres Prentiship* is complex. On the one hand, the insistent oppositions of different kinds of plot, narrative technique, and style present us with a split world where there is no connection between distinct socio-economic levels of existence. For most readers the two plots never come together. Margaret Schlauch, for example, writes that "in style as well as content the two strands of Chettle's *opus* remain irreconcilable."[20] On the other hand, the distinctions maintained by different styles and tones are constantly being destroyed by narrative juxtapositions, as Rhegius' mind is projected onto the conny-catchers of Thrace, Celinus becomes allied to Ulpian, and so on. The unifying theme of the whole is hypocrisy, which destroys the state in the romance, and breaks up households and men in the low plot. Hypocrisy is the keynote of Piers Plainness, for he says at the outset that if he is dishonest he does "but imitate the most, that whatsoever they say, live as they list," and that, for the

---

[20] Schlauch, p. 204. Schlauch echoes the verdicts of Jusserand in *The English Novel in the Time of Shakespeare*, p. 330 and of Baker (who himself echoes Jusserand) in *The History of the English Novel*, II, 122.

commonality of men, "I gesse them to be hypocrites, which they knowe true" (124).

Chettle's remarkable but difficult technique (a technique which we shall see Nashe exploit to the full) allows him to present a world totally splintered socially and economically, but at the same time seamlessly hypocritical in its motivations, high and low. It is a hopelessly fragmented world whose only point of unity is the corruption common to its inhabitants.

It is from this seamless world that Piers recoils at the end, for he is, as he says, too "plaine by name and nature" (124) for it, his "Plainness" implying a whole range of characteristics including honesty, lowliness, plain dealing, and blunt speech. And his recoil takes him into the pastoral world, where he comes to rest and to narrate his former miseries to Menalcas and Corydon. It is important to realize that *Piers Plainnes* does exploit the old form of pastoral romance, but in such a way as to wrest it from its traditional foundations. Pastoral exists here only as a frame for satire and tragedy, and is touched on only at beginning, end, and in two short breaks in the narrative where Piers pauses for liquid refreshment. As a result, many of the usual pastoral presuppositions are inoperative. The new shepherd is not a disguised prince but Piers, a down-and-outer; though pastoral Tempe contains plenty of food and relative content, there reside in it no ideals that rise above the base level of life's necessities. Chettle's diverse plots come to rest in pastoral revised under the pressure of satire: to go into Tempe is not to change the self by touching an ideal, but only to retreat in pain from a bad world.

⟨ IV ⟩

If the late historiography of Lodge presents the world as unremittingly tragic and the satire of Chettle shows it to be both fragmented and evil, the work of Thomas Nashe, which has been characterized with some justice as exhibiting a "basic nihilism,"[21] comes close to plunging into chaos. That Nashe was ordained from the beginning to be the scourge of outworn ideas and baseless pretensions to nobility appears directly in his first work, *The Anatomie of Absurditie* (1589), where he castigates the romancers thus:

> . . . what els I pray you doe these bable bookemungers endevor, but to repaire the ruinous wals of *Venus* Court, to restore to the worlde that forgotten Legendary licence of lying, to imitate a fresh the fantasticall dreames of those exiled Abbie-lubbers, from whose idle pens proceeded those worne out impressions of the feyned no where acts, of Arthur of the rounde table, Arthur of litle Brittaine, sir Tristram, Hewon of Burdeaux, the Squire of low degree, the foure sons of Amon, with infinite others.[22]

Though this is much of a piece with the Humanist attack on romance spearheaded by Erasmus, Vives, and Ascham, it should be noted that the emphasis is not so much on the immorality of romance ancient and recent as on improbability, on the affront that courtly love and chivalry present to a lively sense of the real. In the prefaces to both Greene's *Menaphon* (1588) and Sidney's *Astrophel and Stella* (1591), Nashe transfers his critique from the matter of romance to its proper style, castigating the unreal hyperbolic high style, of, for instance, tragedians who seek "to embowell the cloudes in a speech of comparison, thinking themselves more then initiated in Poets immortality, if they but once get *Boreas* by the beard and the heavenly Bull by the deaw-lap."[23] To this style he contrasts his own plain "extemporal" style, which calls a spade a spade.

[21] Clifford Leech, "Recent Studies in the Elizabethan and Jacobean Drama," *Studies in English Literature*, III (1963), 274. For an extensive discussion of Nashe as nihilistic artist, see Richard A. Lanham, "Tom Nashe and Jack Wilton: Personality as Structure in *The Unfortunate Traveller*," *Studies in Short Fiction*, IV (1967), 201-16.

[22] *The Works of Thomas Nashe*, ed. McKerrow, I, 11.

[23] Preface to *Menaphon* in *Works*, ed. McKerrow, III, 311.

Nashe's attitudes toward romance, myth, the high style, and even the entire rhetorical tradition behind the high style, are most completely developed in *Lenten Stuffe* (1599). This is a mock-oration in praise of the insignificant red herring, a piece which both gathers up its rhetorical forebears such as Erasmus' *Praise of Folly* and destroys them by presenting a rambling monologue before dinner instead of a well-organized epideictic oration. Most of the fun results from treating the herring in the high style and exalting it by myth, insisting that the golden fleece, the gold Midas ate, the gold in Danae's lap were all really red herrings, or that the Pope had canonized the fish. Romance comes specifically under attack in the burlesque of Marlowe's *Hero and Leander*, where instead of low matter treated in the high style we find high matter treated in a comic mixture of styles.

The casual tone of the opening sentence jars against its heroic diction, while conversely, in the second sentence, the formality of Euphuistic balance is used to convey the commercial value of a best seller instead of the glamor of myth:

> Let me see, hath any bodie in Yarmouth heard of Leander and Hero, of whome divine *Musaeus* sung, and a diviner Muse than him, *Kit Marlow?*
>
> Twoo faithfull lovers they were, as everie apprentise in Paules churchyard will tell you for your love, and sel you for your mony. (195)[24]

As he proceeds, Nashe pulls all the glamorous elements of the story down to one level: the Hellespont is treated as a laundry tub or pickling barrel, and Marlowe's lines on fate—"it lies not in our power to love or hate, / For will in us is over-ruled by Fate" (I, 167-68)—are brought low by a homely image to this: "Fate is a spaniel that you cannot beate from you." Nashe is at pains to exploit every possible ambivalence in Marlowe's poem: Marlowe's epithet "Venus nun" (I, 45), for example, is

[24] Page references are to Vol. III of the *Works.*

mocked consistently, as in this passage which includes an indirect quotation from a Hero who is seen as a froward and rather common girl: "by her parents being so encloistred from resort, that she might live chaste vestall Priest to Venus, the queene of unchastitie. Shee would none of that, she thanked them, for shee was better provided." And the light irony with which Marlowe treats his innocent lovers (II, 235-44) is broadened by Nashe into comic delusion:

> . . . for all he [Leander] was a naked man and cleane dispoyled to the skinne, when hee sprawled through the brackish suddes to scale her tower, all the strength of it could not hold him out. O, ware a naked man; Cythereaes Nunnes have no power to resiste him: and some such qualitie is ascribed to the lion. Were hee never so naked when he came to her, bicause he shuld not skare her, she found a meanes to cover him in her bed, &, for he might not take cold after his swimming, she lay close by him, to keepe him warme. This scuffling or bopeepe in the darke they had a while without weame or bracke. (196)

But the tone of the piece is by no means simple; the movement of the mind, for example, is often treated seriously:

> Hero hoped, and therefore shee dreamed (as all hope is but a dreame); her hope was where her heart was, and her heart winding and turning with the winde, that might winde her heart of golde to her, or else turne him from her. Hope and feare both combatted in her, and both these are wakefull, which made her at breake of day (what an old crone is the day, that is so long a breaking) to unloope her luket or casement. (197-98)

Human thought and feeling are real. What is unreal is the attempt to project these outward into a glamorous context, and so the next clause elevates the style in order to bring it down with a thump at the image of a dead fish: "foorthwith her eyes bred her eye-sore, the first white whereon their transpiercing arrowes stuck being the breathlesse corps of *Leander*: with the sodaine contemplation of this piteous spectacle of her love, sodden to haddocks meate, her sorrowe could not choose but be indefinite." The playful myth ends in the colloquial style, as Hero "made no more bones but sprang after him, and so re-signd up her Priesthood and left worke for *Musaeus* and *Kit Marlowe*"; the sorrow of the gods is treated comically, "*Pomona*, the first applewife" being "dumpt" and Apollo so sad "that it was almost noone before hee could go to cart that day." And Nashe proposes his own myth to counter Marlowe's, asserting that Hero and Leander were transformed into the Cadwalader herring and ling fish, respectively, and "meete in the heele of the weeke at the best mens tables, uppon Fridayes and Satterdayes."[25]

Nashe's attitude toward Marlowe in this burlesque is interesting in its duality; it is quite similar to the attitude taken by Jack Wilton toward another romantic poet, Surrey, in *The Unfortunate Traveller*: "if there bee anie sparke of Adams Paradized perfection yet emberd up in the breastes of mortall men, certainelie God hath bestowed that his perfectest image on Poets. . . . Despised they are of the worlde, because they are not of the world: their thoughts are exalted above the worlde of ignorance and all earthly conceits." On the one hand, he stands in awe of the divinity of their wit, and on the other, as himself a fallen man, he denies them any relevance to experienced reality. For the golden world they create is not a transformation of the brazen world into a striking image which can move men to embrace the ideal, but simply a pleasant dream, a world spun out of their wits with no relation to the brazen

[25] Compare the treatment of myth in *Moriomachia* (1613) by Robert Anton, who, though his main model is *Don Quixote*, took many stylistic devices from Nashe: he first exalts the climactic battle between the Knight of the Sun and the Knight of the Moon by having it cause a solar eclipse, but then undercuts his own myth by detailing the comic confusions it causes for lawyers, bankrupts, brokers, usurers, panders, and other contemporary rogues (*Short Fiction of the Seventeenth Century*, ed. Mish, pp. 73-77).

world at all.[26] And so Nashe insists on pulling brazen and golden matters, images, and diction close together, so that we can feel fully the fact of their disjunction.

We have seen how Henry Chettle brought romance down to the level of satire through destructive juxtapositions of various segments of his dual plot. Destructive juxtaposition in Nashe can occur in the quick turn of a sentence, for he is the master of this technique. The technique reaches its peak of development in *The Unfortunate Traveller* (1594), whose scope is immensely broader than that of *Lenten Stuffe*; for there Jack Wilton's experience of reality throughout Europe constantly gives the lie to ennobling formulations of the real, be they literary conventions, intellectual aspirations, or codes of life.

That Nashe clearly felt the novelty of his attempt in *The Unfortunate Traveller* appears in his dedicatory epistle to the Earl of Southampton, where he writes, "All that in this phantasticall Treatise I can promise, is some reasonable conveyance of historie, & varietie of mirth. By divers of my good friends have I been dealt with to employ my dul pen in this kinde, it being a cleane different vaine from other my former courses of writing." It is a "cleane different vaine" from that of any other work in the entire corpus of Elizabethan fiction, too, despite the fact that it owes some suggestions for its narrative voice and its jest materials to Greene's *The Blacke Bookes Messenger*. The models of this new kind of fiction, be it noted, come from the literature of recorded fact, rather than from romance or even (as in Chettle) literary satire. A great deal of history flows in this new vein, since the book is set in the reign of Henry VIII, and alludes to such actual events as Henry's siege of Térouanne in 1513, his meeting with François Premier at The Field of the Cloth of Gold in 1520, the battle of Marignano in 1515, the rising of the Anabaptists at Münster in 1535, the outbreak of the sweating sickness at London in 1517,

[26] See David Kaula, "The Low Style in Nashe's *The Unfortunate Traveller*," *Studies in English Literature*, VI (1966), 45.

Luther's debate with Carlstadt at Wittenberg in 1519, the
composition of More's *Utopia* and Erasmus' *Praise of Folly,*
and so forth. All this historical matter, some of which perhaps
stems from an intention to burlesque Lanquet's *Chronicle,*
has tempted some critics to label *The Unfortunate Traveller*
as something which it certainly is not, our first historical
novel.[27] Rather, the history in it arises from the new demand
for verisimilitude that we have seen operating in Lodge and
others in the mid-1590s. Its other nonfiction models satisfy the
same demand: its subtitle, "The Life of Jacke Wilton," together with its vivid first-person narrator, links it with autobiography of the sort exemplified by Greene's repentance
pamphlets and fictional derivatives such as Breton's *The Miseries of Mavillia*; and its main title, indicating as it does the
thread of travels undertaken by our "outlandish chronicler"
(from Térouanne to Hampton Court, Maregnano, Münster,
Middleborough, Rotterdam, Wittenberg, Venice, Florence,
Rome, Bologna, and Guisnes), links it of course with outlandish travelogues such as *Coryats Crudities* (1611).

In the clear light of this mass of recorded experience (combining fact and pseudo-fact), formulations and theories are
constantly revealed as illusions. The main technique of revelation is, as we have said, destructive juxtaposition, and this
juxtaposition is effected through Nashe's persona, Jack Wilton.
Jack's position as a court page places him in a socio-economic
no-man's-land; though his position is respectable, it is ambiguous enough to leave him totally in the hands of chance and
uncertainty (similarly, Piers Plainness, Margarite, Egeria, and
Mavillia are more victims of action than actors themselves).
The very rhetoric with which he presents his position at the
outset expresses incertitude at his marginal condition: "I, *Jacke
Wilton,* (a Gentleman at least,) was a certain kind of an appendix or page, belonging or appertaining in or unto the con-

---

[27] See G. R. Hibbard, *Thomas Nashe, A Critical Introduction* (Cambridge, Mass., 1962), pp. 145-46.

fines of the English court" (209).[28] As a page, Jack's status lies somewhere between the low and the high, the bourgeoisie and the aristocracy, even though his origins link him to the latter. He knows the great world and is at home in it, but he is not yet *of* it, and cannot wholeheartedly share its values. The effect of this position on his attitudes is to produce a certain amount of awe at the grandeur of high place combined with a genuinely critical view of it which often spills over into ridicule. The position is reflexive, ironic, and skeptical. The style of the page is frequently therefore mock-heroic, as in "The Induction to the dapper Mounsier Pages of the Court," where he exhorts the "Gallant Squires" his companions to defend this "Acts and Monuments," this "Chronicle of the king of Pages," as they discuss it in their symbolic position of "waiting together at the bottom of the great chamber staires, or sitting in a porch (your parliament house)." When the page adopts the manners of his betters, as he frequently does, he does so with the kind of self-conscious parody typical of a little girl wearing her mother's high heels—as we see in Jack's impersonation of Surrey or in his exaggerated Hampton Court foppery, with a "feather in my cap as big as a flag in the fore-top; my French dublet gelte in the bellie as though (like a pig readie to be spitted) all my guts had bin pluckt out," and so on. When Jack Wilton assumes a dramatic role, he does so with less seriousness and a fuller awareness (so full as to be grotesquely comic) of the figure he is cutting than any of the histrionic heroes of the 1570s and 1580s.

It is important that we as readers are forced to interact with this persona, for Nashe has given us a fictional part to play as well. He has, in fact, created a normative fictional audience whose concerns approach those of the persona and whose point of view is the same as his. For in place of the usual epistle to "the Courteous Reader" or "the Gentlemen of Both Universities," he has prefaced his book with "The Induction to the dapper Mounsier Pages of the Court":

[28] Page references are to Vol. II of the *Works*.

Gallant Squires, have amongst you: at Mumchaunce I
meane not, for so I might chaunce come to short commons,
but at *novus, nova, novum,* which is in English, newes of
the maker. A proper fellow Page of yours called *Jack Wilton*
by me commends him unto you, and hath bequeathed for
wast paper here amongst you certaine pages of his misfortunes. . . . Heigh passe, come alofte: everie man of you take
your places, and heare *Jacke Wilton* tell his owne Tale.

The relation between the hero-narrator and his imagined audience, established in the easy reciprocal mockery of this induction, is kept alive throughout the book by all those means for
establishing the immediacy of spoken discourse that we found
in the pamphlets: by Jack's pose as the audience's drinking-
companion, by his sudden questions to his audience, imagined
interlocutions, calling attention to direct hits, and so forth, as
in this typical passage:

What is there more as touching this tragedie that you would
be resolved of? say quickly, for now is my pen on foote
againe. How *John Leyden* dyed, is that it? He dyde like a
dogge, he was hangd & the halter paid for. For his companions, doe they trouble you? I can tell you they troubled
some men before, for they were all kild, & none escapt, no,
not so much as one to tell the tale of the rainebow. (241)

There are, moreover, constant allusions to contemporary London topics—such as Jane Trosse, Mother Cornelius' tub,
Banks's ubiquitous horse, and the "Ballad of the Whipper"—to
keep the relation between narrator and audience flowing and
vital.

The development of persona of Jack creates the narrative
curve of his book, which starts by showing him scraping for
sustenance and merriment among the low life of Henry VIII's
camp, proceeds to his adventures as servant and companion of
the noble Earl of Surrey, and eventually elevates him to an assumed identity as the Earl of Surrey. To these three phases of

Jack's movement from low to high corresponds the three-part structure of *The Unfortunate Traveller*. The structural divisions, as provided by the travelogue frame, rest on the three main places visited: the English camp, northern Europe, and Italy. These three places naturally define the subjects of the three parts: comic incidents from army life, the main historical and intellectual events of the day, and the courtly love and dark villainy for which Italy was famous. The narrative procedure changes slightly from section to section, ranging from a loose string of jests that might well have come from Scoggin's jests, to a proper travelogue describing places and events, and finally to a long connected narrative exhibiting an involved skein of evil deeds. But the most striking distinctions are those of style and tone, and they depend upon the theme of the story as it gradually unfolds. The theme common to all three sections is excess, which, it is constantly pointed out, is really *pretense*. It is the conscious exaggeration of a position beyond the limits of mere belief or fitting action, so that it acquires the status of an autonomous principle to which the poseur demands unwavering allegiance. Such a theme can draw all sorts of activity into its field: personal quirks, pride, styles, or ideas and codes. It is the business of Nashe's hyperbolic style to mock this excess by going beyond it in grotesque exaggeration of every action, feeling, or appearance; it is the business of his plot to deflate it at every turn. And it is the business of his persona to dramatize this theme by himself assuming grandiose roles in self-satire, and by drawing his audience into these roles as well.

But excess assumes various avatars in each section, as its further forms are summoned up, and in response to each new guise, style and tone change also. The targets of Jack's wit in the English camp are personal quirks rather than principles, and so there we observe a small gallery of humor characters, each representing a mode of excess or pretense: the old tub of guts who usurps the hereditary name of lordship, the foolish *miles gloriosus,* the womanizer, the stingy and fanatically sanitary clerks who even scorn "a Lowce (that was anie Gentlemans companion)." Jack exposes the members of his comic gallery mainly through the gestures which epitomize their pretenses, their poses—as, for instance, in this bravura passage, which ends by evoking the audience's gesture in response:

> Oh my Auditors, had you seene him how he stretcht out his lims, scratcht his scabd elbowes at this speach; how hee set his cap over his ey-browes like a polititian, and then folded his armes one in another, and nodded with the head, as who would say, let the French beware for they shall finde me a divell: if (I say) you had seene but halfe the actions that he used, of shrucking up his shoulders, smiling scornfully, playing with his fingers on his buttons, and biting the lip, you wold have laught your face and your knees together.
> (219)

Jack's purpose is to lay bare the true natures of these characters, his technique that of the prankster. He aims to make them reveal themselves to others for what they are: the innkeeping lord for a gluttonous craven, the captain and the clerks for arrant cowards, and so forth. He plays his role with gusto and enthusiasm, constantly turning to us to see if we are laughing as heartily as we should, calling our attention to the skill of his pranks (for he is himself both author and hero of this jest book): "My masters, you may conceave of me what you list, but I thinke confidently I was ordained Gods scourge from above for their daintie finicalitie." The tone of this section is light, as befits slapstick comedy, for the matter here is jest rather than satire.

It turns to satire when Jack reaches Germany, for there Jack's wit exercises itself on important religious and intellectual movements. This is the heavily historical section of the book, consisting largely of name- and date-dropping, and built of brief interludes concerning François I, John Leyden, Erasmus, More, Cornelius Agrippa, Luther, and Carlstadt. Three of these episodes are developed at some length for satiric pur-

poses, and it is clear that the targets are now to be rigid intellectual positions rather than mere quirks. One such mark is
the debate between Luther and Carlstadt at Wittenberg, which
Jack links with Ciceronianism as a kind of sterile and elaborate
formalization of the trivial. Totally ignoring the doctrinal
matters at hand, Jack presents us with this description: "*Luther*
had the louder voyce, *Carolostadius* went beyond him in beat-
ing and bounsing with his fists. *Quae supra nos, nihil ad nos:*
they uttered nothing to make a man laugh, therefore I will
leave them" (250)—and leave them he does, after a comic
catalogue of their gestures. Jack is here observer rather than
actor; but he is all the more important to the story, since mockery proceeds not from an action ridiculous in itself but from a
serious action made ridiculous to us by being filtered through
Jack's point of view, with its surprising overlay of the manners
of a barroom brawl onto an academic debate.

In Jack's all-important juxtaposing mind, the debate is practically indistinguishable from the ridiculous academic ceremony welcoming the Duke of Saxony to Wittenberg to hear
it. There, too, excess achieves the form of pompous phrases out
of Tully ("Some three halfe penyworth of Latine") attempting
to hide the emptiness of minds whose only real interest is
swilling beer. In his description of the Anabaptists under
John Leyden, Jack is concerned to make a frontal attack upon
excess, for in the religious sphere he sees a rigid position as the
outer crust of the sin of pride. Their pride is first presented as
pretension to the military code of their betters, for they enter
the battlefield at Münster all tricked out in Hudibrastic arms
and armor, as the very parody of knighthood. Pretense is immediately transferred to the spiritual realm, however: "Verie
devout Asses they were, for all they were so dunstically set
forth, and such as thought they knew as much of Gods
minde as richer men: why, inspiration was their ordinarie
familiar, and buzd in their eares like a Bee in a boxe everie
hower what newes from heaven, hell, and the land of whipper-
ginnie . . . they would vaunt there was not a pease difference

betwixt them and the Apostles" (233). Their spiritual pride, which extends so far as to lead them to curse God if he does not fulfill their requests, so incenses Jack that he inserts an anomalous sermon on the proper humility of a Christian. Since Jack's intent in these German episodes is to castigate as well as to cause laughter, the tone occasionally becomes bitter and satirical. And this intention causes a broadening of stylistic technique which allows editorial comment and direct abuse as well as dramatic presentation.

In the Italian section of *The Unfortunate Traveller* the tone becomes far more subtle—so much so that it is debatabɪ: whether certain episodes are burlesque or merely the victims of unfortunate hyperbole. One reason for this state of affairs is that the subject has become more complex. It might best be defined as rigid codes of behavior conditioned by literary models; therefore the laughter is sometimes directed at manners, sometimes at literary convention. A case in point is Jack's treatment of the Earl of Surrey. When Jack and Surrey try to seduce the delicate trollop Diamante in the Venetian prison, Surrey approaches her in a deluded and ridiculous exaggeration of the Petrarchan mode. Pretending, in the fashion of Don Quixote, that she is his lady Geraldine (he is fooling himself as well as her when he exalts the actual into this charade), he wipes his tears with her hand, kisses the ground in adoration (as did Arsadachus before the throne of Diana before descending into madness), and sighs tragically and incessantly. In Jack's eyes, of course, such fantastic behavior is merely the translation of what was never meant to be more than a literary mode into actual life, and that amounts to self-love: "I perswade my self he was more in love with his own curious forming fancie than her face." Jack's attack then turns from manners to their model. In evidence for the assertions that such posing is merely an excuse for writing poetry and that such poetry presents life as a narcissistic dream-world (where, for example, erotic desire presents itself as transcendent spirituality), Jack quotes a sonnet that Surrey made up on the spot:

In thy breasts christall bals enbalme my breath,
Dole it all out in sighs when I am laide.
Thy lips on mine like cupping glasses claspe,
Let our tongs meete and strive as they would sting,
Crush out my winde with one strait girting graspe.

After this hot erotic activity conveyed in perversely extreme conceits, the attempt at the standard serene spiritual resolution is devastating:

Into heavens joyes none can profoundly see,
Except that first they meditate on thee. (263)

And Jack's own comment completes the destruction of Petrarchism, both by the homely enthusiasm of its response and by the ironic fact it records in plain diction: "Sadly and verily, if my master sayde true, I shoulde if I were a wench make many men quickly immortall. What ist, what ist for a maide fayre and fresh to spend a little lip-salve on a hungrie lover? My master beate the bush and kepte a coyle and a pratling, but I caught the birde."

This kind of direct undercutting of a literary pose pervades the relationship between master and page. In an earlier passage, for instance, when Surrey utters a hyperbolic Latinate oration on his mistress, Jack's response is this:

Not a little was I delighted with this unexpected love storie, especially from a mouth out of which was nought wont to march but sterne precepts of gravetie & modestie. I sweare unto you I thought his companie the better by a thousand crownes, because hee had discarded those nice tearmes of chastitie and continencie. Now I beseech God love me so well as I love a plaine dealing man; earth is earth, flesh is flesh, earth wil to earth, and flesh unto flesh; fraile earth, fraile flesh, who can keepe you from the worke of your creation? (245)

This is scarcely what Surrey had in mind—or thought he had in mind! In this section, the destructive juxtapositions occur between the supposedly high actions and the low mind of Jack recording them.

The tournament at Florence floats between satire of the pretenses of a decadent chivalry and burlesque of chivalric romance. Here is one of the many descriptions (by no means the silliest):

> His armour was all intermixed with lillyes and roses, and the bases thereof bordered with nettles and weeds, signifieng stings, crosses, and overgrowing incumberances in his love; his helmet round proportioned lyke a gardners water-pot, from which seemed to issue forth small thrids of water, like citterne strings, that not onely did moisten the lyllyes and roses, but did fructifie as well the nettles and weeds, and made them overgrow theyr liege Lords. Whereby he did import thus much, that the teares that issued from his braines, as those arteficiall distillations issued from the well counterfeit water-pot on his head, watered and gave lyfe as well to his mistres disdaine (resembled to nettles and weeds) as increase of glorie to her care-causing beauty (comprehended under the lillies and roses). (271-72)

This creaking description—as well as the horse tricked out as an ostrich and armor in the shape of a tree stump topped with an owl, or a mountain, or a caged nightingale in a hawthorn bush—could be either a comic exaggeration of what one actually saw in Renaissance pageants or a burlesque of this kind of description in romance:

> Himselfe in an armour, all painted over with such a cunning of shadow, that it represented a gaping sepulchre, the furniture of his horse was all of Cypresse braunches; wherwith in olde time they were woont to dresse graves. His Bases (which he ware so long, as they came almost to his ankle) were imbrodered onely with blacke wormes, which seemed to crawle up and downe, as readie alreadie to devoure him. In his shielde for *Impresa,* he had a beautifull childe, but

having two heades; whereof the one shewed, that it was alreadie dead: the other alive, but in that case, necessarily looking for death. The word was, *No way to be rid from death, but by death.*[29]

In either case, the villain is chivalric romance, for such stuff could be presented as adequate fighting gear only in books. Jack makes this point clear in the manner of his descriptions, for he presents them all as mounted emblems, breathing literary artifacts; the result is to broaden the gap between illusion and reality. He takes each detail and elaborates it beyond belief, stressing always the artifice which creates the illusion that a helmet is a watering pot. Then he anatomizes each detail, solemnly explaining each point in the allegory (as he did in the mock-allegory of Midas' gold as the herring in *Lenten Stuffe*), and sometimes coming a cropper and thus broadening the comedy, as when he confesses, "What his meaning was herein I cannot imagine" (276).

The criticism implicit in these descriptions hinges on the disparity between pretentious concepts without relation to function and the real needs of battle, a disparity which Jack's presentations force upon our awareness; and it becomes explicit in the battle itself, where concept fails ridiculously in the face of action. Jack begins with cool irony: "To particularize their manner of encounter were to describe the whole art of tilting." He then goes on to show what "the whole art of tilting" amounts to in fact:

Some had like to have fallen over their horse neckes and so breake theyr neckes in breaking theyr staves. Others ranne at a buckle in sted of a button, and peradventure whetted theyr speares pointes, idlely gliding on theyr enemies sides, but did no other harme. Others ranne a crosse at their adversaryes left elbow, yea, and by your leave sometimes let not the lists scape scot-free, they were so eager. Others . . . tilted backward, for forward they durst not. Another had a

---

[29] Sidney, *Arcadia*, in *Prose Works*, ed. Feuillerat, I, 445.

monstrous spite at the pommel of his rivals saddle, and thought to have thrust his speare twixt his legs without rasing anie skin, and carried him clean awaie on it as a coolestaffe. Another held his speare to his nose, or his nose to his speare, as though he had bin discharging his caliver, and ranne at the right foote of his fellowes stead. (278)

The final fillip to this debacle of fantastic purposes is Jack's comment that the only ones who profited from it were the heralds, the underlings who claimed and pawned all the broken armor scattered on the field.[30]

The tone of the Roman "tragical matter" is more difficult to determine with precision. On the one hand, the rape of Heraclide, the villainous machinations of Zadoch, and the bloodthirsty revenge of Cutwolfe are presented with such highly colored hyperbole and gusto that it is difficult not to think of them as burlesques of the tragical rant that Nashe attacks directly in the preface to *Menaphon*. On the other hand, it is difficult to conceive of a writer (even one possessed of Nashe's loose sense of propriety) making sport of a horrendous rape or treating sin and death in a purely comic manner.[31] Part of the difficulty results from the fact that each of the main characters has moments of intense self-consciousness—Heraclide before her mirror, Zadoch before Zachary, and Cutwolfe on the scaffold before the populace of Bologna—and regards herself or himself as being in a dramatic role; and such a situation in Nashe always has a grotesque, if not comic, effect. We can offer some conclusions on the tone of these events by establishing a rough principle of decorum between the actual person

---

[30] The subtle comedy of Nashe's presentation can be appreciated by a comparison with Anton's much broader imitation of the tournament in *Moriomachia* (Mish, ed., *op.cit.*, pp. 67-72).

[31] These opposing views are represented, respectively, by Agnes M. C. Latham, "Satire on Literary Themes and Modes in Nashe's 'Unfortunate Traveller,'" *English Studies 1948* (London, 1948), pp. 85-100, and Hibbard, pp. 146-47.

and situation and the role he assumes, to see whether the tragic mask fits or sits ajar.

Heraclide is a high-born matron and has just been raped over the body of her husband; therefore, when she looks into the mirror and utters a lament like that of Lucrece, the episode remains on a serious and tragic level. And when the style occasionally falls into tragic ranting, we can with some show of probability ascribe it, as Hibbard does, to overwriting pushed so far as to become unconscious burlesque of itself.[32] When Zadoch receives the Pope's edict of banishment, he sees himself as one more poor Jew persecuted by the double-dealing Christians (actually, of course, he is a psychopath who has mewed up Jack for a vivisection and who reaps sexual satisfaction every day from whipping Diamante). His reaction is therefore presented as comic hyperbole, in a mock high style: "Descriptions, stand by, here is to bee expressed the furie of Lucifer when he was turnde over heaven barre for a wrangler. . . . So swelled Zadoch, and was readie to burst out of his skin and shoote his bowels like chaine-shot full at *Zacharies* face . . . his verie nose lightned glowwormes, his teeth crasht and grated together, like the joynts of a high building cracking and rocking like a cradle" (310). And at the unguarded moments when his sense of his own reality pierces through the rant, the effect of the disparity is ridiculous: "Ile goe to a house that is infected, where catching the plague, and having got a running sore upon me, Ile come and deliver her a supplication, and breath upon her. I knowe my breath stinkes so alredie, that it is within halfe a degree of poison" (312).

Cutwolfe is the most deliberate poseur of them all. He is a poor cobbler of Verona, "a wearish dwarfish writhen facde cobbler," but when his brother, the brigand Bartol, is killed, he conceives of himself as playing the tragical role of the noble avenger. He starts with this pretentious assumption: "My bodie is little, but my minde is as great as a gyants: the soule

[32] Hibbard, pp. 147, 168-69.

which is in mee is the verie soule of *Julius Caesar* by reversion. My name is *Cutwolfe,* neither better nor worse by occupation than a poore Cobler of *Verona*; Coblers are men, and kings are no more" (320). Having thus raised his status, he proceeds to unfold his role, his "code" of revenge: "Revenge in our trage-dies is continually raised from hell: of hell doe I esteeme bet-ter than heaven, if it afford me revenge. There is no heaven but revenge. I tel thee, I would not have undertoke so much toile to gaine heaven, as I have done in pursuing thee for revenge. Divine revenge, of which (as of the joies above) there is no fulnes or satietie" (324). The revenge of stage tragedy has be-come an obsessive principle for Cutwolfe, subsuming, as he says, glory, valor, justice, the Italian national character, and even religion in the imitation of a just God: "The farther we wade in revenge, the neerer come we to the throne of the al-mightie." This preposterous acquired principle allows him to transmute the death of a thief in a brawl into the loss of a noble brother, and his poor puny self into the tragic hero, a role he even goes so far as to rehearse assiduously:

> I have riven my throat with overstraining it to curse thee. I have ground my teeth to pouder with grating & grinding them together for anger when any hath namde thee. My tongue with vaine threates is bolne, and waxen too big for my mouth: my eyes have broken their strings with staring and looking ghastly, as I stood devising how to frame or set my countenance when I met thee. I have neere spent my strength in imaginarie acting on stone wals, what I deter-mined to execute on thee: intreate not, a miracle may not reprive thee: villaine, thus march I with my blade into thy bowels. (324)

The nature of Cutwolfe's determination and the grim single-ness of mind with which he has so long pursued it are terrify-ing; his self-conscious posturings are so grotesque as to be-come ridiculous, for his tongue is too big for his mouth in more than one sense. The tone of the episode is therefore a mixture of the comic and the terrible, quite like the "tragic farce" T. S. Eliot found in *The Jew of Malta* and in Dickens.[33] In this, Jack's final example of the excess resulting from pretense, we see a horrifyingly comic version of his theme, whereby the full entrance into a pose results in the unbearable transformation of a human being into a monster. Cutwolfe is too much for the populace: with one voice they demand his destruction. And Jack, who has himself taken on quite a few roles and played them through with lighthearted gusto, retreats in horror.

⟨ V ⟩

The Unfortunate Traveller bears an interesting relationship to pastoral romance and courtly fiction devoted to the inquisition of ideas. From our account, this work might seem to be an encyclopedic treatment of the subjection of principles to the critical test of real experience. Ideas about oneself and life in this book range from the mere exaggeration of a personal quirk to the pomposities of rigid intellectual and religious systems, and finally to the utter madness of acting out a literary role in life. By the end, finicality about clean linen, Ciceronian oratory, courtly love, chivalry, the code of revenge, and dozens of other modes of codifying life have gone the way of the mad Anabaptists. There is very little left. As G. R. Hibbard concludes, "while it embodies nothing that can be called a view of life, it does succeed in conveying a number of discrepant attitudes to morals and to literature with peculiar force and vitality, giving them the quality of immediate sensations."[34]

This encyclopedic destructiveness both epitomizes the fictional mode of the Sidney-Lyly tradition and severs *The Unfortunate Traveller* from it forever. Though ideas and experience continually clash, it can scarcely be said that experience

[33] T. S. Eliot, "Marlowe," in *Selected Essays* (New York, 1932), pp. 104-5.
[34] Hibbard, p. 179.

tests ideas here: rather, ideas appear only to meet with instant ridicule and then disappear into their proper abode of thin air. Moreover, the fact that so many examples of the human propensity for casting a glamorous veil over life appear in the book has a leveling tendency, as it did in Chettle. When Surrey's noble delusions, buttressed by the venerable courtly and Platonic intellectual traditions, appear in the same work with the silly bravado of "Captain Gogs Wounds" and are treated from the same point of view, any distinctions between them—even those of degree—are annihilated. Beneath this critical bent appears a thoroughgoing and even doctrinaire skepticism which does indeed come close to complete nihilism. "Nashe habitually focuses his attention on isolated particulars. He tends to conceive human action not as evolving through a continuum of cause and effect or of past, present, and future, but as violent, fragmentary, and accidental."[35] Consequently, role-playing holds none of the promise of transforming the self that it held for Rosader or Euphues; rather, it is merely the central form of pretense, and is therefore treated as a form of play, with a grotesque, reflexive awareness of the figure one cuts.

Several elements of Nashe's style contribute to this leveling of all. One is the recurrent imagery of torture and other forms of physical violence applied to high and low, which, as David Kaula writes, represents "in meticulous detail the painful extinction of a humanity suffering either from an impersonal levelling process or from its own brutality,"[36] and perhaps suggests the infernal on earth. Another such element is his reduction of action to gesture, as in the description of the braggart soldier or of the tournament at Florence, or this description of a performance of *Acolastus*:

One, as if he had ben playning a clay floore, stampingly trode the stage so harde with his feete that I thought verily

[35] Kaula, p. 55.
[36] *Ibid.*, p. 44.

he had resolved to do the Carpenter that set it up some utter shame. Another flong his armes lyke cudgels at a peare tree, insomuch as it was mightily dreaded that he wold strike the candles that hung above their heades out of their sockettes, and leave them all darke. Another did nothing but winke and make faces. (249)

To reduce supposedly purposeful action to empty gesture and then derive from this gesture comically different purposes than those supposedly intended serves to deprive bodily movement of any connection with intellect and to pare the human actor down to the scale of a posturing marionette. Such a reduction is explicitly what Jack intends in his rendering of the debates at Wittenberg, where he writes: "They uttered nothing to make a man laugh, therefore I will leave them. Mary, their outwarde jestures would now and then afford a man a morsel of mirth. . . . A third waverd & wagled his head, like a proud horse playing with his bridle, or as I have seene some fantasticall swimmer, at everie stroke, train his chin side-long over his left shoulder" (250-51).

Nashe knew how to use syntax for an effect of comic bathos, especially in what we might term "bombast" passages, where he stuffs detail after detail, interjections, even lists into the sentence until the line of thought has been redirected so many times that it seems ready to break the bounds of syntax entirely; then, as in many an episode, he will bring it to a brief close with a careless predication. In the example below, part of the bathetic effect results from the deliberate throwing away of the rich metaphoric content of the three variations on his dicing prowess:

I had the right vayne of sucking up a die twixt the dints of my fingers; not a crevise in my hand but could swallow a quater trey for a neede; in the line of life manie a dead lift did there lurke, but it was nothing towards the maintenance of a familie. (217)

In the following, more extended, example, the collapse is assisted by the list of bare monosyllables at the end:

> A bursten belly inkhorne orator called *Vanderhulke,* they pickt out to present him with an oration, one that had a sulpherous big swolne large face, like a Saracen, eyes lyke two kentish oysters, a mouth that opened as wide every time he spake, as one of those old knit trap doores, a beard as though it had ben made of a birds neast pluckt in peeces, which consisteth of strawe, haire, and durt mixt together. (247)

The most extended example of this "bombast" style is the magniloquent opening of the book, where epithet is piled on epithet, and attention dislocated time after time, until the fall from the deeds of Henry VIII to those of Jack Wilton is completed in the slangy close:

> About that time that the terror of the world and feaver quartane of the French, *Henrie* the eight (the onely true subject of Chronicles), advanced his standard against the two hundred and fifty towers of *Turney* and *Turwin,* and had the Emperour and all the nobilitie of *Flanders, Holand,* & *Brabant* as mercenarie attendants on his ful-sayld fortune, I, *Jacke Wilton,* (a Gentleman at least,) was a certain kind of an appendix or page, belonging or appertaining in or unto the confines of the English court; where what my credit was, a number of my creditors that I cosned can testifie: *Coelum petimus stultitia,* which of us al is not a sinner? (209)

David Kaula, in his excellent analysis of Nashe's style, points out that not only does the periodic rhythm collapse into parataxis here, but that the passage descends from a high heraldic style to low style, with its word play and tone of "impudent self-assurance." Kaula finds this kind of movement from high to low typical of the whole book, and the main means by which illusions are deflated: "his narration characteristically moves, like the opening sentence of the novel, from a more elaborate rhetorical mode to the low style, the former embodying the illusion under attack, the latter conveying the elemental response to reality which constitutes the final commentary."[37] Furthermore, he discovers constant parody of a whole range of elaborate styles resulting from "a searching scepticism toward the attitudes implicit in these styles, since they assume a reality more highly ordered and grandiose than is warranted by the elementary facts of experience."[38] The style of *The Unfortunate Traveller,* like the episodes burlesquing literary forms, becomes an implicit rejection of the rhetorical tradition which subjected life to intellectual form with standard value judgments embedded in its generalities. The attack on rhetoric is part and parcel of the overall attack on ideas of order, and so through style as well as narrative, Nashe "calls into question any notion of order but the most securely grounded."[39]

The fictional mode of the inquisition of ideas has collapsed under its own weight in *The Unfortunate Traveller.* With imagery that levels all, the reduction of action to gesture, stylistic tricks that deliberately undercut rhetorical formulations of reality, constant burlesque of ennobling literary forms, and a plot composed of jarring fragments, Nashe has gone further than Greene in insisting that not only do idea and act never influence each other, but also that they exist in entirely divided and distinct worlds which never meet. The poet or any other promulgator of ideas of order ranges within the zodiac of his own wit and nowhere else, for the world whirls in quite another fashion, on its own.

But any work of fiction by its very existence makes some statement about reality (though not necessarily a rigid formulation), and so it is with Nashe's, even while he is attacking such a process. While the plot of *The Unfortunate Traveller* is

[37] *Ibid.,* p. 55.   [38] *Ibid.,* p. 49.   [39] *Ibid.,* p. 57.

not really picaresque, it resembles the *Lazarillo* in its boundlessness. It has no clear beginning, middle, or end, for Nashe could have gone on to add several further adventures of Jack Wilton without disturbing the form of his book. Albert Cook, in delineating the major qualities of novelistic fiction, has made a helpful distinction between the "design" plots proper to drama, where causation is contained in the beginning and where the action proceeds in patterned form to a foreseen end, and the "process" plots proper to the modern novel, where causation seems to generate itself or metamorphose anew at several points in the middle so that "we move as we read into ground both unknown and unexpected."[40] In terms of this distinction, pastoral romance and courtly fiction, which usually state in the beginning the ideas to be acted out, are plots of design, while *The Unfortunate Traveller* is an anomalous example in Elizabethan fiction of the plot of process.

In fact, surprise, sudden shifts in the bases of probability, is an effect Nashe deliberately strove for here as well as in *Lenten Stuffe*. There is, for example, the set of very surprising tonal reversals at the execution of Cutwolfe. The first surprise is that, after the "tragic farce" of Cutwolfe's oration has been cut off by the populace's horrified demand for justice, the description of the execution is rendered neither with horror nor with satisfaction of justice done, but rather with Jack's mere amoral delight in a job well done, precisely performed. The lively speech rhythms and the deliberately neutral comparisons to the skilled trades tell us that:

> The executioner needed no exhortation hereunto, for of his owne nature was he hackster good inough: olde excellent he was at a bone-ach. At the first chop with his wood-knife would he fish for a mans heart, and fetch it out as easily as a plum from the bottome of a porredge pot. He would cracke neckes as fast as a cooke cracks egges: a fidler cannot turne his pin so soone as he would turne a man of the ladder.

[40] Albert Cook, *The Meaning of Fiction* (Detroit, 1960), p. 17.

> Bravely did he drum on this *Cutwolfes* bones, not breaking
> them outright, but, like a sadler knocking in of tackes, jar-
> ring on them quaveringly with his hammer a great while
> together. (327)

Yet this passage, where Cutwolfe appears as a grotesque in-
animate object and Jack comments with cool connoisseurship,
turns to horror and shocks Jack into pure fright:

> In this horror left they him on the wheele as in hell; where,
> yet living, he might beholde his flesh legacied amongst the
> foules of the aire. Unsearchable is the booke of our destinies.
> One murder begetteth another: was never yet bloud-shed
> barren from the beginning of the world to this daie. Morti-
> fiedly abjected and danted was I with this truculent tragedie
> of *Cutwolfe* and *Esdras*. To such straight life did it thence
> forward incite me that ere I went out of *Bolognia* I married
> my curtizan, performed many almes deedes; and hasted
> so fast out of the *Sodom* of *Italy*. . . . (327)

The execution has become suddenly the motive for a totally
new and unexpected turn in the action.

Similarly, at the defeat of the Anabaptists, after pages of
scathing ridicule and direct criticism, Jack turns to the actual
slaughter with pity:

> Pitifull and lamentable was their unpittied and well per-
> fourmed slaughter. . . . such compassion did those over-
> matcht ungracious *Munsterians* obtaine of manie indifferent
> eyes, who now thought them (suffering) to bee sheepe
> brought innocent to the shambles, when as before they
> deemed them as a number of wolves up in armes against the
> shepheards. (240)

So, too, with his description of a Roman summer house counterfeiting Eden by artifice. Inserted as it is in the midst of an
account of Roman pretentiousness, it seems slated for comic
exaggeration but turns out instead to be the basis of Jack's se-

rious critique of the postlapsarian world. The exiled English earl's long harangue on the evils of Europe, delivered as it is after Jack's sudden release from the scaffold, seems at first to fix the moral of the book in the terms of Ascham and Eubulus. But Jack's curt response shows that he is really mocking the admonitory tradition:

> Here he held his peace and wept. I, glad of any opportunitie of a full poynt to part from him, tolde him I tooke his counsaile in worth; what lay in mee to requite in love should not bee lacking. Some businesse that concerned me highly cald mee away very hastely, but another time I hop'd we should meete. . . . Heeres a stir, thought I to my selfe after I was set at libertie, that is worse than an upbraiding lesson after a britching. (303)

But the tone turns once again, for the harangue has created a new ground of causation: "God plagud me for deriding such a grave fatherly advertiser. List the worst throw of ill luckes." And Jack falls into Zadoch's cellar to experience for himself the truth of all the earl has told him, and more.

The construction of a "process" plot with constantly shifting grounds of probability is of the utmost importance to Nashe's endeavor to confront reality directly, without recourse to systems or the testing of ideas. That the result of this endeavor is largely a mass of negatives—demonstrations of what the real is not—is not surprising in view of the fact that the only concept of an unformulated reality available to Nashe was that of a mere chaos of events. But by focusing on rapid shifts in our sense of what is or what is not likely to happen, Nashe recovered one positive element from chaos, the probable. It might be said that his book celebrates the temporary liberation of fiction from ideas, for the existing dominates here, rather than the unrealized but possible. At only two places in the book does possibility find a voice: in Jack's sermon and in the description of the Edenic summer house; and both occasions serve momentarily "to underline the contrast between what should be and what is"[41] in this postlapsarian world. For the rest, we have for once a piece of fiction which records the proliferation of character creating a variety of probable situations. The fictional world that results is shimmering if confusing. None of Nashe's contemporaries was willing to follow him into it.

[41] Hibbard, p. 166.

CHAPTER 7

Thomas Deloney and Middle-Class Fiction

The only point of positive contact between the university wit Thomas Nashe and the silk-weaver turned balladeer whom he scorned is their common reliance, probably through the influence of Greene, on material from the sixteenth-century jest books.[1] Nashe presented Jack Wilton at the outset of *The Unfortunate Traveller* as a witty rogue like Scoggin or Peele, and went on to document by a string of witty jests Wilton's pride in his ability to cozen his companions. The opening of Thomas Deloney's first work of fiction, *The Pleasant Historie of John Winchcomb, in his younger yeares called Jacke of Newberie* (ca. 1597), reads like a homespun paraphrase of Nashe's hyberbolical beginning. As he writes elsewhere, "expect not herein to find any matter of light value, curiously pen'd with pickt words, or choise phrases, but a quaint and plaine discourse."[2] Absent is all the comic stuffing we found in Nashe, and instead of a comic contrast between Henry VIII's high deeds and Jack Wilton's low jests, we have Henry providing a concrete context for John Winchcomb: "In the daies of King *Henery* the eight that most noble and victorious Prince, in the beginning of his reigne, *John Winchcomb,* a broad cloth Weaver, dwelt in *Newberie*, a towne in *Barkshire*: who for that he was a man of a merry disposition, and honest conversation, was wondrous wel-beloved of Rich and Poore, especiallie because in every place where hee came, hee would spend his money with the best, and was not at any time found a churle

---

[1] For Nashe on Deloney, see *Works*, ed. McKerrow, I, 280 and III, 84.

[2] Epistle to *The Gentle Craft,* Part II; in *The Novels of Thomas Deloney,* ed. Merritt E. Lawlis (Bloomington, Indiana, 1961), p. 174.

of his purse" (5).[3] There is nothing of the jest-book tone here; Jack Winchcomb lays claim to our attention not by his wit in overcoming his companions but by his harmonious relation with his society, by his tact and a popularity based concretely on the prudent use of money. Nashe took jest material as part and parcel of a view of life as essentially ridiculous; the sober Deloney used it for quite different ends.

There is abundant jest material in *Jacke of Newberie,* one third of the book being in effect detached jests: the ruse by which Sir George Rigley is made to marry one of Jack's maids (Chapter XI); the gulling of the Italian merchant Benedick (Chapter VII); the flouting of Mistress Frank (Chapter X); or the maidens' avenging themselves on Will Summers (himself the hero of a jest book)[4] for damaging their looms by flinging fistfuls of dog turd in his face in the manner of *Owleglasse* (Chapter IV). Moreover, the first chapter is largely a reworking of "the burnynge of olde John" in *A C. Mery Talys* (ca. 1545), transposing the man's attempt to get into his mistress' bed into the widow's attempt to get Jack into hers.[5] Yet for all this, the tone of the whole book is far removed from that of the jest books, partly because Deloney's hero is himself seldom the perpetrator of the jests, and partly because Deloney emphasizes social comment and comic justice in the jests, whose victims, usually proud and haughty, richly deserve their comedowns.

Such a modulation of tone can frequently be observed in several books that exhibit the interrelationships between the jest book and serious fiction at the end of the sixteenth century. For example, some of the "jest biographies," wherein jests are gathered around a single hero like Skelton, Owle-

[3] Parenthetical page references to the works of Deloney throughout this chapter are to *The Novels of Thomas Deloney,* ed. Lawlis.

[4] *A Pleasant History of the Life and Death of Will Summers,* the earliest surviving edition of which is dated 1637.

[5] See Merritt E. Lawlis, *Apology for the Middle Class: The Dramatic Novels of Thomas Deloney,* Indiana University Humanities Series, Number 46 (Bloomington, 1960), pp. 39-45.

glasse, Scoggin, Tarlton, or Peele, often in a rough chronological sequence, approach the kind of biographical fiction we find in *Jacke of Newberie*.[6] This fact has tempted some critics to label *Dobsons Drie Bobbes* (1607), the most unified of them, as "one of the truly significant Renaissance novels."[7] A movement in another direction appears in *The Tinker of Turvey* (1630), an interesting revision of a Chaucerian jest book, *The Cobbler of Canterbury* (1590), which by embracing the novella manages to rise in an unbroken chain of tonalities from jest through romance to tragedy. Some nominal works of fiction, on the other hand, might just as well as be classified as jest books, such as Part II of Deloney's own *The Gentle Craft* or Nicholas Breton's *Grimellos Fortunes* (1604), which is really a series of jests framed by a satire on the five professions of scholar, courtier, soldier, lawyer, and farmer.

Moreover, it is not uncommon to find middle-class sentiment infiltrating some jest books so completely as to convert their heroes from witty rogues like Jack Wilton to admirable merchants, whose jests are not scurrile pranks but rather, as in *Jacke of Newberie,* witty exhibitions of common sense or comic justice. The hero of Richard Johnson's *The Pleasant Conceits of Old Hobson the Merry Londoner* (1607), for example, is "a homely plain man" admired for his equitable temperament as well as for his wit. A kind man, Hobson frequently uses the jest as a means of giving the haughty their well-deserved comeuppance or (as in his fifth jest, which is merely a humorous method of ensuring his prentices' attendance at church) for doing good. Long Meg of *The Life and Pranks of Long Meg of Westminster* (ca. 1590), who reappears in Part II of *The Gentle Craft,* is a widely celebrated folk-heroine. She is a militant champion of the distressed lower classes, "for whatsoever she got of the rich (as her get-

---

[6] See F. P. Wilson, "The English Jestbooks of the Sixteenth and Seventeenth Centuries," *Huntington Library Quarterly*, II (1939), 121-58.

[7] *Novels*, ed. Lawlis, p. xvii; see also Wilson, p. 143.

tings were great) she bestowed it liberally on them that had
need,"[8] and most of her jests involve raising the actual toward
an ideal state by such charitable deeds as succouring poor
soldiers, redressing the wrongs of highwaymen, putting down
the proud oppressors, and so forth; her final act is to establish
her own inn as a hostel for the oppressed.

Deloney's debt to the jest books extends beyond the incorpo-
ration of jest episodes, the use of the jest for social or moral
commentary, and the establishment of a folk-hero. It extends
to something more pervasive, a structural method. We might
say that Deloney used the technique of the jest books not as a
tool for criticizing or even destroying ideals, as Nashe had
done, but as a means to structure an ideal.

Though Anthony Munday was the first writer of Elizabethan fiction to divide his book into distinct parts by chapters,[9] Deloney was the first to make each chapter a discrete
unit, and to build up an entire book by means of such units.
Deloney thought in terms of the individual chapter, and he
conceived of it in a peculiar way, as a miniature drama or
dramatic scene. In *Jacke of Newberie* we have, instead of
continuity, several vignettes from his life distinct from each
other in time, place, and cast.[10] Frequently a chapter will
amount to little more than a brief sketch of the situation or
setting followed by lengthy colloquial dialogue; on occasion it
will be even more scenic, as in the abrupt opening of Chapter
VIII, where we do not even know who is speaking:

> Good morrow Gossip, now by my truely I am glad to see you
> in health. I pray you how dooth Maister *Winchcombe?*
> What never a great belly yet? now fie, by my fa your hus-
> band is waxt idle.

---

[8] *Long Meg of Westminster,* in *Short Fiction of the Seventeenth
Century,* ed. Mish, p. 92.

[9] In *Zelauto* (1580), Part III.

[10] See Lawlis, *Apology for the Middle Class,* p. 38: "If the medium
of Deloney's novels is dialogue, the structural unit is the scene."

Trust mee Gossip, saith mistresse *Winchcombe,* a great belly comes sooner then a new coate. (69)

A major result of the fact that Deloney thought in terms of scenes is that each of his chapters has a distinct, well-rounded structure of its own. One of the most explicit instances of this is the eleventh and last chapter, whose structure is frequently mirrored in its verbal texture, as here: "to become high, she laid her selfe so low, that the Knight suddenly fell over her, which fall became the rising of her belly" (82). It is a structure based on reversal: the knight Sir George Rigley gets Jack's maid with child and abandons her. In order to see justice done, Jack exalts the maid by disguising her as the wealthy widow Mistress Lovelesse, and then encourages Sir George to become her humble suitor. Her rise and his humbling meet in marriage and solidify when the two join Jack's household; Jack gives the whole action social significance by assuring Rigley "that I account the poorest wench in my house too good to be your whore" (86). A structure of reversal from high to low or from low to high position in fortune is common to most of the chapters: the king's jester Will Summers is brought low by Jack's maidens (Chapter IV), the courtly Italian merchant Benedick is foiled when he joins a pig in bed (Chapter VII), the haughty Mistress Frank is made the laughingstock of the town (Chapter X), the bankrupt Randoll Pert is raised by Jack's help to the position of Sheriff of London (Chapter IX), and Jack himself is always rising, as when, within the compass of a chapter, he progresses from the position of a humble suitor of Henry VIII to his host, and overcomes Cardinal Wolsey in the process (Chapter III).

Deloney's chapter headings—such as "How *Jack* of *Newberies* Servants were revenged of their Dames tattling Gossip" or "How *Jack* of *Newberie* went to receive the King"—indicate quite clearly the origins of his structural technique, for their wording reflects the standard headings of jests: "How Tarlton plaid the drunkard before the Queene," "How *George*

Peele became a Physician," or "How *Scogin* was shriven and hosted." The jests are short, dramatic, and telling, as are Deloney's chapters; and, moreover, their standard technique, like that of many jokes, is reversal, whereby the intended victim, who stands on his dignity at the beginning, is brought low by the rogue in a sudden turn of events. Such reversals abound in the jest biographies of Skelton, Scoggin, and others, for example in the jest in which George Peele gets revenge on a gentlewoman who had mocked him by seating her beside him at dinner: "as she put out her arme to take the Capon, *George,* sitting by her, yerks me out a huge ****, which made all the company in a maze one looking upon the other: yet they knew it came that way. Peace, quoth *George,* and jogs her on the elbow, I will say it was I. At which all the Company fell into a huge laughter, shee into a fretting fury."[11] Another conveniently succinct example is afforded by Number 42 of *Tales and Quicke Answeres* (which, because of its verbal emphasis, should be categorized as a quick answer rather than a merry tale): "A courtier on a tyme that alyghted of his horse at an Inde gate sayde to a boye that stode therby: Ho, syr boye, holde my horse. The boye, as he had ben aferde, answered: O maister, this a fierce horse; is one able to holde him? Yes, quod the courtier, one may holde hym well inough. Well, quod the boye, if one be able inough, than I pray you holde hym your owne selfe."[12] What Deloney essentially did with the structure of jest was to clarify it by extension: to prolong the reversal beyond a moment by dialogue and other means, to fix the reversal by making it important in the character's life, and to give it significance by introducing and stressing its social dimensions.

Deloney's inheritance from the jest books included a prob-

---

[11] *Merrie Conceited Jests of George Peele* (1607), in *Shakespeare Jest-Books: Reprints of the Early and Very Rare Jest-Books Supposed to Have Been Used by Shakespeare,* ed. W. Carew Hazlitt (3 vols.; London, 1864), II, 310.

[12] *Tales & Quicke Answeres,* p. 57, in *Shakespeare Jest-Books,* ed. Hazlitt, Vol. I.

lem, that of total structure. By what means could a series of detached scenes be welded into a satisfying whole? The only one of the jest books that attempted to deal with this problem was *Dobsons Drie Bobbes: Sonne and Heire to Skoggin* (1607). This is genuine biography, in that it begins with George Dobson's childhood adventures and ends with his reform, and attempts continuity, especially near the beginning, by supplying purely narrative links between one jest and another. Most importantly, it attempts to trace the growth of a rogue's character by showing how one jest begets another, chiefly in that one jest is seen as revenge for another. The jests do not progress in complexity, but their motivations do, as Dobson progresses from victim to revenger and finally to a young man who commits his bobs merely in order to uphold his reputation as a merry wag.

Deloney devised a bolder way to create a whole out of detached scenes. He chose to retain the integrity of the distinct scene of dramatic reversal that he developed from the jest books, but emphasized the social consequences of each reversal to such an extent that a rise or fall represented not merely success or failure but a character's advancement or frustration in his progress toward a concretely realized social status. By doing this, he gave a thematic function to structure—as we saw, for example, in our examination of Chapter XI, where the emphasis on status in the verbal texture made Sir George's defeat and the maid's success issue in the establishment of a new social arrangement. In the main, *Jacke of Newberie* proceeds to reveal a world of values by means of a single repeated structural and thematic pattern.

This narrative pattern is set up at the outset in the wooing of Jack by his widowed employer in the cloth-weaving trade. Since love and marriage are presented throughout as social problems (this is true not only of Jack's marriage to his mistress, but of his second marriage and that between Sir George and the maid as well), the accomplishment of marriage consists in overcoming successive obstacles in order, hopefully, to rise to a higher position. Jack's mistress therefore seeks to establish in his mind by degrees the probability that he is meant to be her husband, and she does this by means of a stepwise or spatial motif. She has him sit beside her while she describes each of her current suitors—a tanner from Wallingford, a tailor from Hungerford, and the parson of Speenhamland—and then dismisses each in favor of "one neerer hand" (8), each time making it more apparent who that "neerer" one is. She repeats this pattern in a banquet scene, where, after all have eaten their fill, she sends the tanner, the tailor, and the parson packing, so that only Jack remains. The obstacles having thus been overcome, the way lies clear for Jack to climb into his master's bed and then to solidify his position; as he says to his former companions, "by Gods providence and your Dames favour, I am preferred from being your fellow to bee your Master" (21). This level having been reached, there now ensues the age-old struggle for sovereignty. Jack is technically his mistress' husband, but she still treats him as her laborer. In a series of tricks, he first locks her out of the house, then she locks him out (marital relations having centered on possession of goods), and they finally agree to treat one another as equals, each respecting the other's will.

The pattern established in the first chapter infuses theme into structure by making reversal a matter of overcoming obstacles in order to rise to a new level of action, and then, on that level, of redefining (or really creating) a new field of action, after which a new step "upward" will occur. At the beginning, the context which defines Jack's actions is a purely personal one: he has power over his own life only, and therefore seeks to improve his personal fortune. When he succeeds in doing this by rising to the position of husband and master of both the household and the home industry, the sphere of action broadens into a domestic context and Jack can expand horizontally (so to speak) by consolidating the marriage and improving the industry. The boundaries of this new level of operation are reached when, a few years after his wife's death, he has so improved the industry as to make it his own little community, containing well over four hundred laborers in livery, with its own butcher, brewer, baker, and so forth. Instead of finding his place in his wife's world, Jack now resides in a world of his own which reflects his concerns. It is a model community with plenteous food and lodging for all, and filled with singing.

In the security of the new context that Jack has created for himself, he can repeat his pattern of good fortune by raising one of his workers, a girl from Aylesbury in Buckinghamshire, to the status of his second wife. The moment of their wedding is also the moment when Jack takes a further step upward out of the domestic context and into a civic and county-wide one, for the local nobility as well as his neighbors grace the wedding; now Jack can operate more powerfully in the county affairs of Berkshire as magistrate and representative.

The final step upward will come when Jack faces Henry VIII, and his ultimate field of action will be the nation rather than the county. Such a rise must be accomplished with circumspection, and Jack chooses to rise chiefly by means of shows that draw the attention of others to him. By making himself into an emblem (as it were) he both solidifies his own opinion of his nature and status and holds it out to others, in the hope that they will grasp it and draw him into their orbit. The emblems he presents show an interesting progression. His first pageant is played before the queen on the way to Flodden Field with his "fiftie tall men well mounted in white coates, and red caps with yellowe Feathers, Demilances in their hands, and fiftie armed men on foot with Pikes, and fiftie shot in white coats also" (30). The dual stress on neatness of clothing and featness in arms shows Jack as the clothier-soldier, the humble merchant striving to show his sovereign that he can operate in the field of war as well as many another. When the envious spurn him, Jack smears his white coat with blood and the queen, grasping the nature of the case, takes him under her protection.

Protection having been established, he next strives for a more equal footing. He interrupts the king's progress through Berkshire by a show of himself as Emperor of Ants defending his anthill against the Prince of Butterflies, an emblem that both directs satire at Wolsey (who is oppressing the commons) and presents Jack as a kind of mock-image in his small context of what Henry represents in his larger one. Jack is really striving for a delicately balanced relation between himself and the king, for while he refuses to be absorbed into the court as retainer (he later refuses a knighthood), he still wants the kind of equal treatment such a position would entail; he wants the commons and the nobility separate but equal, as it were. He gets what he wants, for Henry comes to him and then promises, "God a mercy good *Jack* . . . I have often heard of thee, and this morning I mean to visite thy house" (37).

The visit of the King of England to the home of the Emperor of Ants constitutes the apex of Jack's career. In the highly favorable position of host, Jack can present to Henry another emblem, a golden beehive as the image of a commonwealth wherein each part labors harmoniously for the benefit of all:

Loe here presented to your Royall sight,
The figure of a flourishing Common-wealth:
Where vertuous subjects labour with delight,
And beate the drones to death which live by stealth. (38)

It is notable that this image of an almost Edenic egalitarian commonwealth is reflected concretely in the orderly operation of Jack's household, and is announced clearly in the song that Jack's weavers sing to Henry:

When Princes sonnes kept sheep in field,
    and Queenes made cakes of wheaten flower,
Then men to lucre did not yeeld,
    which brought good cheare in every bower.
    Then love and friendship did agree,
    To hold the bands of amitie. (40)

What has happened here is that Jack has created for himself
a sphere in which the domestic world he has created and the
national situation he dreams of have merged, so that the household which before illustrated an ideal community now expresses the ideal commonwealth. With this, Jack finally takes
the step up into a national context, where the field of possible
actions again broadens. Now, as a figure famous throughout
the nation, Jack can attack the national problems of the cloth
trade and foreign affairs instead of local ones, and can even
enlist Henry's help against the oppressions of Wolsey. Jack's
major effort in this field is to lead the clothiers to London to
seek repeal of Wolsey's edict against trade with the Low Coun-
tries. The terms in which Henry grants their suit show how
persuasive Jack's image of the commonwealth as beehive has
been: "As the Clergie for the Soule, the Souldier for defence
of his Countrie, the Lawyer to execute justice, the husbandman to feede the belly: So is the skilfull Clothier no lesse
necessary for the clothing of the backe, whom wee may reckon
among the chiefe Yeomen of our Land" (58).

At this point, the possibility of rising further is blocked and
the field of vision firmly fixed in its limits, for Jack refuses the
knighthood that would lift him into the realm of the court and
politics. This plateau has been reached about halfway through
the book, in Chapter III; what follows is a rather static and
disjointed set of episodes illustrating Jack's activities in his new
position. Though there is no sense of progression in this latter
part, it achieves a kind of unity by repeating the thematic and
structural motif used throughout Jack's rise to this final field
of action. Chapter IV, in which Jack's maids requite the king's
jester Will Summers, is a kind of low-life parallel to Jack's
social defeat of Cardinal Wolsey in the anthill tableau and in
the entertainments at his home. The fifth chapter, succeeding
the king's visit, universalizes Jack's rise by pointing out parallels to it in chronicle history and by inviting imitation of the
hero. Here Jack is presenter: "Of the pictures which *Jacke* of
Newbery had in his house, whereby hee encouraged his serv-

ants to seeke for fame and dignitie." The theme of each of the
fifteen portraits is Jack's theme:

> In the first was the picture of a sheepheard before whom
> kneeled a great King named *Viriat,* who sometime governed
> the people of *Portugal.*
> See heere quoth *Jacke,* the father a Shepheard, the sonne
> a Soveraigne. (52-53)

The series of emblematic analogues includes seven emperors
of Rome and two popes, as well as sundry European kings.

In the series of episodes from Jack's later life which follows,
the theme takes both comic and serious forms. There are the
social comedies of Sir George coming down to the level of the
maid and the carting of the haughty Mistress Frank, for example. The exposure of the Italian merchant Benedick by an
ordinary English weaver has many levels of satire: the mere
laborer overcoming the wealthy man, the simple, honest Englishman overreaching the subtle Italian, the triumph of honest
virtue over courtly love, even a stylistic battle between good,
simple English and Benedick's mad farrago of dialect and
Euphuism. The main serious version of the theme is Jack's
only action in his new national position, the successful petition
to revoke Wolsey's edict. Another episode, subordinate to this
one, is Jack's elevation of Randoll Pert from a bankrupt to a
respectable merchant, from which position he eventually rises
to become Sheriff of London. The effect of all these variations
on a theme is to show Jack in the act of creating a set of values
out of his own experience, as in Part II of *Pamela*: raising others to positions analogous to his, drawing the prudent and
hardworking into his orbit, and excluding the proud and
pretentious. It was in this way that Deloney used the standard
technique of the jest books—the emphasis on the single scene
of reversal—to structure an ideal.

With each major narrative step in *Jacke of Newberie,* the
range of possible activities open to its hero expands: at first he
can only work hard and save his money, but finally he is

able to operate in national affairs and safeguard the welfare of his class. At first glance, this may look like the sort of "process plot" we found in Nashe, but it must be noted that while the probabilities change, their *grounds* never change. In *The Unfortunate Traveller* we saw the grounds of probability constantly shifting: rebels are objects of scorn, dead rebels are objects of pity; grave moral advice is nonsense, grave moral advice turns out to be true, and so forth. In *Jacke of Newberie* the possibilities are exactly the same on every level: Jack will show forth his virtue and be rewarded, whether by mistress, town, or king. In *Pamela* (to contrast Deloney's book with the novel that most closely shares its presuppositions), the action depends on our acceptance of the threat that virtue will *not* be rewarded through most of the book; *Jacke of Newberie* never allows us to entertain any such doubts.

Deloney's book is, in fact, an example of "constructivist" fiction, for the process of reading it is equivalent to the process of watching Jack build up a context for himself to operate in. In the terms we have used in examining the bulk of Elizabethan fiction, idea is not tested by action here, but rather action *establishes* idea, proves and elaborates it; and while Jack plays many roles, each is consistently assumed to be his real identity. He is what he plays: the local magistrate, the petitioner to the king, the complete success. The identity of role and actor, of idea and act, is part of the book's notable harmony of tone—and of its dogmatism as well. For *Jacke of Newberie* is essentially a return to the older Humanist mode of fiction, the fiction of building up an ideal out of the actual. What we see in it is the construction of a homespun Utopia, first in the image of the perfect home industry, then (through the emblems of anthill, beehive, and household) the image of the perfect commonwealth with all parts working in harmony. In the latter half of the book, we inspect this Utopia in detail.

Deloney presents the ideal as being constructed by the progress of a character, both because the ideal springs from the empirical experience of the character and because, having no preexisting status in an intellectual tradition, it must be defined as the book unfolds. Reality herein is defined as a thing more simple and exclusive than in many another piece of Elizabethan fiction: it is defined in terms of money and power. Any other factors in reality are either aspects of socio-economic position or qualities that it symbolizes. Love and marriage are means of gaining position, moral virtue is the quality rewarded by position.

John Winchcomb is an ideal of good nature, shrewdness, industry, and piety. He is as exemplary a figure as any of Forde's wooden heroes, and never suffers the kind of failure or even embarrassment (or the rise to wisdom consequent on failure) experienced by Pamela, Tom Jones, Pyrocles, Musidorus, Euphues, or F. J. His narrator dotes on him, and never allows any irony to interfere with his loving presentation. Any criticism of Winchcomb's actions is neutralized by being put into the mouths of the envious. If his ostentatious appearance with his troops before the queen makes him appear a designing *arriviste,* that judgment is immediately given unfavorable presentation by assigning it to "some other envying heereat" who "gave out words that hee shewed himselfe more prodigall then prudent, and more vaine glorious then well advised, seeing that the best Nobleman in the Countrie would scarce have done so much" (30-31); ostentation is turned to patriotism by the unconscious irony of their comment. The only people who accuse Jack of pride are the proud themselves: the haughty prelate Wolsey, who is trying to live down his origins as a butcher's son, and the comically proud Mistress Frank, who gets her comeuppance late in the book.

Merritt E. Lawlis has pointed out one trait that differentiates Deloney's idealized heroes from those of chivalric romance:

The tradesmen heroes are almost as idealized as the kings. They reward virtue and punish vice, but they themselves are allowed only a passive role in the action of the story. Young Jack of Newbury is wooed by a designing widow;

Simon Eyre achieves great wealth through a rather shady plan engineered by Mistress Eyre. In each case the hero reaches a desired goal without having to turn a hand. Presumably if he had turned a hand, he would have soiled it.[13]

Perhaps another reason for the hero's curious passivity can be found in the informal Calvinism which suffuses Deloney's fiction. According to popular expositions, economic success was one of the surest evidences of election; as R. H. Tawney and others have shown, misfortune was a sign of reprobation, good fortune a sign of election.[14] Therefore Jack's rise in the world is in his own eyes providential, each act proving after the fact (as it were) God's good will;[15] as he says to his sometime fellow workers, "by Gods providence and your Dames favour, I am preferred from being your fellow to bee your Master. . . . you shall have no cause to repent that God made mee your master" (21). Because the fictional action partakes of the archetypal action of election, Jack's spiritual value increases as he ascends further up the socio-economic ladder, and makes that rise meaningful. Hence, too, Jack's action is equivalent to self-display, to showing forth his righteousness in prudent spending, in equipping a company of soldiers, or in presenting situations by means of shows; and the advancement of the plot is equivalent to others taking notice of his virtue and rewarding it by raising him to positions of new prominence and greater certitude. Where action is conceived of rather narrowly, as the showing forth of an ideal, the exemplary hero must perforce be passive.

The full force of Deloney's idealistic and constructivist impulse appears in *Jacke of Newberie's* successor, *The Gentle Craft . . . shewing what famous men have beene Shoomakers*

---

[13] *Novels*, ed. Lawlis, p. xix.

[14] R. H. Tawney, *Religion and the Rise of Capitalism* (New York, 1926), pp. 266-67.

[15] Lawlis, *Apology for the Middle Class*, p. 89: "Promotion comes to those whom God elects to give it to, and there is no earthly way for us to know His will before the completely arbitrary promotion occurs."

in time past in this Land.[16] Here the model is not jest biography but chronicle history, and one of some magnitude; for Deloney's ultimate plan was for a trilogy celebrating the shoemaking trade, the first part recording its origins and growth, the second its prominence in London, and a third (never completed) its acts and monuments throughout the countryside.[17] Part I is especially chronicle-like, since it examines myths and origins, attempting to establish the source of the epithets "gentle craft" for shoemaking and "St. Hugh's bones" for shoemaker's tools, of the phrase "A Shoomakers sonne is a Prince borne," and of the annual Shrovetide feast of the London prentices. In three separate tales, arranged chronologically, it traces the honored craft from its first receipt of garlands to its contemporary eminence. Deloney drew upon diverse materials for his tales: the first two stem from *The Golden Legend,* the third from Stow's *Chronicles.*[18] The resultant tales differ even more strikingly in genre, the first being saint's legend, the second romance, the third realistic history. It is interesting to note that in this way Deloney managed to contain in a single book three traditional phases through which literature has often passed: myth, or tales of the godlike; romance or epic, or tales of men in converse with the supernatural; and realistic fiction concerning man in his own human society.[19] The three kinds of tale are so different that their only point of contact is their common goal of glorifying the trade

[16] *Jacke of Newberie* was registered on 7 March 1597 and *The Gentle Craft*, Part I on 19 October 1597; we do not know when Part II of *The Gentle Craft* was published, or whether it was before or after *Thomas of Reading*.

[17] This plan is announced in the Epistle to *The Gentle Craft*, Part II, in *Novels*, ed. Lawlis, p. 173.

[18] See *The Works of Thomas Deloney*, ed. Francis Oscar Mann (Oxford, 1912), pp. 522-23.

[19] See Gertrude Rachel Levy, *The Sword from the Rock: An Investigation into the Origins of Epic Literature and the Development of the Hero* (New York, 1954). Levy's three types are epic of creation (the gods), epic of search (man imitating the gods in a supernatural context), and epic of battle (men fighting among themselves).

and constructing a tradition for it; naturally, the values inherent in the trade and the ways in which these work are seen as entirely different in each tale.

The legend of St. Winifred and St. Hugh (Chapters I through IV) is set in the dim past, in the supernatural world of Winifred's Well and of ritual temptation like that undergone by St. Anthony (Hugh's voyage shows vestiges of the *Odyssey*). It proceeds by a kind of dialectic of love: when Hugh's quite human love for Winifred is thwarted by her conversion of love to *charitas*—"my love is fled to heaven," she avers (97)—he flees to the opposite pole, to the temptations of lust held out by the Sirens of Venice. But he flies from them in disgust. At last able to turn his love for Winifred into disinterested charity, he finally joins her as "a perfect Lover indeed" (109) on the scaffold of martyrdom. Hugh transforms his human love into *charitas* sometime during his sojourn as a shoemaker. His residence among the men of the "gentle craft," marking the period between his return from Venice and his joining Winifred in martyrdom, acts as a kind of catalyst whereby the amorous problems suffered by the prince are solved in the humble capacities of a shoemaker. The gentle craft is for Hugh a kind of retreat, as he says in his commendatory song: "The *Gentle Craft* is fittest then, / For poore distressed Gentlemen" (108). The craft has no intrinsic value in this tale; it is a humble place of retreat, and nothing more.

Hugh, at Winifred's Well, had appealed to his beloved by saying, "content dwells here, or no where: content me, and I will content thee," and she, in an answer, had held out a Bible to him, "read this booke, and there rests content" (97). The romance of Crispin and Crispianus (Chapters V through IX) locates content in a different place. When the two exiled princes hear some shoemakers singing at their work, they "wished it might bee their good hap to be harboured in a place of such great content" (117); and when Ursula, the king's daughter, contemplates marriage with her shoemaker Crispin, she says, "an homely Cottage shall content me in thy company"

(131). Deloney's second tale envisions the gentle craft as a kind of pastoral world, a humble place of contentment to which the noble may retreat to live a happy life. Many of the standard motifs of pastoral romance and its received ideals are incorporated into this plot. The two princes, who must flee for their lives, disguise themselves and enter the shoemaker's trade; there they learn to be content, but thence they issue out again into the great world, in the dual plot of love and war so common to romance (as in Ariosto, Spenser, and Sidney): Crispin wins the love of Ursula, Crispianus wins glory on the field of battle. Aside from substituting shoemakers' virtue for shepherds', the tale glorifies the craft mainly by bringing its motif, the phrase "A Shoomakers sonne is a Prince borne," from metaphor down to the literal level, where it can operate to the honor of the craft. It starts as the inaccurate boast of Iphicratis, a shoemaker's son who rose to the throne of Perisa (128); it is then applied as metaphorical praise of the true nobility of Crispianus, the shoemaker who fights Iphicratis so valiantly (129); finally, it appears in the son produced by the clandestine marriage of Crispin and Ursula, where it becomes literal, "Now will I say and sweare . . . that a Shoomakers sonne is a Prince borne, joyning in the opinion of *Iphicratis,* and henceforth Shoomakers never shall let that terme die" (135).

It is only with the final tale of Simon Eyre (Chapters X through XV) that we get the kind of middle-class "realism" we usually associate with Deloney. The material this time comes not from *The Golden Legend* but from "Our English Chronicles" (139), and it concerns a fully historical person who was Lord Mayor of London in the mid-fifteenth century —a time close enough to Deloney's own and a setting like enough to his London to allow him to surround the hero with concrete contemporary detail. Eyre's story is John Winchcomb's in little, a story of socio-economic success. It is the only one of the three tales to locate virtue centrally in the trade by recording the well-deserved success of a tradesman rather than the condescension of the noble. Eyre, a moderately successful shoemaker, acquires great wealth as a result of deceiving a Greek merchant in linens, and is thereupon taken into higher social circles to become Sheriff, Alderman, and finally Lord Mayor. Like Jack, he attributes financial success to providential election after the fact: "The last day I did cast up my accounts, and I finde that Almighty God of his goodnesse hath lent me thirteen thousand pounds to maintaine us in our old age" (154). Even more strikingly than in Jack's case, his identity changes as he climbs the social ladder: "And now seeing that *Simon* the Shoomaker is become a Merchant, we will temper our tongues to give him that title, which his customers were wont to doe, and from henceforth call him Master *Eyer*" (149); when Eyre is made sheriff, a workman runs home to tell his wife, "you are now a Gentlewoman" (157); and finally, "within a few yeeres after, Alderman *Eyre,* being chosen Lord Maior of *London,* changing his copie, hee became one of the Worshipfull Company of Drapers" (167). It is part of the tale's social naturalism, which of course includes realistic dialogue and abundant reference to concrete things, that Simon Eyre's identity depends on his context, that he is what others think he is.

At the same time that the tale of Simon Eyre converts Part I of *The Gentle Craft* into a more realistic book, it also makes it a more exemplary book. Whereas the first two tales had located no value in the shoemaker's trade other than its worth as a pastoral retreat for the noble, Eyre's tale celebrates openly the tradesman's virtues of industry, thrift, and generosity. Hugh and the others, visitors from another world, are scarcely characters at all; good things happen to them, and they reflect credit on the craft, but they in themselves exhibit no virtues save that of humility. Eyre, on the other hand, is fully characterized and presented as an object for imitation, with his combination of wit, shrewdness, ambition, and piety. And yet, even though he is so fully characterized, he is a more exemplary figure than the saints. Hugh falls prey to lust, Winifred's choice of virginity is treated by the narrator as "over-much superstitious" (96); but so unequivocally must Eyre stand as an ideal that, as Lawlis has pointed out, the one shady deal in his life is conceived and executed by his wife, lest he touch pitch and be defiled.[20] For Deloney, realism and idealism work hand in hand.

Part II of *The Gentle Craft* is the least unified of Deloney's books, being little more than a series of jests gathered around three heroes who in themselves scarcely receive any attention. As Deloney admits in his epistle, his original plan had come a cropper, and he had found so much material on shoemaking in London that he had been forced to gather it all together in a separate volume. To Part II, far more than to Part I, applies his warning that "the beginning shewes not the middle, nor the middle shewes not the latter end" (92); its only unity is unity of place. In the first of the three segments (Chapters I through IV), Richard Casteler merely serves as the motivation for several jests by Gillian of the George, Long Meg of Westminster (herself the heroine of a jest book), and his riming worker "Round Robin" (whose habit of extempore verse owes much to *Tarltons Jests*). The second segment (Chapters V through IX) has a unity approaching that we found in the latter half of *Jacke of Newberie,* for there we see the gallant London shoemaker Peachey becoming the center of a growing world as Tom Drum, Harry Nevell, and Sir John Rainsford gravitate to his shop at Fleet Street. But Peachey's set of values is not germane to his class and trade; rather, it pushes him out of his class, for what is notable in him and his followers is their ability at arms. They are shoemakers who are celebrated not for being good tradesmen, but for being gallant fighting men. The book fizzles out in two chapters celebrating "the merry feats" of a shoemaker called "the grene king" (256).

Along with the sense of total structure, idealism (which

20 *Novels,* ed. Lawlis, p. xix.

for Deloney depended so closely upon constructing a model)
also collapsed. What we are left with in Part II is almost entirely jest-book material for merriment (as the title page
promises) instead of eulogism, a loose string of entertaining
adventures. Here we see the basic interest in telling stories,
which will terminate in the structural masterpiece *Thomas of
Reading*, starting to absorb exemplary interests and intents.

⟨ II ⟩

Many of Deloney's critics have attempted to suggest, by
appeals to his "realism," a link between his work and the
modern novel that grew up a century and a half after his
death. Chevalley, for instance, located in the "primitive and
spontaneous" quality of this "realism" what he felt was "l'en-
fance du roman,"[21] and Lawlis writes, more judiciously, that
"no writer in England has ever had a greater claim to be
called a 'realist.' "[22] Lawlis' is a just verdict and at the same
time a potentially misleading one, for "realism" is one of the
more ambiguous terms of literary criticism. We can single out
at least two quite different meanings of "realism" or two types
of it: there is reportorial "realism," which is mainly a matter
of detailed presentation, of a keen eye for concrete description
of things and a keen ear for capturing actual speech; and then
there is what Ian Watt has termed "philosophical realism,"
which is located in a view of life where particulars are unique
and man is obsessed by time, a view of life at the least detached from absolute ideals and at the extreme totally cynical
regarding values.[23] This distinction between forms of "realism" is not crucial for the modern novel, for there the two

[21] Abel Chevalley, *Thomas Deloney: le roman des métiers au temps
de Shakespeare* (Paris, 1926), p. 133.

[22] Lawlis, *Apology for the Middle Class*, p. 8; see also Schlauch,
Antecedents of the English Novel, pp. 237 and 245 for specific claims
to link Deloney's technique with the modern novel.

[23] Ian Watt, *The Rise of the Novel: Studies in Defoe, Richardson
and Fielding* (London, 1957), Chap. I; see also Wayne C. Booth, *The
Rhetoric of Fiction*, Chap. II.

usually go together. In Elizabethan fiction, however, they never do.

Of reportorial realism, Deloney gives us God's plenty, as a finely detailed passage like the following testifies:

> This man was the first that wrought upon the low cut shoo with the square toe, and the latchet overthwart th'instep, before which time in *England* they did weare a hie shoo that reached above the ankles, right after the manner of our husbandmens shooes at this day, save onely that it was made very sharpe at the toe turning up like the taile of an Island dog: or as you see a cock cary his hinder feathers. (141)

Here the abundance and concreteness of detail, the common-place comparisons (including the specifications of a particular kind of dog), and the interjected "as you see," appealing to the reader's own experience, bring the description to life before our eyes. We can see Deloney's uncanny ability to repro-duce the diction and rhythm of common speech in a passage like the following, where Crispin's mistress is attempting to tell her husband that their prentice has got a maid with child:

> O man (said she) *Crispine!*
> Why what of *Crispine?* tell me. Why speakest thou not?
> Wee shall lose a good servant, so we shall.
> What servant shall we lose foolish woman (quoth he?) Tell me quickly.
> O husband! by Cock and Pye, I sweare, Ile have her by the nose.
> Who wilt thou have by the nose? What the Devill art thou madde, that thou wilt not answer me? (131-32)

Deloney can infuse descriptive detail with significance, also, as in the masterful portrait of Mistress Pert, where identity is made a matter of social status and social status in turn is rendered by the pressure of material things on the flesh:

. . . his Wife which before for dayntinesse would not foule her fingers, nor turne her head aside, for feare of hurting the set of her neckenger, was glad to goe about and wash buckes at the Thames side, and to bee a chare-Woman in rich mens houses, her soft hand was now hardened with scowring, and in steade of gold rings upon her lillie fingers, they were now fild with chaps, provoked by the sharpe lee and other drudgeries. (74)

If we take "realism" to mean accurate and convincing reflection of the material conditions of contemporary life, then Deloney is certainly such a realist; but to the "philosophical realism" that centers on a view of life as conditioned by time and space rather than values, Deloney has no claim at all.[24] To reiterate what we discovered earlier, Deloney has a very palpable design on his readers, and uses his books as vehicles for very simple, even doctrinaire, ideals. To that end, he presents the tradesman's life as an ideal one, his heroes as models of perfection untouched by any but the highest motives—heroes idealized enough to satisfy Ascham's demand for exemplars in fiction, and much more idealized than the heroes of Sidney, Lyly, Gascoigne, and many writers of romance. Lawlis has put the matter well in a suggestive analogy: "All his heroes are romantically conceived. He may remind us a little of Hemingway in that although he gives us many striking details from actual everyday life, his main characters are ideal and highly recommended to us for their

---

[24] Perhaps F. O. Mann's unsupported statement that Deloney "simply holds 'the mirror up to nature' without the interposition of himself or his views" (*The Works of Thomas Deloney*, p. xxxi) results from confusing reportage with a detached and "realistic" view of life; for an opinion directly the opposite of Mann's see Lawlis, *Apology for the Middle Class*, p. 108. In the rather similar case of Defoe, J. Paul Hunter has argued that, in the Puritan context, Defoe's massing of reportorial detail should be seen not as a "realistic" effort but rather a symbolic one, an attempt to find God's hand in all the small things of this world (*The Reluctant Pilgrim: Defoe's Emblematic Method and Quest for Form in "Robinson Crusoe"* [Baltimore, 1966], pp. 84 and 208).

prowess and good instincts."[25] If we seek among the Elizabethans for traits close to the "philosophical realism" or insistence on the primacy of individual over collective or traditional experience which Ian Watt finds so important to the modern novel, we shall find it in the stylized satire of Nashe and Chettle, not in Deloney.

Moreover, reportorial "realism" represents only one side of Deloney's accomplishment, for his books are usually hybrid in form. As Lawlis writes:

> Realism exists in the Renaissance, as Miss Schlauch demonstrates. But the difficulty is that the great artists tend to show little interest in it. . . . Granted, there are a number of "human types" like Randoll Pert and Mistress Pint-Pot, two delightful minor characters in *Jack of Newbury*. But Deloney is no more interested in presenting them for our delight than he is in presenting the euphuistic dialogue of Duke Robert and Margaret-of-the-white-hand.[26]

In this regard, it is well to remember that two of Deloney's four books—Part I of *The Gentle Craft* and *Thomas of Reading*—are generously larded with romance elements.

The true character of middle-class "realism" in the Elizabethan age may be better understood by considering Deloney's coworkers in the production of fiction explicitly intended for the middle class, an audience that Greene had been the first to exploit. There are two such writers, Henry Robarts and Richard Johnson, and both exhibit an interestingly dual relationship to romance and "realism."

Robarts, a Devonshire seaman, shows a direct, almost dialectical, progress from romance to "realism" in his four works of fiction.[27] The first of them, *A Defiance to Fortune*. . . .

---

[25] Lawlis, review of Schlauch's *Antecedents of the English Novel*, in *Journal of English and Germanic Philology*, LXIV (1965), 299.

[26] *Ibid*.

[27] See Louis B. Wright, "Henry Robarts: Patriotic Propagandist and Novelist," *Studies in Philology*, XXIX (1932), 176-99.

*Wherein is noted a myrrour of noble patience, a most rare
example of modest chastity, and the perfect patterne of true
friendship* (1590), betrays the expectations of the exemplary
that its title page arouses. It is really a late example of Euphuistic fiction with heavy debts to Greene.[28] As such, its
subject is experience, its plot the downward path of Andrugio
as he suffers slavery, deposition, and the manifold buffets of
fortune, to end as the usual wiser but sadder man. The
"defiance" of the title is not the stoic virtue of endurance, but
rather refers to the long and bitter complaint the disillusioned
hero utters at the end, where we leave him "with teares ceas-
ing his mournful speeches, bewailing with heavinesse of heart
the worldes ingratitude" (sig. N3v). The model supplied by
Euphuistic plot was in itself inimical to the exemplary, and
from it Robarts turned to a much more fertile field for his
intentions, chivalric romance, in *The Historie of Pheander
The Mayden Knight . . . Enterlaced with many pleasant Discourses, wherein the graver may take delight, and the valiant
youthfull be encouraged by Honourable and worthie Adven-
turing, to gaine Fame* (1595). Robarts deliberately exhorts the
valiant and youthful to the love of fame by consistently hold-
ing up Pheander as a perfect exemplar of chivalric valor and
courtly behavior, a "mirrour of Honeur" (sig. G2).[29] He
entices them by conducting the chivalric enterprise from a
mercantile basis: his hero is a merchant (really the disguised
Prince Dionisius, in love with Nutania, Princess of Thrace)
who, after being knighted as "The Mayden Knight" by
Nutania, defends her kingdom and wins her hand.[30] Robarts
comes close to the everyday life of his audience by showing
Nutania doubtful of the propriety of loving a merchant (sig.
H3), by exhibiting such events as a king's redress of a peasant's

[28] Compare the plot of Greene's *Arbasto, The Anatomie of Fortune*
(1584).

[29] Page references are to the fourth edition of 1617.

[30] Robert Anton mocks the title of "Tom Pheander, the Maiden
Knight" in *Moriomachia* (1613); see *Short Fiction of the Seventeenth
Century*, ed. Mish, p. 49.

wrongs (sigs. N4-O2), and by the unintentionally comic juxtaposition of courtly talk and hardheaded concerns (as in Deloney): for example, when Pheander approaches "that Saint my heart most adoreth" with his equipage, she is impressed by "what cost & rare devises, [with which] each thing by her servant was performed," and immediately assures him that "my kingly Father will recompence . . . your great cost and charge" (sig. G2v).

By moving out of fiction into legendary history in *Honours Conquest* (1598),[31] Robarts came even closer to actual life and the concerns of his middle-class readers, and if his setting was still the romantic East, his hero was a true Englishman. Here he could incorporate virtue in an actual historical personage, Edward of Lancaster, and use the apparent historicity of the events he recorded as a further goad to "the ende of all thy reading," "to attaine true vertue" (sig. A4v). Edward is unlike Pheander in that while he displays the chivalric virtues, what Robarts emphasizes in him are virtues easily attainable by any of his readers: patriotism and piety. On the one hand, Lancaster wades into battle, "putting himselfe amongst the route of them, still crying *Lancaster,* God and Saint George for Englande" (sig. E4); on the other, "our brave English Cavalere playing the part of a heavenly Phisitian, comforted his weake patient, in the promises of Christ Jesus, and his passion" (sig. H2v).

Robarts' progress from chivalric romance to bourgeois "realism" was completed in *Haigh for Devonshire. A pleasant Discourse of sixe gallant Marchants of Devonshire* (1600). Here verisimilitude found its proper sphere: relatively recent times, an English rural setting (in part), and mercantile heroes.[32] In this realistic setting, exemplary virtue is basically a social value, depending on relations with neighbors and the

[31] Only Part II of this three-part work has survived: see sigs. B1 and S4. On Robarts' concern with verisimilitude, see above, p. 195.

[32] On the debts of this book to Deloney's *Thomas of Reading,* see Wright, pp. 196-99.

state: "Faithfull subjects, and good men in the common wealth, were these famous Marchants of whom I intreat, wealthy, charitable and honest" (sig. A3v), and loved by all. The chief exemplar is William, the image of the good master who shows "the perfect love of a Maister to his servants, whom he loved more deare then his children" (sig. I3). The piety which Edward of Lancaster had displayed so outstandingly has faded so far into the background as to be shown only indirectly by a strong anti-Papist bias and by the casual assumption that wealth is blessedness—as when it is said that "These men whom God blessed with wealth, had thankfull mindes to the giver, acknowledging his goodnesse, whose stewards they were" (sig. A4). The central virtue held up for the imitation of youth here is patriotism; it is shown directly when the merchants help put down a Cornish rebellion or outfit ships against the French, and indirectly (in a way strangely reminiscent of some modern international novels) by sexual conquest of foreigners. Robert, for example, manages to overcome both France and the Papistry in the person of an abbess at Rouen: "*Robert*, againe of an humble and thankfull spirit, having strength and ability to performe the office of a man, hath so well pleased the Lady, that shee rather desired private conference with *Robert*, (her new devoted servant) then to heare the sweetest Channon chaunte in the Quire, descant hee never so well, yet the Ladyes devotion is colde to the Church, but burning to the Chamber" (sig. C3v). English virility likewise conquers in the climax of the book, when James (William's factor) so satisfies a Spanish heiress that "she loved ever after Englishmen, better then her owne Countreymen" (sig. H3v). She consequently marries him and pays all his debts, to the great joy of all six heroes.

Robarts was an incessant encomiast, as his various verse celebrations amply show: his welcome to Cavendish (1588), his farewell to Drake and Hawkins "with an encouragement to all Sailers and Souldiers" (1595), and his patriotic celebrations of various exploits on land and sea against Spain. His fiction represents an enlargement of his purposes in verse, for we have seen that it is totally exemplary. Its progress shows Robarts transferring his exemplars to areas increasingly closer to his audience, from chivalric hero to historical personage to several middle-class merchants, but the essential nature of the fiction does not change, whether its trappings be chivalric or "realistic." The exemplary virtues change somewhat in the process, from chivalry to a combination of piety and patriotism to sheer patriotism alone as (perhaps) his sense of his audience broadened. But what is important to note is that Robarts could use middle-class "realism" and chivalric romance quite easily for the same purpose, whatever the virtue he celebrated; both were for him essentially vehicles for presenting ideals.

The same is true of Richard Johnson, the erstwhile tradesman's apprentice, though his path is not as steady as Robarts' and though he tends to combine in single works various elements of romance, history, and realism. His first production, *The Nine Worthies of London* (1592), is a case in point, for it combines many influences; composed of both verse and prose, it carries into prose fiction the kind of verse encomia that Robarts produced. With its allegorical frame of the visit of Fame and Clio to Elisium, where each of the worthies recites his tale in rhymed stanzas, the book forms an obvious bourgeois analogy to *The Mirrour for Magistrates* (which also influenced many of Deloney's ballads, such as those on Rosamond, Shore's wife, and Mistress Page), with the comedy of success replacing tragedy. The title itself indicates the intention of elevating the middle class to the heroic plane of the traditional nine worthies, who had long since passed from history to romance. Johnson's worthies are firmly historical and mercantile: Sir William Walworth, fishmonger; Sir Henry Pitchard, vintner; Sir William Sevenoake, grocer; Sir Thomas White, merchant tailor; Sir John Bonham, mercer; Sir Christopher Croker, vintner; Sir John Hawkwood, merchant tailor; Sir Hugh Caverly, silk-weaver; and Sir Henry Maleveret, grocer. They are all, of course, presented as unexceptionally hardy and virtuous. Only once is a reservation voiced, and that is when, after Sir Henry Pitchard has boasted about entertaining at his house "Foure kings, one prince, and all their royall traine," Clio wonders "at this modest audacitie" and requests Fame henceforth "to proceede altogether with the honourable acts of these memorable men, and onely touch their vertuous endeavours" (sig C3v)—an interesting tonal contrast to Deloney's presentation of Jack's entertainment of Henry VIII.

With a single exception, that of Sir Thomas White, who is celebrated as a peaceful benefactor, Johnson's heroes move up from their class by means of valor on the field of battle; for Johnson seems to have been incapable of conceiving of impressive virtue as anything but chivalric, or of eminence as anything but movement *out* of the middle class into knightly orders. Because he lacked the imaginative scope which allowed Deloney throughout his career and Robarts in his last book to locate virtues in the merchant life itself, he was usually constrained to locate bourgeois virtues in chivalric romance, a fact that goes far to explain why chivalric romance and realism are so closely allied in middle-class fiction.

It was therefore a short step to the chivalric collection of *The Most Famous History of the Seaven Champions of Christendome* (ca. 1597, with additions in 1608 and 1613), Johnson's most popular work. As in Robarts' *Honours Conquest,* the basis of the book is legendary history, which gives it some aura of verisimilitude; the seven champions are naturally held up as mirrors of piety and chivalric honor, and there are heavy patriotic overtones (especially since St. George is the center of interest). But so great is the book's emphasis on the wonderful and improbable that it may well have astounded its readers rather than encouraged them to virtue, as well as nullifying its claims to verisimilitude.

The Most Pleasant History of Tom a Lincolne (published in two parts, ca. 1599 and 1607) shows Johnson turning away from history to romance, and romance of the most fantastic kind. Its only claims to historical verisimilitude are its pseudo-historical Arthurian setting and its celebration of the great bell called "Tom a Lincoln" in the city of Lincoln, "where to this day it remaineth."[33] For the rest, it records a dragon fight, voyages to Fayerie-land and Prester John's land, and other such marvels. Though the book does record the rise of a low-born hero to nobility, its bourgeois idealism is slight, confined as it is to the first few chapters, where Tom is presented as "The Boast of England" and "the perfect patterne of an exquisite souldier; such a one as all martiall captaines may learne to imitate."[34] But after Tom sets out to "eternize his name" in foreign lands, the marvelous takes the center of interest, while the second part contains only dark but interesting tragedy.

Johnson's last work of prose fiction (or his last two, if we accept him as the author of *The History of Tom Thumbe, the Little,* 1621),[35] *The Pleasant Conceits of Old Hobson the Merry Londoner* (1607), belongs to the genre of jest biography. Though the latter part of it is practically plagiarized, jests 12 through 35 being mere repetitions of jests in *Tales and Quick Answeres* (ca. 1535) applied to Hobson, the first eleven jests constitute as close an approach as Johnson was to make to the kind of bourgeois "realism" we find in *The Gentle Craft.* His hero, William Hobson, is historical, being a London haberdasher (d. 1581) about whom a body of legend had developed and to whom several common proverbs had been ascribed. He is not a clown or wag, but a merchant hero like Simon Eyre. His jests are therefore not the usual scurrile rough-and-tumble, but are softened to kind rebukes and usually consist of witty moral justice, as when he gives the proud their comeuppance (jest 2), raises a down-and-outer to success as Jack

[33] Text in *Early English Prose Romances,* ed. William J. Thoms (3 vols.; 2nd edn.; London, 1858), II, 246.

[34] *Ibid.,* II, 249.

[35] See *The History of Tom Thumbe,* ed. Curt F. Bühler (Evanston: The Renaissance English Text Society, 1965), pp. ix-xiv.

of Newbury did Randoll Pert (jest 3), mocks his prentices for missing church (jest 5), or comically reproves his wife's pride (jest 8). The center of attention in this early part is character —the even temper and success of an exemplary and merry old man—as the opening description shows: "He was a homely plaine man, most commonly wearing a buttond cap close to his eares, a short gowne girt hard about his midle, and a paire of slippers upon his feete of an ancient fashion; as for his wealth, it was answerable to the better sort of our cittizens, but of so mery a disposition that his equal therein is hardly to be found."[36] Hobson is presented with the kind of affectionate regard mixed with admiration that we find Robarts according his Devonshire merchants and Deloney his various heroes. It was at this humane ideal that Johnson finally arrived in his unsteady progress from chivalric idealism.

In the work of Robarts and Johnson we can see how fully the idealism of chivalric romance filtered into middle-class "realism." Even though the nature of the idealism was sometimes modified in the process, such a process did give bourgeois "realism" the essentially exemplary form we found in Deloney. It was romance, with its highly idealized heroes, that dictated the motives of realism: the realistic milieu and style were merely the most effective ways of bringing their ideals home to their audience, for while it might have been more fun for a prentice to imagine himself a knight, it was easier for him to envision the fruits of commercial success. That is why, in *Jacke of Newberie*, we find a total reportorial realism surrounding the most idealized of heroes.

Furthermore, once we peek beneath their chivalric trappings, we find that the romances often have plots little different from that of *Jacke of Newberie*, which consists of the rise from low estate to high. Many of them have, beneath their long catalogues of adventures, a "hidden" plot familiar to us from fairy tales, the proletarian dream of discovering that the

[36] Text in *Shakespeare Jest-Books*, ed. Hazlitt, III, 7-8.

peasant youth is really the king's forgotten child. Such plots center on questions of identity, though identity is not figured as social status but as the fact of birth. Emanual Forde exploited this type of plot twice. In *Parismenos* the hero, raised by a lion, confesses that "my name is hidden from my selfe" (sig. D1), but goes from exploit to exploit accruing worship as "the Knight of Fame" (good repute serving as a good substitute for nobility, as in Deloney's and Robarts' books) until at last he is united with his real parents Parismus and Laurana, king and queen of Bohemia. Similarly, Montelyon arises from supposedly obscure origins and goes through several identities before he finally discovers his father Persicles, king of Assyria. *Tom a Lincolne* contains a similar plot concerning a boy raised as a shepherd whose valiant heart projects him into the field of chivalry where he, a king's son in reality, belongs. In these romances—as well as in Middleton's *Chinon* and the Elizabethan version of *Blanchardine* (1595),[37] in both of which the hero must be aroused from stupor to honor—the achievement of socio-economic status is only thinly disguised. We may be sure that their common message was not lost on the prentices for whom they were most profitable.

Elizabethan middle-class "realism" is opposed to chivalric romance in its reportorial technique—and in nothing else. Both kinds of fiction often came from the same pens; they share the aim of exhorting their audience to virtue, the values of piety, patriotism, and thirst for fame, and the consequently flawless hero. These facts explain the severe limitations of Deloney's "realism" and show why, if we seek a realm of slightly more human imperfection than his, we must go, paradoxically but truly, to the artificial fiction of the Euphuists, pastoral romance, and the highly stylized satire of Thomas Nashe.

[37] *The Moste Pleasant Historye of Blanchardine* (1595), a translation of the thirteenth-century romance *Blancandin et l'orgueilleuse d'Amour,* which Caxton had also translated ca. 1489. See the edition of Caxton's *Blanchardin and Eglantine* by Leon Kellner, Early English Text Society, Extra Series No. 58 (London, 1890).

⟨ III ⟩

Ernest A. Baker gave this final judgment on Deloney:

> In truth, there is always something lacking in Deloney which is fundamental, something that cannot be dispensed with in a story, as distinguished from what is at best only an amusing display of manners and peculiarities. There is nothing much going on in his tales; there is no real business, except business in the particular sense, and of that there is too much. Allowance must of course be made for one of his main incentives in writing. He put himself forward as the eulogist and defender of the trading corporations. Hence the economic element, which many writers tend to overlook, essential though it be in the structure of life, all but monopolizes the story interest.[38]

In the main the verdict is a just one; we have seen many consequences of Deloney's sacrifice of narrative interest to eulogistic motives, and several reasons for it. But to this verdict must be excepted Deloney's masterpiece, *Thomas of Reading* (ca. 1600),[39] where the basic, vital impulse of telling a story and locating its own meaning in it rises above any didactic intentions.

In *Thomas of Reading* ideas of value are not established by action, but are discussed, and even modified by experience, as they are in the best work of Deloney's predecessors. A case in point is the minor incident of the Halifax hanging law. When Hodgekins of Halifax persuades King Henry I to issue an edict permitting summary hanging of cloth-thieves, he conceives of it as an economic necessity to remedy the heavy losses the clothiers have suffered at the hands of rogues. But

---

[38] *The History of the English Novel,* II, 192.

[39] On the date, see *Novels,* ed. Lawlis, p. 379; that *Thomas of Reading* appeared after *Jacke of Newberie* and *The Gentle Craft,* Part I is fairly certain, but that it appeared after *The Gentle Craft,* Part II is only probable.

when economics is put to the test, the case is altered: when, in Chapter VIII, the first thieves actually come before the citizens of Halifax, human feeling turns against the death penalty, the people are so moved with pity that no one will consent to be the hangman, and the thieves go free. Then a third and objective point of view enters, and it carries the weight of religious authority: a friar reproves Hodgekins, telling him that "compassion is not to be had upon theeves and robbers: pitty onely appertayneth to the vertuous sort, who are overwhelmed with the waves of misery and mischaunce" (310). We are not done yet, for the resolution of the conflict between economics and feeling by absolute precept is itself submitted to experiential scrutiny, but this time the testing is done indirectly, by analogy and juxtaposition. The chapter immediately succeeding this one is devoted to a short tale of two base-minded, cowardly, and foolish London catchpoles who are successfully bilked of their prey, Tom Dove, by the kindly giant Jarret. In this tale, where the victim of law is a man besieged by debtors rather than a thief, the defeat of the law by kindness is stressed, and much is made of the disgrace of the office of catchpole: "notwithstanding that it was an office most necessary in the commonwealth, yet did the poorest wretch despise it, that lived in any estimation among his neighbours" (312). The final position which Chapter IX reflects back onto Chapter VIII is that justice must be done, but that the just man will refuse to profit by it.

The dual attitude toward justice as both necessary and restrictive of normal human impulse crops up in several places in the book. The fabliau of Cutbert of Kendall and old Bosom's wife Winifred is dispersed between Chapters II and V, and is conducted from two different points of view. In Chapter II the planned adultery, as seen by Cutbert and Winifred, is justified by the naturalness of their desires, by the lighthearted wit they use to hide their intents, and by a view of old Bosom (which the narrator shares) as

> ... a foule sloven, [who] went alwayes with his nose in his
> bosome, and one hand in his pocket, the other on his staffe,
> figuring forth a description of cold winter, for he alwaies
> wore two coates, two caps, two or three paire of stockings,
> and a high paire of shooes, over the which he drew on a
> great paire of lined slippers, and yet he would oft complaine
> of cold. . . . This lump of cold ice had lately married a yong
> wife, who was as wily as she was wanton. (275)

But when the adultery is about to occur, in Chapter V, it is
presented through the eyes of old Bosom, who quite under-
standably sees it as horrible: "O abominable dissimulation,
monstrous hypocrisie" (289). The overdone tragical rant modu-
lates to cool irony as Bosom catches them in the act and, with
full comic and moral justice, hoists Cutbert in a basket, there
to reveal him to all as a villain who buys his mutton too dear
(293).

Deloney's fidelity to a chosen point of view is remarkable
here, as it is in his various presentations of King Henry I.
Henry is rendered in as objective a fashion as possible, mainly
because the narrator refuses to offer comment, and puts opinions in the mouths of a variety of characters. In Chapter I,
Henry's rather Machiavellian plan to support his position on
the throne he has usurped from Robert, Duke of Normandy
by cultivating the lower classes is presented flatly, without
comment. Only in Chapter II do we get an opinion—the
clothiers'—and then it is dual: dislike of the king's enemies
but pity for their distressed families "turned out of doores
succorlesse and friendlesse" (272). In Chapter IV the king
speaks like an exemplar of fatherly concern, and is praised by
Thomas Cole of Reading as "a most mild and mercifull
prince" (287); but then we get his brother's unmediated view
of him as well: "By me he hath received many favors, and
never yet did he requite any one of them: and who is ignorant
that the princely crowne which adorneth his head, is my
right?" (316). In his final action, the pardoning of Margaret

and the blinding of Robert, Henry is said to be "of nature mercifull"; but what we are permitted to see is his cruelty in forcing Margaret to witness her beloved's gruesome punishment—"let her not passe, till she see her lovers eies put out," he instructs his officer (334). Henry is de facto king, and must be obeyed; he is just, but a little cold and cruel. Deloney holds back nothing.

Perhaps enough has been said to show how different the world rendered in *Thomas of Reading* is from that of *Jacke of Newberie*. Few of its heroes are exemplary:[40] Thomas of Reading is likeable but is not held up as a model; Simon and Sutton are mainly seen through their wives, haughty and foolish women like Mistress Frank in *Jacke of Newberie*; Cutbert is a lecher, "for no meate pleased him so wel as mutton, such as was laced in a red petticoate" (274); Tom Dove, though lovable, is a prodigal; and Henry I, as we have just seen, is not undefiled. The only real models of perfection in the book are the tragic lovers Robert, Duke of Normandy and Margaret-of-the-white-hand, and they are wooden figures inherited from romance, not tradesmen-exemplars.

Moreover, Deloney is interested in his characters' fates as human beings, rather than merely in using them to point morals or adorn tales. *Thomas of Reading* is the only one of Deloney's books that is not a story of commercial success; the climax is the death of its titular hero, not his final attainment of status. Thomas Cole's death conditions the tone of the book's latter portions, for there we find a growing sense of life's futility. This tragic tone is a totally new departure for Deloney. Instead of a gleeful acceptance of material felicity as the reward for virtue, there is only contempt for this world, as Robert announces, "Life, why what is it but a floure, a bubble

[40] The subtitle's promise of six heroes, "The six worthy yeomen of the West," is not accurate, there being in fact nine of them. We hear practically nothing of William of Worcester and Martin of Manchester, and most of the action devolves upon three of them: Thomas Cole of Reading, Tom Dove of Exeter, and Cutbert of Kendall.

in the water, a spanne long, and full of miserie" (335-36) and submits to his blinding; as Tom Dove, like Job, discovers "the small trust that is in this false world" (338); as Margaret, smeared with ashes, cries out, "now farewell the world, farewell the pleasures of this life" (343). The book ends with the pious deaths of all. What is important to *Thomas of Reading* alone among Deloney's books is not "business" but the problems of life, love, and death in time.

Only once in his three previous books had Deloney presented his readers with a hero less than exemplary, in the case of the prodigal Green King of *The Gentle Craft,* Part I. And only once before had he stressed tonal complexity, in the Randoll Pert episode of *Jacke of Newberie,* where Pert is first presented as a pathetic fugitive, "ever looking behind him, like a man pursued with a deadly weapon, fearing every twinkling of an eye to bee thrust thorow" (75), and then immediately as ludicrous, when his pants fall down: "his breech, being tyed but with one poynt, what with the haste he made, and the weaknesse of the thong, fell about his heeles: which so shackled him, that downe hee fell in the streete all along, sweating and blowing."[41] What was before the exception is in *Thomas of Reading* the rule: relatively unidealized heroes, undeserved failure, questioning rather than assertions of value-structures, and complex tonal effects.

Perhaps, in the overall context of the middle-class fiction that we examined earlier, it will seem only mildly paradoxical that *Thomas of Reading* achieved its eminence as fiction by pulling romance—romantic matter and romantic structure—into the embrace of a realistic rendering of life. True, *The Gentle Craft,* Part I had contained both romance and "realism," but it had kept them separate, and had proceeded from romance to realism. *Thomas of Reading* combines the two, weaving them together so that they attain a working relation with one another. What we have in *Thomas of Reading* are two distinct levels of plot, the various doings of "the sixe

[41] See Lawlis, *Apology for the Middle Class,* pp. 93-95.

worthie Yeomen of the West" and the noble love-tragedy of Margaret-of-the-white-hand and Robert, Duke of Normandy.

The main concern is the adventures of the clothiers: Henry's admiration of their wealth (Chapter I) and subsequent favor to them (Chapter IV) culminates in his visit to their homes (Chapter VII), and is interwoven with their experiences at various London inns, including Cutbert's seduction of Bosom's wife (Chapters II and V) and the experiences of the clothiers' wives (Chapter VI); the latter part of their adventures is dark, and includes the experiences with the hangman and the catchpoles (Chapters VIII and IX), Thomas of Reading's murder (Chapters XI and XII), and the misfortunes of Tom Dove (Chapter XIV). Interwoven with these adventures is the noble feudal tragedy of Robert and Margaret: her misfortunes as the outcast daughter of the banished Earl of Shrewsbury (Chapter III), his imprisonment (Chapter VII), their meeting and love (Chapter X), and its tragic end (Chapters XIII and XV). To the two plots belong two distinct styles (as in Chettle's *Piers Plainnes,* the book it most resembles). One is a high Euphuistic style: "Consider, faire *Margaret* (quoth he) that it lies not in mans power to place his love where he list, being the worke of an high deity. A bird was never seene in Pontus, nor true love in a fleeting mind; never shall I remove the affection of my heart, which in nature resembleth the stone Abiston, whose fire can never be cooled" (316). The other is the normal low colloquial style, where love can sometimes be conducted in these terms: "Come on, you puling baggage, quoth he, I drinke to you; here will you pledge me and shake hands?" (278).

To the two plots belong quite different views of life. Material things are of necessity important to the clothiers: their wives demand fine clothes, financial success or failure determines their ways of life, and success is achieved by hard work. To these concerns Deloney adds a vital sense of the enjoyment of life, a love of wine, women, song, and jests. In the noble tragedy of sentiment, things are quite different: Robert conceives of his duties in terms of love and honor and, in direct contrast to the sense of the nobility of labor available to the clothiers and to Henry, persists in finding labor demeaning; as he says to Margaret (and in complete ignorance of her nobility), "I muse thou canst indure this vile beseeming servitude, whose delicate limmes were never framed to prove such painefull experimentes" (314). Robert and Margaret sacrifice themselves to an ideal of fidelity in love; Jarman the innkeeper and his wife murder Cole for his money. So distant are the values of the two plots that they can make contact only through convention. Margaret has been taken in by Gray of Gloucester; she waits on table and joins the other maids in spinning. But when she meets Robert, she suddenly is made to seem a character out of pastoral romance: "It chaunced on a time, that faire *Margaret* with many other of her Masters folkes, went a hay-making, attired in a redde stamell petticoate, and a broad strawne hatte upon her head, she had a hay forke, and in her lappe she bore her breakfast" (314). And the scene between them is conducted in terms traditional to pastoral romance, he tempting her to love and high place, she defending the standard pastoral values: "whereas you alleage poverty to be a henderer of the hearts comfort, I find it in my selfe contrary, knowing more surety to rest under a simple habite, then a royall robe . . . such as are indued with content, are rich having nothing els: but he that is possessed with riches, without content, is most wretched and miserable" (316). Historically, of course, the two plots represent two worlds—the medieval world of love, tragedy, and honor, and the new world, where, as Henry says, middle-class wealth counts: "I always thought (quoth he) that Englands valour was more than her wealth, yet now I see her wealth sufficient to maintaine her valour" (270-71).

Lawlis finds the interweaving of these two plots masterful. He points out that scenes from the lives of the clothiers are dispersed through the beginning, middle, and end of the book;

that incidents like the Cutbert-Winifred episode are divided and placed in two separate chapters (Chapters II and V), so that they become part of the structure instead of being isolated like the Benedick episode in *Jacke of Newberie*; and that, "Since all the incidents, even those of a farcical nature, are clearly related either to the main plot or to the subplot, the result is a narrative density that is extremely rare in Elizabethan prose fiction" (though, we might add, it is common in pastoral romance).[42] The two plots are carefully linked by characters: by Margaret, Gray's servant and Robert's mistress, and especially by Henry, who controls both of them by helping the clothiers (thus fostering their general success) and by hindering Robert (thus turning his tale to one of tragedy).[43] Full narrative unity is achieved in Chapters XI through XV, which form "one large climax and ending," tying up, chapter by chapter, the loose ends in the lives of Cole, the wives, Robert and Margaret, and Tom Dove, and "thus completing what no one could have expected from the author of *Jack of Newbury*—a well-made plot."[44]

The book falls into two parts. The first nine chapters trace the growth and solidification of an alliance between the king and the clothiers (excluding the nobility), whereby Henry joins wealth to valor. The essence of this new society is seen as the establishment of order, especially through laws of measurement: the Halifax hanging law, the reform of currency, the establishment of the yard as universal standard of measurement (an interesting egalitarian touch); and these laws are examined, as we have seen, in Chapters VIII and IX. Margaret and Robert scarcely enter into this part of the book, for they—the daughter of the banished earl and the defeated prince—are the outcasts in this new social order.

With Chapter X the new and the remnants of the old begin to interrelate. The love story of Robert and Margaret (Chapters X and XIII) frames the two chapters devoted to Cole's

[42] *Ibid.*, p. 61.   [43] *Ibid.*, p. 58.   [44] *Ibid.*, p. 67.

murder. At first the relation is one of contrast, as noble love (Chapter X) is set against the covetousness and hate of Cole's murderers (Chapter XI); but then it turns to parallel, as Robert's plans for escape fail and the noble plot becomes as tragic as Cole's (Chapter XIII). The chapter on Tom Dove's failure (Chapter XIV) starts as a parallel to Robert and Margaret's, but then, when Cole's will saves Tom from collapse, is turned to a contrast by Tom's regeneration, a regeneration which is continued with a totally new tonality in the last chapter, where Margaret leaves the world for a nunnery and contemplation of the world to come.

More important than the interrelations of these two levels of plot is their interaction, the ways in which each influences the quality of feeling the reader apprehends in the other. The climax of Cole's murder takes place in a nightmare world, and this world is distorted further in the next chapter (Chapter XII), where the wives go so far as to imagine Cole's flesh being eaten. This nightmare quality (so reminiscent of *Macbeth*) seeps into the noble world of Robert and Margaret, so fully that Robert can announce that this life is but a bubble full of misery and then, turning his empty sockets toward Margaret, go "groaping for her with his bleeding eies, saying, O where is my love?" (336). And this tragic view of life, along with its proper high style, infuses as well the purely commercial failure of Tom Dove (perhaps even inappropriately), in a chapter that begins, "Such as seeke the pleasure of this world, follow a shaddow wherein is no substance: and as the adder Aspis tickleth a man to death so doth vaine pleasure flatter us, till it makes us forget God" (337). By means of such qualitative progressions the parts of *Thomas of Reading* become parts of a world where diverse modes of life and value meet to illuminate one another, as they did in the worlds of courtly fiction and pastoral romance.

Different concepts of the real constantly meet and change, as we saw earlier in the case of the Halifax hanging law, the affair of Cutbert and Bosom's wife, and the judgment of

Henry. Deloney's rendering of Cole's murder in Chapters XI and XII is perhaps the finest thing in the book. Chapter XI heightens the normal sense of the real into a nightmarish unreality. Cole is treated like a pig to be butchered, the atmosphere is full of ravens croaking and the like, and Cole himself falls prey to uncontrollable melancholy and weeping, even to hallucination: "With that, *Cole* beholding his hoste and hostesse earnestly, began to start backe, saying, what aile you to looke so like pale death? good Lord, what have you done, that your hands are thus bloudy? What my hands, said his host? Why you may see they are neither bloudy nor foule: either your eies doe greatly dazell, or else fancies of a troubled mind do delude you" (325). But his nightmare turns out to be real, and all the distortions really forebode the actual horror of the death by boiling that he suffers. But even this complex view of the real is not allowed to stand without further distortion. To this succeeds Chapter XII, one of Deloney's masterful little dramatic scenes: amid the merriment of Mistress Sutton's churching the gullible women hear rumors of Cole's death, and in that context the affair appears as gruesomely comic:

> . . . it is reported for truth, that the Inholder made pies of him, and penny pasties, yea, and made his owne servant eate a piece of him.
>
> But I pray you, good neighbour, can you tell how it was knowne? some say, that a horse revealed it.
>
> Now by the masse (quoth *Grayes* wife) it was told one of my neighbors, that a certaine horse did speake, and told great things.
>
> That sounds like a lye, sayd one of them. (329)

In this nonsense-world, death by boiling becomes inexorably linked with eating, and Cole's poor wandering horse becomes an entertainer, like Banks' horse.

This scene in itself constitutes a demonstration of the variability of opinion and the difficulty of establishing a single truth in a world of strange appearances. The book abounds in such passages illustrating the gap between intention and result: Cole cries in amazement, "I did verily purpose to write a letter: notwithstanding, I have written that that God put into my mind," which is his last will and testament (324). The difficulty of sorting out appearance from reality looms large: "What, my nose quoth he? is my nose so great and I never knew it? Certainly I thought my nose to be as comely as any mans: but this it is, we are al apt to think wel of our selves, and a great deale better than we ought: but let me see, (my nose!) by the masse tis true, I do now feele it my selfe: Good Lord, how was I blinded before?" (318). Though of course it is not true, Sir William Ferrers is blinded now by the illusion Margaret has foisted on him that his nose is so long that it sags down upon his lips.

Deloney moved away from a rather narrow form of middle-class "realistic" fiction toward a full exploration of all facets of reality. What is remarkable—and embarrassing to the literary historian enamored of neat categories—is that he did so by moving backward, so to speak: by reaching back to embrace Sidney and the romance, to catch up the traditional romantic themes of love and death, illusion and reality, and to combine them with his vivid sense of the contemporary scene.

Conclusion

In his important essay "Manners, Morals, and the Novel," Lionel Trilling has defined the sovereign task of the novel as an exploration into the nature of reality, an attempt to encourage its readers to sift appearance and reality.[1] The novel does this chiefly by juxtaposing different concepts of what reality is; and this juxtaposition is accomplished by locating such concepts in different societies or social groups, with correspondingly different moral codes and sets of manners, and then setting these groups in conflict. One of Trilling's main examples is *Don Quixote,* where the hero's chivalric idealism and his society's gross materialism clash. At first the conflict seems to destroy the hero and locate reality in materialism alone, but then (in Part II, where Don Quixote becomes more like Sancho Panza and Sancho becomes more like the Don) the two come to modify rather than exclude each other, and thus leave the reader with a more brilliant sense of probability.[2] To novels like those of James and Forster that accomplish such a task, Trilling opposes the novels of Dreiser and Steinbeck, which, instead of questioning reality, present a single "doctrinaire" concept of the real that the reader is expected and encouraged to accept uncritically. In Steinbeck's *The Wayward Bus,* for example, every means at the novelist's disposal is employed to evoke love of the lower-class characters and contempt for the middle-class characters.

Trilling's employment of *Don Quixote* perhaps justifies an attempt to apply his criteria to other kinds of fiction besides the novel. Of the fiction we have examined in this study, the kind that provides the clearest example of juxtaposition of different manners, morals, and concepts of the real is pastoral romance. In its symbolic geography, court and country repre-

[1] In *The Liberal Imagination: Essays on Literature and Society* (New York, 1950).

[2] See Salvador de Madariaga, *Don Quixote: An Introductory Essay in Psychology* (London, 1935), pp. 112-30.

sent directly (not obliquely, through manners, as less highly stylized literature might do) two different concepts of the real or two different metaphysical levels of reality: the pastoral world embodies an absolute such as Platonic vision or ethical imperative or an ideal personal freedom, the world of the court represents its opposite in unreformed actuality. At its best, as in *Arcadia,* the pastoral romance manages to modify the assumptions of both worlds in the experience and mind of its hero. At its worst, it either depicts the court as absolutely villainous and has its hero withdraw into a rigid pastoral ideal, or simply ignores values entirely, as is the case in much of Greene's pastoral work. The usual result is that the courtly hero returns to his own world bearing at least some of the values he met with in "Arcadia"—as in *Rosalynde,* where, although Lodge has delimited his worlds crudely, he still manages, by stressing the hero's ability to play out a role and imagine his life as different from what it had been, to open out reality for his readers instead of closing it in. The courtly fiction of Lyly and his peers comes closer to the modern novel in that it brings together different societies with different codes of conduct (Athens and Naples, Venice and Valasco, Italy and England); at the same time it is in a sense more abstract than the romance, because it presents Humanistic ideals or their opposites which the hero first grasps as intellectual constructs and then puts into practice in a full social context. This kind of fiction is least trenchant when the hero, having failed to find one such construct viable, turns to embrace another, as in *The Anatomy of Wit.* It is at its most poignant when the hero fails completely and finds no new position to sustain him, as in *Don Simonides* and *The Adventures of Master F. J.* It is perhaps at its best as a criticism of life in *Euphues and his England,* where the failure of one given concept of value causes its revision in the light of experience.

It was the commerce between abstract ideas and concrete experience (rather than that between different kinds of society, as in the novel) that fostered the exploration of reality in

Elizabethan fiction. We have traced the collapse of that commerce (and some reasons for it in intellectual history) in the work of Robert Greene, with a resultant bifurcation in the history of fiction: fiction which either breaks down the area of contact between different sets of values entirely, or which upholds a single view against all others. We see both unsatisfactory alternatives in Greene himself. He asserts the traditional morality unequivocally in his repentance pamphlets, yet presents a world where different codes fail to interact in romances like *Menaphon*, which leave us with a vision of human life as a marionette show manipulated by the powers above. After Greene we have, on the one hand, books like *Piers Plainnes* and *The Unfortunate Traveller,* which juxtapose so many mutually exclusive concepts of the real as essentially to destroy them all; and on the other, a return to what Trilling terms "doctrinaire" presentations of reality (whether that reality be conceived simply as corrupt, as in *A Margarite of America,* or as the field for a celebration of middle-class virtues). With the single exception of *Thomas of Reading* (which, as we saw in the last chapter, shows a brilliant interaction of the diverse), Deloney's fiction exemplifies the doctrinaire. Not only are all who disapprove of John Winchcomb and his cohorts presented as envious villains, but all members of social classes other than his are ritualistically humiliated in the interests of industry, piety, and patriotism.

Deloney's first three books bear as close a relation to the tract as does *The Grapes of Wrath*—or, for that matter, as does *Utopia.* For in Deloney and others the fiction of the late 1590s is becoming exemplary again and constructive of single values, like the older Humanistic models (though, of course, with different aspirations at its roots). A brief inspection of literary fashion will clarify the process by which late Elizabethan fiction became what it was.

The years 1575-85 were dominated by the fiction of Gascoigne, Lyly, and the Euphuists, a literature recording the frequent failure of ideas in the face of reality. The years 1588-90, with the publication of *Arcadia* in 1590 and the several romances of Greene and Lodge, are the years of pastoral romance, a less astringent form than its predecessor, and one which accommodates the actual and the ideal. The "philosophically realistic" fiction of Nashe and his fellows does not actually dominate the 1590s; though frequently brilliant, it was never popular. Publication records show this fact clearly: *A Margarite of America* and *Piers Plainnes* received only one edition apiece, *The Unfortunate Traveller* barely achieved two—this in contrast to about twenty-five editions of an exemplary work like Forde's *Parismus* (1598), twenty-two of Johnson's *Seaven Champions of Christendome* (ca. 1597), twenty-eight of Munday's Palmerin romances, and twenty-three of Deloney's *The Gentle Craft*.[3] Readers obviously preferred fiction that asserted new values to that which outlined the ferment of the times. What we in fact find between 1595 and 1600 are two different forms, bourgeois fiction and chivalric romance, growing up side by side in the works of Deloney, Robarts, Johnson, and Forde. The simultaneous birth of a new fictional genre and recrudescence of an old one comes as no surprise when we realize that they were both addressed to the same audience and had the same aim: the use of fiction as exemplum.

Deloney was as retrospective in his concept of the function of fiction as he was forward-looking in some of his techniques. And he can more accurately be regarded as having come near the end of a movement in fiction (a very old movement, as we demonstrated in our first chapter) than at the beginning of a new one. He had few followers in the seventeenth century, and the same is true of Sidney, Greene, Nashe, and others.[4] By and large, the accession of James I sets the limits

---

[3] Statistics are taken from Arundell Esdaile, *A List of English Tales and Romances Printed Before 1740* (London, 1912), and must, in the absence of fuller data, be taken as approximate.

[4] Lyly had become a figure of fun before the turn of the century, and Lodge lived chiefly in the plagiarisms of John Hynde's *Lysimachus and Varrona* (1604). While Nashe's style can be traced in the pamphlets of Dekker and others, his narrative art left its mark on only one work

for the effectiveness of the writers we have studied. It is a curious but undeniable fact that fiction of distinction all but disappears between the death of Elizabeth and the accession of Charles II, and it is the province of a different kind of study from ours to trace the process, causes, and effects of the decline.[5] When original fiction arose in England again in Bunyan and Congreve, and later in Defoe and Richardson, it appeared rewoven on the loom of history, of probable fact, as Congreve affirmed.[6] But it was a new kind of history, not so much that of man facing other men, much less nature or concepts, as of man facing himself, the internal history of the mind as conveyed first by such subliterary genres as the Puritan diary or spiritual autobiography.[7] William Congreve and his contemporaries thought of the novel as a complete departure from earlier fiction, bearing little relation to it other than that of burlesque to its target; we have every reason to accept their judgment in the matter.

---

of fiction, Robert Anton's *Moriomachia* (1613). Sidney's *Arcadia*, together with the quite different romances of Forde and others, continued to be popular into the eighteenth century; but it had·few imitators, most of the elements of its appeal having been absorbed by the popular French romances instead. Similarly, Deloney's popularity won him few imitators beyond his contemporaries Johnson and Robarts, most notably in the latter's *Haigh for Devonshire* (1600). Greene's influence alone appears to have been continuous, since his rogue pamphlets leave a strong imprint on Richard Head's *The English Rogue* (1665) and other works of its type.

[5] One might suggest, among other causes, the rejection of myth and the growing rift between imaginative verse and factual prose: see K. G. Hamilton, *The Two Harmonies: Poetry and Prose in the Seventeenth Century* (Oxford, 1963).

[6] Preface to *Incognita* (1692), in *Shorter Novels, Jacobean and Restoration*, ed. Henderson, p. 241.

[7] See, e.g., Watt, *The Rise of the Novel* and Hunter, *The Reluctant Pilgrim*.

A CHRONOLOGY OF THE FICTION DISCUSSED

For complete listings of Elizabethan prose fiction, see Esdaile, *A List of English Tales and Romances Printed Before 1740* and Volume I of *The Cambridge Bibliography of English Literature*. It may be noted in passing that neither of these reference works lists C. M.'s *The Nature of a Woman*, and that CBEL incorrectly lists *The Moste Pleasaunt Historye of Blanchardine* (1595) and R. C.'s *Palestina* (1600) under "Original Works of Fiction."

1573   George Gascoigne, *A Pleasant Discourse of the Adventures of Master F. J.*

1575   Gascoigne, *The Adventures of Master F. J.* (second version)

1577   John Grange, *The Golden Aphroditis*

1578   John Lyly, *Euphues. The Anatomy of Wit*
       Sir Philip Sidney, The "Old" *Arcadia* (started)

1579   Stephen Gosson, *The Ephemerides of Phialo*

1580   Lyly, *Euphues and his England*
       Austen Saker, *Narbonus. The Laberynth of Libertie*
       Anthony Munday, *Zelauto. The Fountaine of Fame*
       Robert Greene, *Mamillia. A Mirrour or looking-glasse for the ladies of Englande*

1581   Barnabe Riche, *Riche his Farewell to Militarie Profession*
       ———, *The Straunge and Wonderfull Adventures of Don Simonides*

1583   Greene, *Mamillia The second part of the triumph of Pallas*
       Brian Melbancke, *Philotimus. The Warre betwixt Nature and Fortune*

1584   Riche, *The Second Tome of the Travailes and Adventures of Don Simonides*
       William Warner, *Pan his Syrinx*
       Thomas Lodge, *The Delectable Historie of Forbonius and Prisceria*
       Greene, *Gwydonius. The Carde of Fancie*

————, *Arbasto, The Anatomie of Fortune*
Sidney, The "New" *Arcadia* left unfinished (published
1590)
W. C., *The Adventures of Ladie Egeria* (? entered in The
Stationers' Register 15 December 1580)

1585   Greene, *Planetomachia*

1587   Greene, *Penelopes Web*
————, *Euphues his Censure to Philautus*
————, *Philomela. The Lady Fitzwaters Nightingale* (writ-
ten ? published 1590)

1588   Greene, *Perimides the Blacke-Smith*
————, *Alcida Greenes Metamorphosis*
————, *Pandosto. The Triumph of Time*
————, *Greenes Orpharion* (written ? published 1590)

1589   Greene, *Ciceronis Amor. Tullies Love*
————, *Menaphon Camillas Alarum to Slumbering Euphues*

1590   Sidney, "New" *Arcadia* published
Lodge, *Rosalynde. Euphues Golden Legacie*
Henry Robarts, *A Defiance to Fortune*
Greene, *Greenes Never too Late*
————, *Francescos Fortunes: Or, The Second Part of
Greenes Never too Late*
————, *Greenes Mourning Garment*

1591   Lodge, *The Famous, True and Historical Life of Robert
Second Duke of Normandy*
Greene, *Greenes Farewell to Follie*

1592   Richard Johnson, *The Nine Worthies of London*
Riche, *The Adventures of Brusanus, Prince of Hungaria*
Lodge, *Euphues Shadow, The Battaile of the Sences*
Greene, *The Blacke Bookes Messenger. Laying Open the
Life and Death of Ned Browne*
————, *Greens Groats-worth of Wit*

1593   Lodge, *The Life and Death of William Long beard*
Henry Chettle, *Kind-Harts Dreame*
Greene, *Greenes Vision*

1594   John Dickenson, *Arisbas, Euphues Amidst his Slumbers*
       Thomas Nashe, *The Unfortunate Traveller*

1595   Chettle, *Piers Plainnes Seaven Yeres Prentiship*
       Robarts, *The Historie of Pheander The Mayden Knight*
       Robert Parry, *Moderatus, The Most Delectable and Famous
          Historye of the Blacke Knight*

1596   Lodge, *A Margarite of America*
       Johnson, *The Most Famous History of the Seaven Cham-
          pions of Christendome*
       C. M., *The Second Part of the Historie, called The Nature
          of a Woman*

1597   Johnson, *The Seaven Champions of Christendome*, Part II
       Christopher Middleton, *The Famous Historie of Chinon of
          England*
       Nicholas Breton, *The Miseries of Mavillia*
       Thomas Deloney, *The Pleasant Historie of John Winch-
          comb*
       ———, *The Gentle Craft*, Part I

1598   Deloney, *The Gentle Craft*, Part II (?)
       Dickenson, *Greene in Conceipt*
       Robarts, *Honours Conquest*
       Emanuel Forde, *Parismus. The Renoumed Prince of
          Bohemia*
       ———, *The Most Pleasant Historie of Ornatus and Artesia*
          (?)

1599   Forde, *Parismenos*
       ———, *The Famous Historie of Montelyon* (?)
       Johnson, *The Most Pleasant History of Tom a Lincolne*

1600   Deloney, *Thomas of Reading* (?)
       Robarts, *Haigh for Devonshire*
       Breton, *The Strange Fortunes of Two Excellent Princes*

1604   Breton, *Grimellos Fortunes*
       John Hynde, *The Most Excellent Historie of Lysimachus
          and Varrona*

1606   Hynde, *Eliosto Libidinoso*

INDEX